Chicken Soup for the Soul®

From Lemons to Lemonade

Chicken Soup for the Soul: From Lemons to Lemonade
101 Positive, Practical, and Powerful Stories about Making the Best of a Bad Situation
Jack Canfield, Mark Victor Hansen, Amy Newmark
Published by Chicken Soup for the Soul Publishing, LLC www.chickensoup.com

The publisher gratefully acknowledges the many publishers and individuals who granted Chicken Soup for the Soul permission to reprint the cited material.

Front cover photo courtesy of iStockPhoto.com/kirin_photo (© Agnieszka Kirinicjanow). Back cover and interior photo courtesy of iStockPhoto.com/ivanmateev (© ivanmateev).

Cover and Interior Design & Layout by Brian Taylor, Pneuma Books, LLC

Distributed to the booktrade by Simon & Schuster. SAN: 200-2442

Publisher's Cataloging-in-Publication Data
(Prepared by The Donohue Group)

Chicken soup for the soul : from lemons to lemonade : 101 positive,
  practical, and powerful stories about making the best of a bad
  situation / [compiled by] Jack Canfield, Mark Victor Hansen, [and] Amy
  Newmark.

   p. ; cm.

   ISBN: 978-1-61159-914-5

   1. Attitude (Psychology)--Literary collections. 2. Suffering--Literary collections. 3. Attitude (Psychology)--Anecdotes. 4. Suffering--Anecdotes. 5. Anecdotes. I. Canfield, Jack, 1944- II. Hansen, Mark Victor. III. Newmark, Amy. IV. Title: From lemons to lemonade : 101 positive, practical, and powerful stories about making the best of a bad situation

PN6071.A88 C45 2013
810.8/02/0353   2013937409

PRINTED IN THE UNITED STATES OF AMERICA
on acid∞free paper

22 21 20 19 18 17 16 15   03 04 05 06 07 08 09 10

Chicken Soup for the Soul®

From Lemons to
Lemonade

101 Positive, Practical,
and Powerful Stories
about Making the Best
of a Bad Situation

Jack Canfield, Mark Victor Hansen
& Amy Newmark

Chicken Soup for the Soul Publishing, LLC
Cos Cob, CT

www.chickensoup.com

Contents

❶
~From Victim to Victory~

❷
~From Rat Race to Relationships~

3

~From Pausing to Pursuing~

4

~From Adversity to Acceptance~

5

~From Problem to Purpose~

❻

~From Sickness to Success~

❼

~From Heartbreak to Healing~

❽

~From Bleak to Blessings~

❾

~From Apprehension to Appreciation~

⑩

~From Fear to Faith~

Introduction

We can complain because rose bushes have thorns, or rejoice because thorn bushes have roses.
~Abraham Lincoln

Wow. I am still reacting to these 101 stories, from some of the most inspiring people you'll ever meet. I'm thrilled to introduce you to these men and women, who took huge challenges and turned them into life-changing benefits through positive thinking, creativity, and hard work. This is what we love about Chicken Soup for the Soul stories—the opportunity to learn from the example of people like us, ordinary people, who have *extraordinary* experiences. We focus on finding stories for you that are uplifting and helpful—ones that show how you can implement the same practices and improve your own lives.

What struck me the most in these stories is the resilience of the human spirit, whether our contributors are fighting health, financial, career, or relationship battles. They don't complain about their situations—they just get up off the floor and deal with them—and that's how you make lemonade after being handed a bunch of lemons.

You'll read many stories from contributors who suffered through near-death experiences or health crises that ended up leading to new careers, improved relationships, and self-discovery. Jo Eager is an example. She is a TV reporter who had to learn to walk again after a near-fatal rattlesnake bite, and now has a new lease on life with the addition of part-time work as a fitness trainer. You'll also be inspired by Esther McNeil Griffin, who gave away most of her possessions when she was given one year to live, pursued all her dreams, and now, a quarter century later, continues to live each year as if it is her last. You'll read about Alicia Bertine, who decided to flaunt her bald head after chemo and became a successful bald fashion model. You can watch her YouTube videos to see her in action.

I was also inspired by the courage it took many of our contributors to leave dead-end or unhappy relationships, at home or at work, and start over again. Successful novelist Margaret Nava has one such tale. She left an abusive marriage with nothing, and rebuilt her life slowly but surely as a writer who has had several books published now. You'll love the stories in this collection by people who changed their lives after leaving, usually involuntarily, their jobs, and now realize they are much happier with a new career path or with no job at all. W. Bradford Swift reveals in his story that he was contemplating suicide when he realized that he was unhappy as a veterinarian and needed to change his occupation. He now guides other people on their own paths to happiness through his Life on Purpose Institute.

You'll read about how Dr. Jennifer Arnold, who stars in TLC's *The Little Couple* with her husband, overcame prejudice against little people and was accepted by the renowned Johns Hopkins School of Medicine. You'll read how pain-management specialist Dr. Rita Hancock finally figured out her own diagnosis—her constant pain was related to her feelings about her inability to care for her out-of-state aging mother.

I'm always amazed by the good cheer of regular contributor Cindy Charlton, who lost three limbs to flesh-eating disease, and writes a funny story about having to get all her errands done one morning while one of her prosthetic legs, with a broken foot, sits on the car seat next to her. She shows the detached leg to people to explain why she can't get out of the car and needs them to help her. And I never knew that our contributor Karen Hessen had adopted the most severely abused child in America. Her story relates how she learns a lesson about forgiveness from him when he wants to tell his former abuser that he is okay now.

We also have bittersweet stories from contributors who can't erase the losses in their lives but do find the best possible way to get through them. You'll read about Julie Cole, who had to simultaneously plan her older daughter's funeral and finalize her younger daughter's wedding arrangements. She and her family managed to make the wedding a joyous event during a time of mourning. And in a really dramatic lemons to lemonade... to lemons story you'll read about how grieving widow Carol Goodman Heizer got to spend a month "on vacation" hanging out with her son when she was unfairly suspended from her job, only to have him unexpectedly die at the end of their time together. She was so grateful that she had been given that time off, despite the unfairness of it, and had that month of freedom to spend with her son.

I come away from this project feeling energized and encouraged. These contributors tell stories that put our own problems and stresses into perspective. If they can overcome these challenges, certainly we can handle ours! We all want to go about our days with a positive outlook, but we don't always know how to do it, and there are lessons in these pages for all of us.

As the father of positive thinking, Norman Vincent Peale, said, "Change your thoughts and you change your world." I'm pretty sure that after you read these stories, you'll feel empowered to use positive thinking to navigate your own difficult situations, reorient your lives, and improve your personal relationships. And you'll see that there is always the possibility of a bit of sunshine behind the next cloud, even during the worst storms of your life. Thanks for reading.

~Amy Newmark

From Lemons to
Lemonade

From Victim to Victory

No Food for Alligators

A happy person is not a person in a certain set of circumstances,
but rather a person with a certain set of attitudes.
~Hugh Downs

freely admit that I am a Pollyanna. I look for rainbows after the storm. I point out silver linings. I am accused of having a perennial smile on my face, seeing the good in everyone, and sometimes being "annoyingly" happy. On most days, I live up to my reputation. And most days, I get the proverbial swamp drained even when I'm up to my eyeballs in alligators. But there are those days when the alligators are unrelenting, snapping at my every move. They lick their chops in anticipation of taking a bite out of my Pollyanna spirit. I remember one such day when they almost devoured me.

I was the homeroom mom for my son Colin's fifth grade class. It was the morning of the end-of-semester holiday party. Colin and I were loading the car with bags of porcelain cups filled with candies, teachers' gifts, and food and games for the party scheduled that afternoon. After several trips from the house to my car, I started one last time for the house to get my purse and keys. Upon turning on my prosthetic leg, I found myself falling forward and landing on my very cold cement driveway.

I rolled onto my side and sat up like a seasoned pro linebacker hardly realizing I was down. I spotted the lower half of my prosthesis, with my foot attached, three feet away from the rest of me. Colin was terrified that I had hurt myself and was on the verge of tears. I assured him that I was fine—it was one of those rare moments when I felt grateful for well-padded hips—and instructed him to get the rolling desk chair from my home office.

The words of my physical rehab doctor, "Cindy you will need to make friends with your wheelchair," were swimming around in my head. I had not made friends with my wheelchair, and in fact two years after becoming a bilateral below-the-knee amputee, I donated my wheelchair to an organization that was in desperate need of one. My office chair had to suffice.

With Colin and my neighbor's help, I got into the chair and was pushed to my car. I transferred myself into the seat right behind the steering wheel. Luckily, it was my left foot that broke. It was sitting on the passenger seat right next to me. My right foot was securely in place where it belonged, at the end of my right prosthetic leg working the gas and brake pedals.

When we arrived at school, I noticed one of my friends in the parking lot. I waved her over to my car.

"Can you help Colin take some bags into the school? I broke my foot this morning and can't get out of the car."

She gasped. But after I swept my arm across the passenger seat and pointed to my foot, Vanna White style, she began to laugh.

"Oh my gosh Cindy, I forgot that you don't have real feet."

We all laughed and agreed it could have been worse—a real broken foot.

I phoned Chris, the guy who makes my prosthetic limbs, on my cell phone and left a message asking—I may have sounded a little desperate—for his help.

"I need to be back at school this afternoon for the party," I explained.

I said a silent prayer that my leg could be fixed.

Boy the alligators are biting today, I thought as I started the engine to make the trek to Chris's office in downtown Denver.

When I turned my key, I found that I was riding on empty. Rolling my eyes, and shaking my head, I uttered a forlorn, "You've gotta be kidding!"

I then remembered that there was a service station only a few blocks from school with an attached auto repair garage. I hoped that it would be open, and that someone would be there to pump gas for me. It was still pretty early in the morning. Most businesses had not yet turned on their lights.

I drove into the station and up to the garage doors. The doors were closed, but I could see people moving around inside. I began to honk my horn. As I waited for a warm body to emerge, I tried to reach Chris again. Bingo! I got him on the second ring. He told me to come to his office as quickly as possible.

"Call me when you get here, and I'll meet you in the parking lot. I'm sure it will be an easy fix."

"Yes!" I pounded my fist on my dashboard. "Ha! The alligators haven't gotten me yet!"

I may have said these words out loud.

Finally, after several toots of the horn, a grouchy looking man emerged from the garage, obviously not thrilled to have been beckoned in such a rude manner. I rolled down my window, and began to explain that I had broken my foot earlier that morning and needed his assistance at the gas pump.

"You broke your foot?"

As he looked into my car, I once again swept my arm across my seat where my left foot sat. He looked down at my leg. His eyebrows went right up to his hairline. He literally laughed out loud.

"Well there's somethin' ya don't see every day."

On my way to Chris's office, I was listening to the radio and heard something that I felt compelled to impart to a friend... immediately. During our two-minute conversation, my phone died. I was out of battery power. I exhaled heavily, wondering how I was going to alert Chris to my arrival.

As I turned into his parking lot, Chris came out. He had been watching for me. He took my foot and the rest of my left leg into his office. Ten minutes later he emerged with my leg—foot attached. I put it on and hopped out of the car. He tweaked the alignment of the foot a bit, making sure that I was walking well. I left the parking lot, waving happily over my shoulder.

"Not on your menu today, alligators!"

I drove to the grocery store. Snow was predicted to start falling that evening, and by all accounts the storm was going to be a doozey. No one would go hungry at my house. After putting away my groceries, I sat down with a cup of coffee.

I looked up at the clock and started to laugh. It was not yet ten o'clock. I took stock of all the morning's events. If I had given in to those alligators at any point, I would have never been able to find the help I needed to get me back up on both (fake) feet.

I arrived at the party with time to spare. Colin's teacher could not believe that I had made it. I assured her that it would take more than a broken foot (and a swamp full of alligators) to keep me away from a good party.

~Cindy Charlton

Rescuing Myself

Follow your passion, and success will follow you.
~Terri Guillemets

Within two weeks of our wedding, I began noticing that my husband humiliated me in front of friends by criticizing or ridiculing everything I did. Nothing I did was good enough—his way was the only right way. When he criticized or ridiculed me, I thought it was because I had actually done something wrong. When he humiliated me, I believed I deserved it. I lost what little confidence I started with and I lived in fear of making mistakes. When chastisement turned into abuse, I told myself I was wholly to blame and prayed for guidance to mend my ways.

For our tenth anniversary, I cooked my husband's favorite meal and chilled a bottle of champagne, but my husband never came home from work. The following morning he called to say he had worked late and slept at the office rather than disturb me. I accepted his excuse. But when the nights away from home became more frequent, I began to question what was really happening.

One fall weekend, we went for a drive in the country to view the changing colors. I don't know if it was the crisp air or the beautiful sunlight but something gave me the strength to ask my husband if he was having an affair. It felt like a bomb went off in the car. My husband started yelling at me and pounding the steering wheel with his fists. When the back of his hand connected with my nose, I grabbed the door handle and attempted to open the door and jump from the moving car.

My life was in ruins and my twelve-year marriage was over. I spent several weeks pondering what to do. My options were few: I could stay with my husband and subject myself to further abuse; I could suggest we go to a marriage counselor, which I didn't think would work; I could file for divorce and try to pick up the pieces of my life. I had only one clear choice—divorce.

In order to assuage my husband's rage, I filed a "No-Fault" divorce and asked for nothing more than my clothes, a box of high school memorabilia and a beat-up car. It wasn't much but I knew I wouldn't need much as long as I was free. Surprisingly, my husband didn't oppose the divorce; in fact, I think it made life easier for him. On my own and almost penniless, I rented a small apartment, took a job as a receptionist and began my new life.

On and off during our marriage, I had tried my hand at writing. Whenever I asked my husband to read what I had written his response was always the same: "A third grader could do better." Fortunately, my desire to write hadn't dissolved like my marriage. I started writing short stories about nature, camping, and religion—things that were important to me. I spent a lot of time studying magazines to determine what kind of articles they printed and sent my work off to potential publishers. Although many of those stories were returned, some were published. Checks were few and far between but I was gaining confidence that I could actually do something right. I went to the library, checked out books about the mechanics of writing and submitted more pieces. I have now had five books published, and another is in the works.

My story isn't unique nor is it about writing. It's about what motivated me to write. Like many others, I allowed myself to be dominated and abused because I believed my husband had the right to treat me as he saw fit and because I thought I was inferior to him. Neither was true but it took a near disaster to wake me up to the reality of the situation.

For all those years, the signs of domestic violence had been obvious enough for me to see but, for whatever reason, I denied them. As long as I ignored my husband's abusive actions and infidelities, they didn't exist. If they didn't exist, they couldn't hurt me. But all of that backfired when I tried to jump out of the car.

Leaving my marriage was not an easy thing to do. I was psychologically beaten and physically threatened. I was confused, uncertain and torn. I hated my husband; I loved my husband. One moment I felt like running away; the other, all I wanted to do was stay and make things better.

Of course, not everyone is a writer, or an artist or an actor. But that's not what is important. Facing up to the facts and knowing there are ways out of situations like mine is what is important. When faced with verbal, mental or physical abuse, know that you are not alone, you are not at fault, you don't have to take it and there are things you can do to make your life better.

Writing was my path to rescuing myself. What's yours?

~Margaret Nava

Jane Doe No More

Courage is not the absence of fear, but rather the judgement that something else is more important than fear.
~Ambrose Redmoon

Life was good. My husband and I had been married for twelve years, had busy careers and were raising two young children, who were our world. Our lives changed in an instant in the wee hours of the morning on September 11, 1993.

My husband was away overnight for the first time in our marriage. I had taken our son and daughter, ages five and seven, to dinner and a children's concert earlier that evening; we were back home and fast asleep by 10:00 p.m. In the early morning hours, I awoke to the sound of footsteps in the hallway; when I opened my eyes, I saw a masked man entering my bedroom. The intruder tied my wrists and forcefully bound me. He cut my clothing with a knife, put a gun to my head, and raped me. Miraculously, he let me live and my children never woke.

In a matter of minutes, I went from unimaginable terror to survival instinct to immense gratitude. Gone were the days of taking things for granted. I was treated for a scratched cornea at the hospital, lacerations were noted on my wrists, and a sex crimes kit yielded DNA from the perpetrator. It was all a bit surreal, but I knew that I had so much to be grateful for: as long as I had survived and my children were untouched we were going to be okay. I have a strong faith in God, and with my loving husband by my side and the wonderful support of family and friends, I was back to work and well on my way to healing a few weeks after the crime. Little did I know that the worst days were still ahead.

In the weeks and months that followed, I was thrown into a world I knew nothing about. I quickly became aware of the stigmas associated with the crime of sexual assault—stigmas that even those sworn to protect and serve carried with them into the investigation of my assault. The re-victimization that I suffered at the hands of the officers initially in charge of my case was, in many ways, more damaging than the rape itself. You see, someone went to the lieutenant in charge of my case with a rumor—a vicious lie, actually—that changed the course of the investigation. Someone who knew nothing about me or the circumstances of my assault suggested to the lieutenant that I might have concocted the rape to cover up an illicit affair. And instead of investigating this rumor using standard, tested and mandated police protocols, the officer tried to break me emotionally, threatening me with arrest and everything I held dear unless I confessed to falsely reporting my rape. Though I had done nothing but tell the truth about this horrific event from the start, I was challenged and accused. I was left feeling frightened, ashamed, intimidated, and humiliated.

Through dogged persistence and the help of my incredible legal team, we saw the investigation turned over to a new team of officers. This team believed me; they gave me—and my family—the precious gift of hope. Amazingly, eleven years after the crime, my perpetrator was found through a DNA match. He was clearly a man leading a double life. To those who thought they knew him best, he was a happily married, church-going father of three. He was also a good friend of my husband's, and had been since they were in kindergarten. The betrayal my husband feels to this day is gut-wrenching. Even more maddening was the fact that the perpetrator could not be arrested for sexual assault in my case because a statute of limitations had run out.

This life-changing experience has taken me on a journey for justice, and challenged me in ways I never thought possible. I had to go from victim to warrior to survivor, something no one should have to do.

The experience awakened my passion to fight for meaningful and lasting change. There were, of course, difficult days when I felt I could not continue the fight. On those days, I reminded myself that every two minutes someone in this country is sexually assaulted, and that most victims are so very young—under the age of twenty-four. Something had to be done, and the more I learned about this misunderstood and under-reported crime the more passionate I became.

I channeled this passion into the 501c3 charity I founded in 2007: Jane Doe No More. At the same time, I made a very big, but important decision: I would come forward publicly, on national television, to put a name and a face on the crime of sexual assault. In every sense, I would be Jane Doe no more. In doing so, I hoped to break some of the stigmas that had compromised my case. I hoped that people would understand that sexual assault is a crime that does not discriminate. That victims come from all walks of life. That victims are our friends, our family, our neighbors. That there is no shame in being a victim. I became Jane Doe no more during a two-hour primetime piece on Dateline NBC. And at that time, I introduced my organization, Jane Doe No More, to the world.

To build Jane Doe No More, I sought help from the best and brightest people I knew. I wanted to create an organization that provides information and education to both sexual assault survivors and the community at large. That same year, I successfully advocated for a change in the law that had prevented my perpetrator from being charged with sexual assault: my case was the impetus for a governor's bill in the state of Connecticut that removed the statute of limitations on sexual assault cases involving DNA evidence.

Today, Jane Doe No More offers educational programs for college students, for law enforcement and other first responders, and for a wide-range of community organizations. We offer classes and support for survivors, engage in advocacy initiatives, and provide self-defense classes for women and girls. We have a staff and hundreds of volunteers that share my passion. Together we are improving the way society responds to victims of sexual assault. No more shame. No more blame. No more fear.

Looking back, I am grateful that something so tragic put me on a path to something wonderful—something that has become my life's work. I dared to dream big, to follow my moral compass, and to let God do the rest. I collaborated with M. William Phelps to tell the world my story in the book *Jane Doe No More*, published in 2012. The priceless gift of hope is shared freely in the pages of the book, and through the smiles, words of encouragement and acts of kindness of the hundreds that share my passion. Watching other victims gain confidence, hearing them find their voice, and ultimately seeing them become strong survivors has been awe-inspiring; it has carried me through my darkest days. As *Jane Doe No More* grows in strength and numbers, our collective voice gets louder. What started as a whisper, when I was barely able to speak, has grown to a roar. There is no stopping us now.

~Donna Palomba

The Return of My Son

Life is very interesting... in the end, some of your greatest pains,
become your greatest strengths.
~Drew Barrymore

t was late at night when I received the phone call from my neighbor about my son. "Travis is in an ambulance on the way to the hospital. He's been in an accident."

My one and only child was twenty-four.

"Is he all right? Is he hurt?"

I wanted to ask if he was alive, but dared not say that out loud.

I had lost Travis's father Danny in a car crash fourteen years earlier. It had devastated me. I couldn't lose my son too.

My neighbor's son was in the accident too, along with another young man, but they had minor injuries. Travis had been a passenger in the back seat.

"I'll drive over and pick you up," my neighbor offered. She knew I had night blindness and couldn't drive in the dark.

I prayed while I paced the floor and waited for her.

Please, God, let him be okay. Let him live.

When my neighbor arrived, I phoned my mother and nephew to let them know.

When I got to the emergency room, I wanted to see Travis immediately, but the doctors told me I had to wait.

Finally a doctor came out to talk to me. "He's being airlifted to the University of Kentucky Medical Center."

"Can I ride with him?"

"There isn't room. You'll have to follow by car."

I went with my mother and nephew to the University of Kentucky Medical Center. Metal from the car had cut Travis's face around his right eye, and he had over fifty stitches.

The injury would leave a scar, but he had full use of his vision and would otherwise recover.

The doctor sent him home with pain medication, and that's when I began to lose my son.

He took the medication as prescribed, because he was in a lot of pain from his injury. Not only was he dealing with the physical pain, but emotional pain from carrying a scar on his face, and PTSD from the crash.

He wore a wool cap low over his forehead to hide the scar, and refused to go outside at first.

He was always a very handsome guy who was attractive to girls, but one of those guys who didn't realize how handsome he really was. It wasn't vanity that kept him inside; it was self consciousness.

I told him nothing could change his beauty, because it comes from within. I told him all the things a mother could say to help her son, but he had his own way of dealing with it.

Little by little, the cap came off, and he began to go outside.

His PTSD wasn't noticeable until he rode as a passenger in someone's car. He cringed or looked away whenever he passed by the site of the accident, and he became so agitated and tense at the way other people drove that he told them when to apply the brakes, turn on the signal, speed up, or slow down.

"It's normal for you to feel this way," I told him gently. "Do you think some counseling would help?"

"No," he replied quietly. "I know I overreact. It's just something I have to work out myself."

But his way of working it out was with prescription pain medication, funded by his insurance money. I didn't know this at the time.

Travis has a big heart and isn't very materialistic, so I naively thought he was spending his money on other people, because he bought his family and friends nice gifts. Week by week he bounced back, but he wasn't the son I had known before the accident. This new version of Travis was secretive, sullen, temperamental, and distant. He lived with me at the time, so his personality changed right in front of me. I attributed it to PTSD, not pills.

Then one day he came to me and asked for money. "You know I'm on a budget," I reminded him. He didn't say anything, but started selling off the things he'd purchased with his insurance money — TV, computer, game system, DVD player, DVD and CD collections, even shoes and clothes. I knew something was wrong, but I hadn't figured out what.

He continued to act in uncharacteristic ways: being gone for days at a time with friends, holing up in his room, and avoiding conversations with me.

And then one evening I went into his room and was surprised to find him packing clothes into a suitcase.

"What's up?" I asked innocently. It looked as though he were packing to stay with a friend.

He closed the flap and buckled it.

Matter-of-factly he said, "Look around, Mom. I've sold everything I have. I don't have anything left."

I didn't have to look around. I knew his room was almost empty except for a bed, a sofa, and a computer desk.

He continued quietly, "I'm on pills and I'm going to detox."

The truth nearly knocked me down. Why didn't I see it? So many emotions ran through me — pain, guilt, shame, sympathy, anger — but the most powerful was love.

I walked up to him, my son of six feet two inches, and reached up and hugged him, pulling him down to sit on his bed next to me. I held him in my arms and rocked him a little, and we both cried.

"I love you," I whispered. "I'm so proud of you."

His decision to go to detox was as sudden as his accident.

I was astonished at his honesty and courage.

"I'm here for you," I told him. "I'll do all I can to help you. I can't be there with you physically, but you already know I'm with you in spirit."

I had watched the TV show *Intervention* many times, never dreaming that my own son would be in the same type of situation.

So, having been a social worker, and still his mother, I arranged for my mother and nephew to phone him that very minute to encourage him to go and let him know they were behind him too.

When he got off the phone with them and picked up his suitcase to meet his ride to detox, Travis smiled at me and said, "So you made your own little intervention, huh?"

I smiled back. "Well, sort of."

He gave me a goodbye hug and went outside to catch his ride.

My son's return wasn't without a hitch. Travis relapsed once and started using prescription medication again, but was determined to get clean once and for all. So, with another effort, he finally managed to stop using and he has been clean ever since.

~Tammy Ruggles

Making the Change

Reach high, for stars lie hidden in your soul.
Dream deep, for every dream precedes the goal.
~Pamela Vaull Starr

t was mid-April and cooler than normal for Florida, which meant the A/C unit wasn't running. That left the apartment very quiet that night. I was awakened by a noise coming from the living room at 2:30 in the morning. I looked next to me to find an empty spot where my husband should be and found the cat sleeping on his pillow. I slid out of bed to check and make sure what I heard was him and not something else. As I opened the bedroom door and headed down the hallway to the living room, I could sense something wasn't right. The closer I got to the living room, the more an overwhelming feeling of dread came over me.

When I looked into the living room, a rush of emotion hit all at once. Disbelief at first, followed by disgust with a side of betrayal topped off with a big scoop of heartache. There in our living room I found my husband naked, on all fours, searching for his crack rock. It was happening all over again. I stood there watching him as he searched in the carpet and under the couch cushions for his precious drug. I stood there thinking, "What have I done? Why is this happening? Why did I put myself back in the situation?" I didn't say a word; I just slowly and quietly backed away from the living room and went back to bed. I realized that this was never going to end; he wasn't going to change, so I had to.

A few days later, I left my husband for the last time; I packed what I could and left twenty years of my life behind. It wasn't easy to do. I had to move back in with my mother, with no money, no job, and no car. I had nothing except some clothes and a few personal items to my name.

After living in Mississippi for almost a year, unable to find work and with my unemployment running out, my future looked pretty bleak. I was becoming more depressed every day, second-guessing my decision of leaving my husband. I started to think or "convince," myself that maybe my old life wasn't so bad. I had my own home and a job. Now I lived with my mother in a rural area with no public transportation and no jobs.

I went to the job center, as I had so many times since I arrived, and I learned I could receive help to go back to school. I had heard my sister-in-law's lawyer tell her if she went to school and obtained her degree as a paralegal, he would hire her to work at his firm. She was in the middle of a real estate dispute. I had helped her do much of the research to save her some money, and her attorney said we did a good job. She wasn't interested in his offer, but it made me think that I could do this. I had always been interested in law. I felt that I was too old to go to law school and become a lawyer, but I could certainly work for one.

That's what I did, with a little research and help from the job center. I filled out a federal aid grant application, took an entry exam at Northeast Community College, and a few months later I was enrolled in the paralegal program. I started to feel better about myself, like I had a purpose again. After my first year, I had learned enough to draw up and file my own divorce, which cost me a fraction of what most lawyers charge. Within sixty days I was divorced and moving on with my life. I have since met a wonderful man who accepts me for me, who encourages me instead of discouraging me, and who after months of dating says he loves me… for just being me.

~Elaine Cartwright

6

Abandoning Anger

Forgiveness does not change the past,
but it does enlarge the future.
~Paul Boese

"Forgive and forget," Mother always said. I thought I was forgiving. It took more energy to be angry than it did to just get over it.

Then I adopted Kurtis—the most severely abused child to survive in the United States at the time. With hair the color of Rumpelstiltskin's spun gold, eyes like warm caramel and skin the texture of silk, it was hard to imagine what crime this angelic toddler could have committed to warrant such violent abuse. At fifteen months of age, he had been hit over the head with a chair for not cleaning his plate. He had been placed naked on hot stove burners and dipped in boiling water for soiling his diaper. The abuse took place at the hands of a biological uncle who had adopted him and become his father.

The burns left large, red, itchy keloid scars on his buttocks, legs and back.

The traumatic brain injury left him totally blind, deaf and paralyzed on the left side until swelling was released in his skull. Kurtis was comatose for eight weeks. The right side of his brain was damaged to the extent that it didn't provide enough stimulation for growth to his left arm and leg. One month before his second birthday he functioned at the level of a nine-month-old.

My nursing background made me a good candidate to adopt Kurtis. As much as I understood his medical history and rehabilitation needs, I knew there would be challenges ahead for him emotionally and socially. I recognized his disabilities and, at times, they overwhelmed me. I believed if Kurtis grew up angry, anger would be the biggest disability of all. My job was to teach him to forgive his abuser.

My life changed the day Kurtis moved into our home. During the first four days, I just enjoyed his presence. I worked at exercising his left foot and ankle the way his foster mother had shown me. I rubbed vitamin E oil on his buttocks and legs in an attempt to smooth out the ugly burn scars. He tried learning to walk. His heavy leg brace banged against the ornately carved wood of my Victorian antiques. I replaced the antiques with plain, functional furniture. I left plenty of space for gross motor development activities between furnishings. Mostly, I just let his wounded spirit meld with ours—his five-year-old sister Tina's, his father's and mine.

On Monday, I had to start locating resources to deal with the complex issues ahead. The phone had not been installed in our new country home. While Tina was in school, I loaded Kurtis into the child safety seat in the Jeep Cherokee we had purchased to travel the mountain roads, and headed into town. We first stopped at the pediatrician's office where I told Kurtis's story and made an appointment. The pediatrician referred us to our next stop... Easter Seals. They were the resource to provide Kurtis's physical therapy. I filled out numerous forms and told Kurtis's story. Easter Seals sent me to the local ophthalmologist and orthopedic surgeon. We were also set up with a home teacher who would stop by the house on Thursday to get acquainted. At the eye doctor, I told Kurtis's story again and scheduled an appointment. Three times I told Kurtis's story and he listened in. People's responses were a mixture of horror and disbelief. I knew this was not the way for Kurtis to learn forgiveness.

By the time we pulled into the parking lot of the orthopedic surgeon, Kurtis was worn out. Everything in his environment, including me, was new. I had lifted him in and out of the car seat numerous times and carried him into unfamiliar places with strange people. He was heavy. I was tired. We both needed lunch and a nap.

A few minutes before noon, I sat Kurtis down on the green Formica countertop. The familiar alcohol smell hung in the air. The waiting room was mercifully empty and so quiet it seemed my footsteps echoed off the gray slate flooring. Soon, the receptionist stepped to the window and asked how she could help me. Tears started to flow down my cheeks. "I just adopted this little boy. He has this brace on his leg and I don't know what to do," I managed to get out between sobs. My nurse's training abandoned me and left me just a mom.

So quickly, it seemed she had been transported, the receptionist appeared at my side, took Kurtis in her arms and led us to an exam room in the back. "The doctor will see you now," she said. I had not filled out a form or even given my name. It was then I realized everyone should be at lunch, but they were making time to see us—a small, blond, fragile child with leg braces and his desperate, teary-eyed mother.

Again, I told Kurtis's story. The doctor reacted with outrage and anger saying, "If I were your husband I would be out hunting this guy down with a gun."

For the first time, I found the courage to say, "We don't feel that way. We don't want Kurtis to grow up with hate and anger. We think those would be the biggest disabilities of all."

Over the next few years Kurtis had many painful surgeries. He endured ongoing mistreatment, injustice and ridicule from classmates. His schedule was filled with therapy and doctors' appointments. I deplored the abuse Kurtis suffered and the disabilities it left him with. I made excuses for his abuser; he was an abused child; his wife had adopted Kurtis while he was overseas; he asked for help from the military and was turned away. All the while, for Kurtis's sake, I kept stuffing my own anger back down inside where I tried convincing myself it had vanished. I said I wasn't angry, so, I wasn't angry... right?

This was our life: doctors' appointments and therapy in town on Mondays and Wednesdays, doctors' appointments in Reno and Sacramento on Tuesdays and Thursdays. On Fridays, I worked in Tina's classroom so she would not feel left out.

One afternoon, when Kurtis was eight, he looked up from his playing and said, "Mom, do you think you can find the man that hurt me?"

Kurtis's request took me by surprise. I wondered if I located the abuser if I could be as forgiving as I wanted Kurtis to be. "I think I can, Kurtis. Why do you want to find him?" I asked. While I waited for his response, I searched my soul and found the feelings of anger that had once churned within my gut were gone. A peace had filled me instead of hatred. Kurtis, Tina, their father and I were family—forever. This was my life. It was good.

Kurtis' answer confirmed my thoughts. "I want to tell him I'm okay."

~Karen R. Hessen

Learning to Fly

If you're going to be able to look back on something and laugh about it,
you might as well laugh about it now.
~Marie Osmond

Life is not remembered in days, it is remembered in moments. There are embarrassing moments we would like to forget, and spectacular moments we always want to remember. This momentous day held a little bit of both.

May 19th, 1990, dawned bright and clear. Spring, with the flowers blooming and the sweet song of the birds overhead, usually holds the promise of new beginnings. However, for me on that day, a phase of my life was ending as well. That was the day I graduated from Emporia State University with my bachelor's degree in English, and a minor in Creative Writing.

The ceremony was to be held on the football field. Seats were set up for the graduating class on the grass, while family, friends and other spectators overflowed from their designated section in the stadium. My proud family had traveled from out of state to see me graduate.

A few weeks beforehand, the Director of Disabled Student Services had asked me if I would like to have someone push my wheelchair up the ramp onto the stage for the ceremony. Because the field was often wet, and I am not strong enough to push myself on soft surfaces, I gratefully accepted his offer. It was a perfect plan. Well, almost.

I asked my good friend Carolyn to do the honors. For the two years I had known her, I had observed her caring and generosity on countless occasions. Even though she wasn't actually graduating for another semester, she agreed to put on a cap and gown so that she would "fit in" while helping me through the ceremony.

It started off without a hitch. A folding chair was removed at the end of a row of graduates, and my wheelchair fit into the space nicely. The commencement address was appropriately inspiring; the speaker encouraged us to work hard and dream big, to remember our goals and not get lost in the details. Although the speech dragged on a bit, I was amused by the seniors. Several graduates had written massages in masking tape on their caps, "THANX PA" and "I HAVE A JOB" dotted the crowd.

Finally, the procession for the diplomas began. My fellow graduates glided effortlessly up the stairs and across the stage in their gowns. They smiled briefly for the cameras, and returned to their seats to the spontaneous cheers from their supporters.

At last it was my turn. Carolyn began pushing me across the field toward the ramp and the stage. The grass was a little bumpy, and it slowed us down. The gap between me and the flowing gown in front of me widened more and more. We both felt the eyes of the crowd. Then, within three yards of the safety of the ramp, one wheel sank deep into an unlikely rut on the edge of a low spot.

Oh yes! I took a nosedive into the deceptively green grass that actually covered a mud hole at the end of the stage. My gown was covered with mud. The cold wetness soaked through to my skin as I lay there in front of the whole crowd. Humiliated! Embarrassed! I couldn't believe it. Was this really happening? No way!

Time stood still. Quickly, my assessment began. Was I hurt? No, not physically. Were people staring? Yes. Everyone. Even though my disability had desensitized me to stares to a certain extent, on this day, in this moment, I had expected positive attention celebrating my victory. Not this. I vaguely fantasized about hitting the rewind button and doing the whole thing over.

Suddenly, I heard my name over the PA system. There was a long pause, followed by a flurry of activity. The gap in front of me now extended to the podium, and even those exiting the stage had turned and could see my muddy spectacle. Almost instantly, several ushers rushed to get me back into my wheelchair. Although they were well intentioned, I just wanted to be left alone to settle and adjust myself. Somehow, the cushion I was supposed to sit on ended up behind my back and the foot pedals on my wheelchair were backwards. Carolyn kept apologizing. I dusted myself off, both literally and figuratively, the best I could and continued on the trek to receive my diploma with as much poise as I could possibly muster. Maybe the crowd clapped for me, too. Honestly, I cannot remember.

In the minutes that followed, I realized that I had a choice to make. Part of me wanted nothing more than to leave my pride on the ground where I fell, and sink into the black hole of negative thoughts. On the other hand, I knew I could choose to move on, focusing on the humor instead of the humiliation. I could look at what happened as a tragedy or a triumph. Whatever choice I made would color the memory of my college graduation for years to come. There was only one way for me to go.

At the conclusion of the ceremony, Carolyn was not finished apologizing. With an endless chorus of "I am so sorry I ruined your graduation!" she seemed to think that her repetitions might erase what happened.

But that wasn't what I wanted to do. With a conscious decision and perspective, I reassured her. "Are you kidding me? I must have been the subject of about 500 conversations today! How many other people can say that? It was awesome! Hilarious, even! You couldn't possibly script stuff like this. I won't ever forget it, and I'm sure lots of other people won't either."

I gave her a big hug. It really was okay.

I learned many things in college about academics, friends, and my own independence.

Unfortunately, I didn't learn how to fly. Or did I?

~Lorraine Cannistra

New Vision

Beauty is how you feel inside, and it reflects in your eyes.
It is not something physical.
~Sophia Loren

At fifteen years old, a teenager growing up in 1980s Africa, I was as confident as they get at that age. I possessed self-esteem in bucket loads; I had the looks and the attitude, was very smart and opinionated and didn't suffer fools gladly. I was determined to set my own pace and people had better be ready to keep up; it was my way or the highway!

You see I had it going on: parents who cared, siblings whom I loved and friends with whom I enjoyed life. I loved going to school and loved more coming home at the end of each day. Unbeknownst to me, my secure world was about to come crashing down around me.

My transformation started in the kitchen, the one place where I never liked to spend any time. One minute I was trying to get the bottled gas to work, the next: Boom! From nowhere a fire exploded in my face. I fumbled in the dark, trying to navigate the flame-engulfed kitchen, praying that I was the only one in the room. No one else deserved to suffer the consequences of my carelessness and disobedience. After all, hadn't our mother always warned us to be careful not to bring any kind of naked flame into the kitchen where the bottled gas would feed off it? Unfortunately, I had minutes before I dragged my younger brother, by the scruff of his neck, into the kitchen with me. We managed to attract the attention of neighbours who came to our rescue, helped to douse the fire and arranged emergency medical attention. Although we survived the fire, the damage, for me, was permanent.

Within a month, I went from a beautiful teenager with flawless skin to a shrivelled-up old lady, at least that was who I saw looking back at me in the mirror. I had aged decades and now had physical scars on my face and hands. How was I expected to look the world in the face without feeling ugly? How was I expected to shake hands with people with my scarred hands? How could I go back to school and face the other students?

I spent most of my time in the hospital reflecting, wondering what sort of life I would go on to have. I remembered how my friends and I used to make fun of the physical appearance of others and wondered if I would still have any friends left. My family might be able to express the same love they had before the fire, but I doubted that my friends would be gracious enough to tolerate amongst them one not so perfect-looking. I should know! Eventually, I withdrew into myself, turned my thoughts inward, and was convinced that life didn't matter anymore. I just couldn't see past the physical. I struggled to imagine what good could come out of this most painful experience. I was only fifteen!

The tables had turned. I used to stare unkindly at people with my friends and now I would be the object of people's stares! How was I expected to survive in a world that judged people mostly on their physical appearance, where any kind of disfigurement was tacitly considered to be grounds for social exclusion? The worst part was that there was nothing I could do about it. Actually there was—I could either hide away from the world by becoming reclusive, or I could reclaim my life, go out and stare the world back in the face. Being a self-conscious teenager, I of course chose the former approach, initially. I hid from the world.

After several months of persuasion I decided to try the second approach, if only to get my mother off my back. I agreed to go back to school and complete my secondary education, albeit without the dedication I had exhibited prior to the fire incident. For a fifteen-year-old, it was pretty hard going. I found it difficult to raise my head and look people in the face. I was scared that I would only see pity or disdain in people's eyes. I was right. Some people stared at me and shook their heads in pity, some looked away as if in disgust at the disfigurement, trying not to let their eyes meet mine; some others saw the colour patchwork on my skin (that's what it looked like in the early stages) and concluded that it was a result of a botched attempt to bleach my skin white! Oh the emotional pain of it all.

With time I gained strength and confidence, and began to gradually lift my head up and look people in the face again. My self-esteem improved when I came to the realization that I first had to learn to accept myself if I wanted to be accepted by others. Once past this hurdle I grew stronger and was able to find myself again. Instead of wanting to hide from the world, my presence and demeanour forced the world to pay attention to and take notice of the person behind the scars. So I snatched victory from the jaws of defeat and formed one of the tenets of my life that states: "nobody can put you down without your permission." I completely withdrew the tacit permission I had given the world. I got my groove back!

That near-fatal experience changed me completely and forever. Suddenly, I started to see beauty with new eyes. Not because my physical eyes had been improved by the fire, but because my inner, spiritual eyes had gained better vision and perspective. Now, more than three decades later I am a more gracious adult. Who would have thought that such a painful experience could turn out to be a force for liberation?

~Tope Songonuga

All's Well That...
You Know

All misfortune is but a stepping stone to fortune.
~Henry David Thoreau

Ten years ago I picked up a monthly newspaper on community games, at the grocery store. Having been raised in a household of five brothers, I am a sports fanatic. As I sat down with a coffee to read up on the different events, I noticed an ad stating the paper was in need of a sports writer.

Up to that point I had had little success as a writer, having sold an essay here and there to smaller publications with what little free time I had as a mom of four young children. On a whim I e-mailed my résumé to the sports editor. Three weeks later I was on assignment.

I had never done an interview before, but I've always loved asking questions. My first assignment was the local ladies' curling team. When I entered the rink with my half dozen questions on an index card, I found the curlers were grateful to have any publicity whatsoever. They were prepared to tell me anything.

My second assignment was a dream come true—to talk with Martin Biron, who was then back-up goalie for the Buffalo Sabres. Once I cornered him in the locker room, Biron couldn't have been sweeter. Brand new to the pros, he was thrilled to be interviewed.

I wrote for that paper for four months. Every month I would invoice them for my three or four articles. No response. Every month

I would call to see if something was wrong with my work and I would hear a song and dance about advertisers not paying up, but the check would be in the mail soon. The paper eventually folded and the owner/editor disappeared.

Thankfully I was able to rewrite my article on Biron and sell it to another publication for five times what that first paper would have paid, if it actually had paid. And I was able to use the springboard of my first "paying" job to get assignments from other local papers. I was off and running.

For all of his sleaziness, the editor of that defunct paper did me a huge favor. He got me inside the Sabres' locker room. I not only met Biron but also their media representative, who allowed me re-entrance to the arena at the beginning of the next season. I interviewed Curtis Brown, who was playing well, and I sold the resulting article to an international sports magazine. From there, I discovered I could get other media reps from other teams on the phone, who in turn, once they heard that I'd interviewed other NHLers, connected me with their player of choice for some exposure.

While my first editor lacked integrity, he made up for it by offering me experience, confidence and contacts, which are priceless. I've been happily asking questions ever since.

~Jayne Thurber-Smith

From Abandoned to Attorney

Goals are dreams with deadlines.
~Diana Scharf Hunt

t was one of those smoldering July afternoons, with the temperature pushing 100 degrees. At five o'clock I was in the kitchen, as usual, preparing dinner for my family. Then eight and a half months pregnant with our third child, I was hot and miserable.

As I stirred the vegetables, I heard the happy squeal of my three-year-old daughter greeting my husband as he walked in the house from work.

"Hi there!" he greeted me a few seconds later, placing a kiss on my forehead as he opened the fridge and popped the top of a beer. "How are you feeling today?"

"Hot and pregnant," I replied with as much of a smile as I could muster.

After listening to his daughter chatter on about her day for a few minutes, I heard him say, "Why don't you go play in the back yard with your brother; I need to talk to your mom."

"Okay," she replied, happily skipping out the door.

I turned to face him, wiping my hands on a dishtowel. "What's up?" I asked.

"Come sit down," he invited and I joined him at the kitchen table. "I've met someone."

"What do you mean you've met someone?"

"Last weekend, when I was at the lake with my friends, I met this girl. I realized I am not really into this whole own a home and have a family thing. She has an apartment and says I can move in, so I am going to pack a bag of my clothes now. She's waiting for me. I'll come back for other stuff once we decide how to divide our property."

I just sat there and stared at him in disbelief as tears started to flow down my face. This had to be a joke. I had been very content with having two children, a boy and a girl, but Mark had begged me to have just one more. I had acquiesced, if we could have another child before I turned thirty-five. So here I was two weeks from the delivery of that child, three months from turning thirty-five, and he wanted out.

"But you were the one who wanted this baby," I stammered.

"Well, I've changed my mind," he said matter-of-factly as he rose and went upstairs to pack his clothes.

The next minutes are still a blur. I remember Mark walking down the stairs with his bag, getting in his truck and heading down our small, quiet residential street. I remember the humiliation of me running out the door and chasing his truck down the block in my bare feet screaming for him to come back, with all of our neighbors looking on in disbelief. But he never came back.

I survived those next days, but I'm not sure how. Two weeks later, I delivered a healthy, wonderful baby girl; a month after that, Mark and his new girlfriend left town in the middle of the night to parts unknown.

I had grown up as a child of the 1950s and 60s, my mother and all of her friends were highly educated, stay-at-home moms. It was all I ever wanted to be. Despite the fact that I graduated at the top of my high school class and had always gotten straight A's, I was happy to quit college after two years to get married and become a mom. Since my marriage, I had helped my husband with the bookkeeping for his business and waitressed part-time to bring in some extra cash. Now, all of a sudden, I was left with three kids, no hope of child support, and no way of supporting us. I needed a plan, fast!

I did much soul searching about what I wanted to be, besides a wife and mother. After much thought and prayer, I realized that I had always been fascinated with the law; surely I could support my kids and myself as a lawyer. I did some research and calculated that I could go back to college part-time, finish my degree in three years and then go to three years of law school. We could survive on student loans, and in just six years I would be an attorney.

I enthusiastically broached the subject with family members, friends and co-workers, and got less than enthusiastic responses. "What?" they all said. "You can't do that; you would be forty-one years old before you became a lawyer. You should go back and get a teaching degree or something similar that will only take a couple of years." The trouble was, I didn't want to be a teacher. I wanted to be a lawyer, but after hearing the same thing over and over, I started to doubt myself. Then one day, I repeated my desire and the responses I'd gotten to a wonderful friend, who also happened to be a therapist. I'll never forget what she told me.

"It's true that if you do this, you won't be a lawyer until you are forty-one, but in six years you will be a forty-one-year-old lawyer! If you don't do it, in six years you will be a forty-one-year-old waitress."

My mind was made up and I plowed ahead. Three years later, I graduated *summa cum laude* from our hometown college with a degree in political science. That fall I packed up and moved out of state with my now thirteen-, seven- and four-year-old children to attend the University of Nebraska College of Law. Those three years of law school flew by as I juggled parenting and studying. You could frequently find me on the sidelines of a soccer game, cross country or track meet, playing law tapes through headphones, while cheering on my kids. I discovered the true meaning of "it takes a village" as many amazing friends and neighbors stepped up to help me parent.

One of the proudest moments of my life was walking across that stage on a May afternoon almost exactly six years after that fateful afternoon, and receiving my law degree as the song "One Moment in Time" by Whitney Houston silently played in my head.

That fall, after moving back home to Colorado and passing the bar exam, I began my career in a law firm as an associate attorney. Now, almost twenty years later, I have my own law firm and the satisfaction of having helped countless women, men and children get through the difficult divorce process as painlessly as possible. I have also watched my children grow into happy, well-adjusted adults. What had seemed like the end of my world at the time has turned into a blessing for myself, my children and all of those I have been able to help along the way.

~Jill Haymaker

Chapter
2

From Lemons to
Lemonade

From Rat Race to
Relationships

We Make Our Own Choices

The trouble with learning to parent on the job is that your child is the teacher.
~Robert Brault

Many years ago, I had a busy health care practice and was commuting two hours a day. I didn't get to spend much time with my family. At the time, our son Gabriel was almost three, and our other son Noah was nine months old. In addition to the practice and the young family, I was president of my professional association. Life was very busy.

Colleagues looked upon me with respect, asking, "How do you do it all?" Well, "it all" was about to collapse around me. My wife had suffered postpartum depression after Gabriel's birth and after Noah's it was even more severe. I ignored the clues that things weren't going well for her. I was busy, so I encouraged her to stay positive, read inspirational books, eat well, and exercise. I was so committed to my work that I dismissed her concerns, expecting her to make do.

When my wife admitted herself to hospital, the medical staff suggested she stay over the weekend for further evaluation. I didn't voice my protest, but I was thinking about the professional work I had to do.

After the weekend, I met with the medical staff and my wife. I listened quietly as they described that my wife needed to be admitted for several weeks. I defiantly told the psychiatrist that "you do not know my wife... she's not depressed!" Somehow I remained oblivious to my own observations and concerns regarding what I had seen and heard at home over many months.

I encouraged my wife to resist, believing the psychiatrist "crazy" for wanting to institutionalize her. I secretly panicked over missing my work and not meeting my financial obligations. The psychiatrist persisted, and stated my wife would not be free to leave until she was feeling better.

I remember the long walk down the overpass to the hospital parking lot. The children were with me and were quite fatigued from being at the hospital during their naptime. I still couldn't believe what was happening. I tried to remain calm for my older son, Gabriel, stating that Mommy had to stay with the doctors for a little while.

Later, when my mother joined us, I broke down. I cried for days—unusual because all my life I had concealed my emotions. I had developed great defiance towards a bullying father and refused to show vulnerability. Now, I couldn't hold back my feelings.

I arranged for all my appointments to be cancelled until further notice, and I made arrangements to take a leave of absence from the board of directors. I felt very alone for several days, crying whenever I had a short break from the all-encompassing duties of caring for our children. We visited my wife in hospital and I felt a deep ache in my gut every time we had to say goodbye.

My good friend Scott listened to my shock and despair. "How will I get through this?" I asked. "You have to... you have no choice," he compassionately replied.

Before this incident, I'd never been alone with the children for more than eight hours at a time. Now, I was their primary caretaker. Noah had still been breastfeeding, so we had to wean him onto a formula during my wife's hospitalization. This meant I had to awake in the night to feed him, change him, and care for both of them... all things my wife had done before.

I struggled to learn new skills, but over time I gained confidence as I realized I could care for my children. I actually enjoyed being home and spending time with them. My mother was a great help, and afforded me time here and there to go for walks to ruminate on my situation and process my feelings. I was beginning to understand and appreciate how challenging my wife's role had been.

The hospital visits were rough. My wife expressed anger over my former absences due to my professional pursuits. I was angry over the upheaval of my life. The social worker and hospital staff helped us to express our emotions and heal as we experienced many painful feelings.

I remember the day that was the turning point, when my hope was renewed. I realized that life had not stopped, but was in fact evolving for us. My wife had been in the hospital for about three weeks at this point, and I was playing outside with my older son. As we climbed atop a huge rock, Gabriel said "Daddy…"

"Yes, Gabriel." I turned to look at him, and was absolutely captivated by the young brown eyes that seemed far older and experienced than the boy that held them. As I gazed into these brown eyes, Gabriel said, "Daddy… we make our own choices."

I stared in disbelief. How could a boy so young say something so profound? I responded, "What… what did you say, Gabriel?" He realized my surprise and laughed with glee. He said again, "We make our own choices!"

The full impact of this message did not resonate within me at the time. I was not expecting to hear such words from a boy not yet three. But as I relayed the story to friends and family, I understood the clear message.

I was justifying my long hours and professional position as being best for the family. I realized my family had not been my first priority, but instead my status, prestige and desire for more material things were. I would have to change if I wanted to experience the home life I desired, and that my family deserved.

My new experience showed me I could be a competent and loving father and husband, and that I could miss several weeks of work without financial disaster. I made the decision to choose balance and happiness. I learned to let go of things that seemed important, but in the final analysis were not.

My life has far greater integrity now, and people no longer ask me "How do you do it all?" My wife is strong and vibrant, and the happiest I've ever seen her in our marriage together. The boys recognize the stability in our family, and are confident, healthy, and loving. I am aware that every day I make my own choices.

It may be interesting to note that the name Gabriel translates into "messenger of God." And on that sunny day in February many years ago, for me... he was.

~Donald Quinn Dillon

The Gift of Limitations

It is possible at any age to discover a lifelong desire you never knew you had.
~Robert Brault

loved my business more than anything. I was twenty-one years old and so proud when I opened my first hair salon. Being a hairstylist allowed me to do everything I enjoyed: I was able to meet and talk with people on a daily basis; I got to be creative; and I had the opportunity to help people feel better about themselves. I was very lucky to do what made my heart sing.

My days were so fulfilling and fun that I never felt like I was at work. My co-workers and clients had become like family to me and that made the atmosphere in the salon feel like home. There was always someone to laugh and share stories with. It's where I gave and got support.

So when I had to give up my salon because of a health crisis, my whole world turned upside down. I felt like I was living someone else's life, because I couldn't wrap my brain around what had transpired. I had always had a bad back, and at thirty-eight years old it got so bad that I needed surgery to repair a fractured disk. The surgery didn't go well and life as I previously knew it came to a screeching halt. After the surgery, I felt as if I had entered another person's body. It certainly didn't feel like mine. I wasn't sure how to navigate this new life with many limitations.

Doing anything physical was out of the question. I could no longer work. I couldn't walk, stand, or sit for any length of time because of the chronic pain. I missed my clients and co-workers. Losing them was like losing friends and family. I missed being a productive part of society. I missed having a purpose, and most of all I missed me — the me I used to be. I soon realized that my entire identity was wrapped up in my career, and without it I didn't know who I was.

I kept asking myself, "How can I incorporate all that I am and all that I still love into this new life that's filled with so much limitation?" I had to learn how to embrace this new way of living. What was once a full and active life had turned into one filled with silence. There were no more clients, and no more co-workers. It was just me, alone with my thoughts and prayers.

After years of struggling with chronic pain and the losses that came from that, I noticed things had started to change. Good things were happening. Even though I could no longer work outside my house, I discovered I could work on myself, which was something I never had the time to do when I had a career. My identity as a hair salon owner had become a thing of the past but I found that being a wife, a loyal friend, and a writer not only fit me better but captured me at my core.

I started a journal. After writing in it for a few months, I realized I had something to say and that I could possibly write for others. Inspiring people had been a constant in my life and at the heart of everything I loved to do. Even with my physical problems, I found a new venue that would allow me to do what I loved most.

I hadn't lost myself after all. In fact, I was coming into my own. I realized I didn't need my hair salon to feel valuable or give me a sense of identity. I started to understand that my purpose couldn't be extinguished.

I still missed the group dynamic in my salon, where my clients confided in me and trusted me with their personal stories of love and loss, triumphs and defeats. I watched their children grow up, their marriages fall apart, and everything in between. They taught me so much about life. Having them share with me on a personal level was what I liked best about my career. So I thought a new group of people would fill that void.

I had a lot of single friendships but I didn't have a group. Out of the blue I heard from an old friend who I hadn't seen in over thirty years, and she invited me to go to lunch with a bunch of old high school friends. We all turned fifty the year I joined the group, and it was just what we all needed at just the right time in our lives. We get together often. Our time together is filled with laughter and support that's rich with a history of having known each other from our youth. It's become an extended family for all of us. It's a treasured part of my life that gives me far more joy than any job could.

Most importantly, in the midst of my transformation, my marriage became better because I have more time to devote to my husband. He tells me, "I like you better now. You're kinder than you used to be. And now you have time to cook!" My career had taken all my energy in my prior life, and once it was gone, I was able to focus my attention where it really mattered. My marriage has become a gift of such enormity that I feel blessed beyond words to have been given the opportunity to realize that.

I found that when I could no longer chase after my old life, all the right things had a chance to chase after me. What I originally thought was a limitation turned out to be an answer. My true desires had been buried under the demands of a career. Now without it, I'm able to see what really matters.

It took a major life change to get my attention but now I have what I wanted all along—a life of substance and purpose. It's a life that matters. The old me that I thought was lost forever had just been waiting for the real me to catch up. I finally have all my heart's desires and carry a deep expectation for my life to continue unfolding in more wonderful ways than I can imagine.

~Marijo Herndon

Riding Out the Storm

A successful marriage requires falling in love many times,
always with the same person.
~Mignon McLaughlin,
The Second Neurotic's Notebook, 1966

My ten-year-old son said it best: "Mom, I know Hurricane Katrina was a bad thing. But I never had so much fun with my family." We live an hour north of New Orleans. Where the city got flooding, we in the country got tornadoes—an estimated two hundred twisters that spun off from the hurricane, taking down hundreds of thousands of trees, blocking roads, obliterating power lines that took more than a month to repair, and making towns like our little country village inaccessible for days.

We found ourselves barricaded in our home and, even after we were able to make it outdoors, found our quarter-mile-long driveway covered by a horizontal forest of pine trees. So there we sat. We had no electricity, no running water. What we did have was each other. Evenings that would have involved my husband, David, watching TV, me fiddling on the computer and the kids doing various solo activities had us huddled together by candlelight talking and laughing (and swatting mosquitoes and doctoring the scraps and cuts we sustained trying to hack our way to freedom). David and I told the kids stories from our childhoods and taught them games we'd played when we were their age.

Without the distractions of civilization, my eyes were opened to the blessings in my life—not the least of which is a very capable and devoted husband. It was in those days after the storm that a long overdue metamorphosis in my marriage began.

It began in a hallway where we spent nine hours clinging to each other while listening to the storm rage around us. Something happens when we fear for our lives. When life hangs in the balance the way ours did that day, all our intellect, all our reasoning, all our worldly wisdom is stripped away leaving only the bare, naked truth.

I required more breaking than most. My biggest challenge as a wife has been reconciling the feminist ideals I was raised with in the '70s and '80s with the way I feel I should act as a wife and mother now. Most days I'm Rosie the Riveter, steamrolling right over my husband anytime he tries to make a decision or express his point of view, while my inner June Cleaver shakes her head and clucks her tongue.

Then there we were on August 29, 2005, huddled with our four kids in a hallway listening to windows exploding, the roof tearing away and dozens of trees collapsing around us—all miraculously avoiding the house. I've never been so relieved not to be in charge. In an instant, listening to my husband felt like the most natural thing on earth.

When the storm finally stopped, our land looked like the aftermath of war. There were decisions to be made about where we'd live for the time being, whether we'd send the kids to school out of state and whether David should accept a transfer that meant we'd live apart for a while. I'm sure the kids were stunned to hear me say, "We'll do whatever Daddy decides"—words they certainly never heard from their mom before.

That storm opened my eyes to see that I had a stable, intelligent husband fully capable of leading his family without having to fight his wife to do so. As we spent days trying to track down family and friends, as we watched the TV coverage of what had happened to our beloved Gulf Coast, as I got the news that two of my sisters and four of my cousins had lost everything, as I found out my teaching position had been "discontinued," I felt an unexplainable peace knowing I was finally following my heart where my marriage is concerned.

It's been eight years since Katrina and this region still has a long way to go to recover. But in the time since the storm, this sassy, big-mouthed Southern woman has learned to value her partner in marriage and trust him to lead the family without being second-guessed.

~Mimi Greenwood Knight

Those Were the Days

While we try to teach our children all about life,
our children teach us what life is all about.
~Angela Schwindt

During my quiet moments I often think back to the days when my children were young. Life was busy for me then. I had a demanding job that I hated. Most mornings I cried as I drove to work and then cried all the way home. But we needed the money—or at least I thought we couldn't live without it. So I went to work in spite of the fact that every moment there was spent in misery.

I had to have minor surgery. Believe it or not, I looked forward to it because I would not have to go to work for a couple of weeks. I realize today that nobody should keep a job they hate more than surgery.

The Friday before I was to go back, I received a call from the office. The office manager wanted to set up an appointment for me to meet with my employer Monday afternoon. Since I was scheduled to return to work Monday morning, I knew something was up. I called my boss and told him I wanted to talk to him after everyone else left for the day. He agreed, and my husband and I met with him that afternoon.

As I suspected, I was losing my job. They had budget cuts and needed to lay off employees. I was the last hired and the first to leave. I was devastated. Usually when I left a job on my own, my employers wanted me to stay. Even though I didn't like the job, I didn't want to lose it.

After a long conversation, my employer handed me an envelope.

I was pleasantly surprised when I opened it and saw the check I had received. It was large enough to get us over the hump. I filed for unemployment and immediately started looking for a job.

In the meantime, my children and I had the time of our lives together. I saved a great deal of money on childcare, and we discovered how much fun we could have on a shoestring budget. We went on nature hikes, joined the local recreation department, and saw matinees at a nearby theater at least once a week. We began checking out books at the library and discovered a weekly puppet show that the kids loved. We saved cans and cashed them in periodically. On those days we'd stop to get ice cream cones. We had picnics by a pond at the local college. We had a blast.

Time quickly passed, and I had yet to find a job. The week before my unemployment benefits ended I received a telephone call. I was offered a part-time bookkeeping job at a local pharmacy. I took it and worked during the hours my twin sons were in school. I was able to take my daughter, who was younger, to work with me.

I worked at that pharmacy for eight years before we moved to another town. Then, I commuted back and forth. I kept the job for another ten years. The experience I received there enabled me to find a similar job in our new hometown. And seventeen years later, I'm still employed with that pharmacy. I will probably stay there until I retire.

When I think back to the day I lost my job, I realize that as upset as I was, it was the greatest thing that could have happened to me. I enjoyed my children more than I ever had before and we were able to spend quality time together. I have memories of those months I stayed home laughing and playing with my children that will last a lifetime. Those were truly the best days of my life, and then I found the perfect job and never cried on the way to work again. I am truly blessed to have worked for some of the nicest people I've ever met. Getting laid off was one of the best things that ever happened to me.

~Nancy B. Gibbs

The Gift of a Lifetime

While earning your daily bread,
be sure you share a slice with those less fortunate.
~*Quoted in P.S. I Love You, compiled by H. Jackson Brown, Jr.*

I have been a competitive distance runner since elementary school. As a high school freshman, however, I suffered a hip stress fracture and was sidelined for my sophomore year. Although I was devastated by my injuries then, today I consider them true blessings. They made me realize how deeply I love running and all it has given me: the purity of racing, yes, but also the camaraderie and inside jokes with teammates, the feeling of improving every day to reach the goals set at the beginning of the season, the balance provided by a good run in the middle of a busy day.

Running is hard, but NOT running is harder.

My parents and especially my older sister Dallas—herself a track and cross-country runner in high school—have always taught me that the best way to overcome personal adversity is to help others with their challenges because it brings us joy and puts our own problems in perspective. In this light, I empathized with disadvantaged kids who couldn't enjoy running—not because of injury, but because they could not afford running shoes.

I turned adversity into opportunity by creating Give Running, a non-profit organization that teaches youth, through running, the character traits and skills that serve as a foundation for success in all aspects of life. Since 2006, Give Running has collected, cleaned, and donated more than 14,200 pairs of running and athletic shoes to youth in developing countries and local inner-city communities. To further promote a love for running and the benefits it fosters, Give Running also holds youth running camps that include leadership development and community service components emphasizing the broader application of lessons learned through sports.

In December 2009, I traveled to Mali in West Africa as part of the USC Africa Health Initiative and spent three weeks in the small village of Sikoro (population 450) building an irrigated community garden to provide fruits and vegetables that are severely lacking from the villagers' nutrient-poor diets, while also economically empowering women with a new source of income from produce sales. In Malian culture, we learned, men and women are each expected to have their own source of income; women would use their income to purchase food for meals and other necessities. Before we helped build the community garden, the women in Sikoro mainly earned money by cutting down trees to sell as firewood—an unsustainable practice that was contributing to deforestation in the region.

Furthermore, we raised funds prior to our travels and purchased materials for building a desperately needed bridge. During the four-month rainy season, the river bordering Sikoro floods, isolating its residents from the secondary school, larger markets, and medical clinic in the larger town across the river. Less dramatic but equally sincere, I brought along 113 pairs of running shoes—as many as I could squeeze into five extra duffle bags—to distribute to our generous hosts.

For many of the Sikoro villagers, these were the first shoes they ever had! Indeed, so precious were the shoes that if we at first guessed wrong and gave a person footwear that was a half-size—or even more—too small, the villager would scrunch up his or her toes and insist the shoes fit just fine! Painfully too small was better than none at all; they would not let us take the running shoes off their feet until we brought over larger replacement pairs. Recalling it still gives me goose bumps.

As special as it was to honor the Chief with the first pair of running shoes given out, lacing up each pair on recipients' feet was equally meaningful. However, one gift pair of shoes stands out in my mind and heart as distinctly as does the most memorable run of my life.

The day before leaving Sikoro, I went on a six-mile run circling through the village. The first few laps of my quarter-mile loop I ran in solitude, but then several children began to run with me. They would keep me company for one or two circuits, then drop out and take a rest, only to rejoin me the next time I came around. Before I knew it, my running group had swelled from three to ten to twenty-plus smiling kids—many of whom were wearing the gift shoes they had received the previous day.

During this most cherished run, one training partner stood out because he had to stop—not out of exhaustion, but because of a rocky section of the trail and due to the fact that he was running barefoot. Lameen Sacko, I learned, had not received a pair of Give Running shoes the day before. The following day, my last in the village, I met Lameen at his tin-roofed mud hut and asked him to try on my running shoes—the only pair of shoes (besides flip-flops) I had brought for my own use in Mali.

My size 11.5 Adidas Supernova Glides fit Lameen perfectly.

"*I ni che, Amadou* (Thank you, Greg)," he said, using my adopted Malian name.

"*I ni su* (You're welcome)," I replied, smiling.

As we shook hands in friendship, adrenaline again surged through my body and my heartbeat raced. I realized how each pair of Give Running shoes serves as a bridge between two lives. While the giver and receiver of each pair of shoes may not meet face to face as did Lameen and I, through the shoes they nevertheless meet foot-to-foot.

Visiting Africa, I found, breaks your heart—and opens it wider than ever before. I am certainly a better and more fulfilled person for the experience. The following holiday season when I sat down to a feast of Christmas foodstuffs, I thought of the wonderful companionship I was treated to in Sikoro. I gave thanks for all I have and for all I learned from those who have so much less. I also thought of Lameen and laced up my new Adidas to go for a run.

When the USC Africa Health Initiative returned to Sikoro in the summer of 2011, our dear friend the Chief was wearing his bright white running shoes — still in excellent condition — when he greeted the visiting contingent. While I could not return this time, before the USCAHI cohort left Los Angles, I gave one of my friends going on the trip another pair of my size 11.5 Adidas Supernova Glides for Lameen.

~Greg Woodburn

Changing Gears

Put your future in good hands — your own.
~Author Unknown

I had a great job at a local company. Interesting work. Great salary and benefits. Enjoyable co-workers. My career was sailing along quite nicely. Life was good.

The only concern I had was for my mother. Several visits to doctors didn't turn up anything. But I felt that something was wrong.

Persistence paid off, but the answer was not good. My mother was diagnosed with progressive supranuclear palsy — a rare neurological disease that is similar to Parkinson's disease. There was no cure and in fact there was little available to treat the symptoms that include frequent falls, swallowing difficulties, slurred speech, and body stiffness.

As the months passed, my mother experienced all of these symptoms and more. Not a week would go by without a medical incident. Because of this, it became increasingly clear that she needed a lot of personal care.

I was very confused about how best to help my mother through this trying time, so I drove to the beach and sat on the sand. The ocean has always held a spiritual connection for me. The salty air, the cry of the gulls, the waves' rhythmic dance as they are greeted by the shore. It's where I feel most at home.

I sat quietly by myself — my thoughts focused on my mother. A seagull landed on the sand a few feet away. We stared at each other. He was probably looking for food—which I did not have. He soon took to the air. As I watched him fly away, a sense of peace came over me. I knew that somehow things would work out and that I just had to have faith.

The solution to my problem came the following week. I went to work at 8:30 a.m. By 9:30, I was back in my car, laid off. It came as a complete surprise.

Now I would be available to care for my mother, whose health continued to deteriorate as the months progressed. She needed help with everyday activities like brushing her teeth, getting dressed, and feeding herself.

Caring for someone who is seriously ill was an eye-opening experience. It was the hardest job I've ever had, but also the most meaningful. I dealt with issues that I thought I would never face: The brakes on my mother's wheelchair needed to be fixed; prescriptions needed to be refilled; medical appointments had to be scheduled; health insurance forms needed to be filled out and submitted.

When my mother passed away, she was at home in her own bed. I sat by her side holding her hand as she went on her final journey. It's a moment that I will always remember.

Although the years caring for my mother were challenging, they taught me much about myself. I learned that I was much stronger and more capable than I thought. This newfound confidence continues to help me each and every day.

~Maryanne Curran

Rattled

Take time today to appreciate beauty — natural beauty, art, people.
Slow down, breathe deeply, smile. It's a beautiful world.
~Jonathan Lockwood Huie

The deafening sound of the rescue helicopter sliced the still, spring air. The chopper got into position, lowered and hovered over a San Diego hilltop, dropping a member of a rescue crew to the ground. I'd seen this scene unfold many times in my career as an airborne news and traffic reporter. This time, though, was different. I was the person being rescued! They lifted me into the harness. I was hoisted — dangling in the air — to the waiting aircraft. The chopper flew me to an ambulance waiting nearby. Then one of the most difficult journeys of my life began.

It had all started earlier that afternoon as I set off to hike my favorite trail. About a half-hour into the hike, a short portion of the path became very narrow, covered with thick, waist-high grass. I knew the trail well so I always scurried quickly through this part since I couldn't see what might be lurking. Making fast tracks, I suddenly heard a rattle. Like an antelope racing from a cheetah, I turned around and ran as fast as I could to reach my hiking buddy, JP, who was a bit of a distance behind me.

"I heard a rattlesnake," I gasped.

He eyed my bloody ankle. "I'll call 911."

"No, I'm okay. I hit a branch or something," I said, annoyed that he'd want to freak me out.

"Okay." He flipped his cell phone shut.

My ankle did hurt—it felt like someone had hammered thorns into my leg. Despite the fact that I'd heard a rattle, I was in denial that a snake had bitten me. It didn't take long to grasp the situation, though. Within ten seconds, my hands and fingers were tingling and numb.

"Call 911." My voice shook.

JP stayed on the phone giving directions as we waited for the helicopter.

"Keep the heart above the injury and don't panic." JP repeated what the person on the other end of the phone said. Don't panic? I felt my insides swelling; my breathing was labored and difficult. Closing my eyes, I thought about my kids: a twenty-four-year-old in college and a twelve-year-old still living with me. Don't panic? I could die here!

Terrified, I wanted to cry. Determined to keep cool, I sat down and became aware of my breath. Deep breath. Inhale. Exhale.

My stomach cramped. My tongue swelled. My entire body was under attack.

"Where are they? Why are they taking so long? Are they almost here?" I asked every few minutes.

Twenty minutes later, the sound of the helicopter gave me hope. JP and two hikers waved their arms to help the pilot spot us. It's not easy to find little specks of people in a wide-open space from a helicopter.

A few minutes later, I was in the ER asking, "Doc, I'm going to be okay now, aren't I?"

"I don't know yet," he said.

Not the answer I was looking for—the only time in my life I actually wanted a man to lie to me.

It wasn't long before complete sedation took away any fears.

From the ER, I moved to intensive care. A large area around the bite turned black and blue. There was bluish discoloration under my nails. My muscles twitched. Doctors stated there was "severe envenomation."

"That first night was trying," JP later told me. "We figured if you got through the night, you'd make it. When I first saw you, there were three tubes down your throat and four people working on you. Your throat and tongue were very swollen."

"Critically ill in a life-threatening situation," stated my medical records.

My mom had groups praying for me. JP sent out an e-mail asking for prayers.

I had my own little mantra: "Dear God, please make this nightmare end."

I figured some good would come out of this. But while I waited for that silver lining, my leg was turning black! Temporarily paralyzed, I was helpless and dependent.

The venom attacked every system in my body, causing bruising and swelling from my toes to the top of my head. The texture of the skin on my abdomen, thighs, and groin became extremely stiff and painfully hard. It felt more like hard leather. I gained sixty pounds from swelling!

My side and ribs were bruised. The top of my foot blistered badly. I was anemic and had several blood transfusions. Seven days later, more antivenin. Who knew a snake could do so much damage?

"I was so scared when I saw you in the ICU. You were yellow," a friend later said.

During those two weeks, my son brought me a grand slam baseball he'd hit and two homerun balls!

"I'm going to need a trophy cabinet if they don't get me out of here pretty soon," I told my nurse.

Fifteen days and at least twenty-eight vials of antivenin later, I went home. I had to learn to be more patient, as my physical healing was going to take time. I practiced gratitude more than ever—for everyone and everything. I became more compassionate.

Life can change in a split second. I could have died and never seen my kids again. The importance of always keeping peace with my loved ones became very obvious after this ordeal.

I looked for something positive in my daily progress—first

walking one house length, the next day two. Within a few weeks I walked, albeit slowly, for a half hour. From the feeling I had inside, you'd have thought I ran a marathon.

My body healed. My leg has a couple of issues, but I am able to do anything and everything I want with that leg. I couldn't even move that leg for a few days. I had to learn how to walk again, but less than two years later I started training to get my fitness certifications and now teach several Zumba and senior fitness classes at various gyms.

Taking the first step is the start — then looking for the good all around — like the perfect day for a hike — with my new snake-proof boots!

~Jo Eager

Working for Peanuts

Being good is commendable,
but only when it is combined with doing good is it useful.
~Author Unknown

The New York State Fair. Twelve humid days of funnel cake and cotton candy, bloated goats and scouring calves. A vibrant landscape of family and friends all gathered together to soak up the last remaining drops of summer. For a Cornell veterinarian like me, this two-week field trip was an annual reminder that veterinary medicine can, in fact, be practiced without the help of an MRI, EKG, or COP. I was there to be served a hearty bite of the life of a country vet — with a side of kettle corn.

The call came at around midnight — a gruff voice breathed into the line, "I think we've got a sick cow in the dairy barn, can you come and take a look?" I slipped coveralls over my pajamas, grabbed my keys and stethoscope, and steered the sputtering golf cart toward the dairy barn. The concerts had long finished, the gates were locked, and the swarms of meandering fairgoers had been replaced by the flurry of the late-night cleaning crew. Working under the neon glow of the carnival lights, they furiously erased the remnants of the day in preparation for the next.

Upon arrival at the dairy barn, I was surprised to find not a gruff man and a cow, but a ten-year-old boy and his six-month-old heifer calf. His name was Matt. Her name was Peanuts. He looked stressed. She looked awful. Awfully dehydrated, that is. With eyes so sunken they practically touched inside her skull, she was the bovine version of a potato chip. Rumen was dry and hard. Heart rate was high. Not ideal. He reported that she had been a little colicky earlier after a five-hour haul from home in the heat of the day. Doing his best to help her, he had given her antibiotics, since that is what his dad did when his cows were a bit "off" at home. He had also walked her—for hours. Totally exhausted, she now stood with her head and her ears drooping, kicking at her belly just often enough to say that she hurt there, too. There was anxiety in his eyes when he said, "I did everything my dad does, but I think she's gotten worse!" No kidding, kid.

Step one: rehydrate. I tubed her with water and electrolytes and was contemplating in which side to place the IV catheter when he popped the million-dollar fair question: "Is Peanuts still going to be able to show tomorrow?" Crud. The obvious answer was no; the day was almost upon us and this calf was about as likely to make it into the show ring as a college kid is to finish a marathon after a week in Cancún. She needed rest—and fluids. With "No" forming on my lips, I watched him gently stroke her ears and I was reminded of my own small-town roots and childhood state fair experiences. This week was a big deal. A really big deal. So much time and hard work, so much of summer break went into preparing for the final hurrah that was the state fair. I decided to ride the fence: "Well, Matt, I don't know. Let's see what we can do."

Knowing an IV catheter would be a sure way to get the night supervisor's attention—and Matt's name scratched from the entry lists—I headed to the vet office to see what I had. I surveyed my stash of supplies and returned to the dairy barn packing hypertonic saline and two five-liter bags of fluids. By this time we had drawn a small crowd of concerned observers—boys from Matt's 4-H group—which was good because we were going to need their help.

Matt held Peanuts while I guided a fourteen-gauge needle into her jugular. One boy held the bottle of hypertonic, another held the fluids; still another held a pocketknife. Two other boys, both a bit older, supervised. We gave Peanuts most of the bottle of hypertonic, and then dumped out the remainder. With me still manning my position at her neck, the boys cut the base off the bottle and then carefully poured in the fluid from a punctured bag. They worked with absolute focus: pouring carefully to avoid spilling, lifting the bottle high above their heads, then bringing it back down for refilling just before it emptied and let air invade the line. Soon, we were finished. Now it was time to wait. We called it a night and agreed to meet first thing in the morning.

Pulling up to the dairy barn through the early morning fog, there was already a steady flow of bovine traffic to and from the wash rack. The sounds of blow dryers and clippers resonated from inside. It was show time. As I turned down Peanuts' aisle, I said a little prayer under my breath. Please let her be better. Please don't make me wreck this kid's state fair. Please. I headed toward her stall, but as I drew nearer, it was not Peanuts that I saw first. It was Matt. He was sound asleep on a cot, with no blanket, less than a foot from his calf. He must have slept with her all night. He was out cold, one hand dangling limply in the hay at her side. Peanuts, on the other hand, pricked her ears and turned her head to greet me. She was happily chewing her cud. Eyes bright and no longer sunken. Water buckets half empty. Thank goodness. Matt's class wasn't until 3 p.m., so I woke him just enough to tell him his calf was going to be okay to show before letting him drift back into exhausted slumber. His 4-H leader, who was by now aware of the previous night's festivities—thanks to Matt's comrades—walked by and mouthed the words "thank you."

I returned at 11 a.m. to check on the pair. Matt, looking freshly pressed and ready for action, greeted me with a smile. He was already fully dressed in his showmanship attire: boots polished and number neatly pinned to his front. I glanced at my watch and smiled; he still had four hours. Peanuts chewed her cud contently and appeared oblivious to the ruckus she caused merely a few hours earlier. I turned to go and Matt stopped me.

"Don't I need to pay you?" he asked.

I was astounded that a ten-year-old kid would show such responsibility. I had a bill in my pocket, a mere $37.00 thanks to special fair pricing, but I had planned on asking his 4-H club leader for his parents' phone number and settling with them directly.

When I offered my plan to him, he simply said, "No ma'am, I can pay for it," and whipped out a little wallet from his crisply starched Wrangler jeans. He counted out $37 in mostly fives and ones, and then handed them over decisively.

"Do you have enough money for the rest of fair… for food?" I asked.

"Yes, ma'am, I have lots." He began brushing the already immaculate Peanuts and said, "You know, I think she just wanted some extra attention!"

Four hours and a blue showmanship ribbon later, all was well again in the dairy barn. As I sat in the stands watching Matt's class, I couldn't help but grin and once again be reminded that we vets are so fortunate to do what we do. In an unlikely place at an unlikable time, I bumped into a boy and a calf that left my heart feeling full and made my day — all by just doing my job. There's a reason we don't do this for the money — our return is cash for the soul. I'll take that any day of the week and twice on Sunday.

~SallyAnne L. Ness, DVM

Press Start

When you look at your life,
the greatest happinesses are family happinesses.
~Dr. Joyce Brothers

When my husband lost his job in 2012, it wasn't a private family matter. It was all over the news under clever headlines like "Looks Like It's GAME OVER for Curt Schilling's Game Company, 38 Studios." The end of the company happened quickly and terribly for us, and for the hundreds of employees who found themselves very suddenly unemployed. We had no warning until suddenly there were no paychecks, and then there were daily meetings, and then the doors of the company were closed. One of the items locked inside and lost for good was our daughter's ultrasound photo.

Zach and I had just bought our house on May 7th, the company-wide missed paycheck was on May 15th, and our daughter, Madeline, was due May 29th. In the two weeks following the 15th, when I was nine months pregnant and the collapse of the studio was detailed on every news station in New England, I was told to take it easy. I was told not to stress (for the baby's sake), to relax with my feet up (for the baby's sake) and to calm down. The problem was that I have never been a very calm person. When something catastrophic happens, I cry about it. I stress over it. I had just finished grad school, and I was unemployed. My husband's job loss meant that we were about to welcome our first child into a household with no income. On top of the stress from this nightmare situation we found ourselves in, I now had to stress over what my stress was doing to our unborn baby. I remember curling around my enormous belly and wanting to stay in bed forever—to keep our daughter inside me where she wouldn't have to deal with any of what was happening to our family.

I woke up with the strangest cramping pains on May 27th. When they became stronger and closer together, I realized that I was in labor. We left for the hospital around noon, and Madeline was born seven hours later. My delivery was better than fine, and my husband and I greeted our beautiful, dark-haired daughter at 7:39 that night. She was perfect, and we spent the night in this lovely fog of new parenthood, waking up every few minutes to peer into the bassinet where our baby, only hours old, slept. The next day, our happy fog was cleared away by the billing department at the hospital. We didn't have health insurance, because my husband wasn't laid off—his company simply didn't exist anymore, and it was discovered that they had not been paying for their health insurance. One of the most awful, vivid memories I have of that day is my husband crying in the chair by the window of my hospital room. He held his face in his hands and said, "I don't know what we're going to do."

We took Madeline home the next day. For the next few weeks, I spent most of my time feeding, reading to, and napping with our baby, and Zach spent his time interviewing for new software development jobs, changing diapers, and relaxing with our daughter, who was enamored with her daddy from the very beginning. When Zach napped, Madeline napped on his belly. When Zach cooked or cleaned, Madeline watched him as though he were the most interesting person in the world.

Zach found a job at another game company, and he started work at the end of June. While May and June of 2012 were the most terrifying months of our lives, Zach was able to spend an entire month with his new daughter, and that time was precious.

Madeline is nearly eight months old now, and our family isn't haunted by what happened to 38 Studios last May. Some families still are—Curt Schilling himself looks like a ghost whenever he makes a television appearance. We are always thinking of those families, and hoping that they are able to overcome such an enormous obstacle, too. What happened was terrible, but a happier byproduct was the time that Zach had with our newborn. It was time he wouldn't have had with her otherwise, and it contributed, I am certain, to the wonderful closeness they have now. At seven months old, Madeline's first word was "Dada," and I don't think that was a surprise to anyone.

~Renee Beauregard Lute

Chapter 3

From Lemons to
Lemonade

From Pausing to Pursuing

Who Would Have Thought?

Nobody can go back and start a new beginning,
but anyone can start today and make a new ending.
~Maria Robinson

grew up in a family of seven children in a wonderland near Wolf Lake, Michigan. We enjoyed acres of woods, streams, the lake, and wildlife. Also located on the property where we lived was a motion picture production studio. My dad wrote scripts and directed scores of films in that place for the then-fledgling Gospel Films.

I'll never forget the day he told me, "It'll be safe on this road. Just ride your bike, and make sure you stay inside the line." Well, that dark night, I was struck and "killed" by a hit and run driver while riding my bike. But... since the movie I was in was being shot in black and white, the blood that ran from my nose, ear, and mouth actually came from a chocolate syrup bottle. Any time children were needed for background extras, I was all too willing to volunteer.

There was never any doubt in my mind that one day I'd follow in my father's footsteps and enter the world of film production. There was something magical about the whole process and I found myself hanging around the studio, in the shadows, whenever I could. It was there that I learned about characters, timing, humor, dialog, scripting, and directing. I can still hear my father calling out instructions and then announcing "Action" at the start of each scene and "Cut" at the end.

After high school, I began working in the film company full-time while attending a local college. This was a normal transition because I'd grown up in and around the business and knew how the process worked. After being drafted into the army, I returned to my film production roots. There was one year when I was out of the country, on productions, almost more than I was home. Our travels took us to many different countries, cultures, and exotic locations.

At the same time that I lived in this environment, I also grew up as a struggling, reluctant reader. In such a large family, it's easy for something like that to go unnoticed. To complicate matters further, my father was also the author of more than seventy books during his lifetime, and I never read any of them. Of all my siblings, it was a pretty safe bet that I would never follow in my father's footsteps as an author. I had no idea that these two elements in my life—film production and writing—would come together in the future.

In addition to dramatic and documentary film productions, my work expanded into corporate video production and television commercials when I joined a new production company. Then something happened that would dramatically affect the rest of my life—9/11. Within days after September 11, 2001, my clients began cancelling projects. Most of these were for industrial video projects or client TV commercials.

"Let's just wait and see what happens," one client told me. "We'll give it thirty to sixty days."

The video production landscape changed rapidly after that. Marketing people I'd worked with for years lost their jobs. Promotional budgets were slashed, companies left town or went out of business, and my phone went dead as far as any future production work. What's a person supposed to do after devoting a lifetime to a career that ends so abruptly?

Then for some reason, a little voice inside me suggested children's books. At first I tried to ignore it, but it wouldn't go away. After all, I didn't know anything about writing books because my life had been devoted to visual communication. But after I gave in to the prompting, and began to walk this new path, it became obvious that all my previous training had uniquely prepared me for this new challenge.

Without even realizing it, I had been a student of the elements of story, plot, characters, setting, and more. All of these impressions had made an indelible mark on my mind. They were locked in my subconscious only to surface again after I began the transition into writing.

For the next three years, I wrote manuscript after manuscript without an agent, a publisher, a contract, or even the hope of seeing anything published. But I couldn't help myself, because story ideas bombarded my mind. The process was amazing. A title always came first. This was quickly followed by characters, setting, plot, and other details.

Next, I told myself the story, into a recorder, and transcribed the notes. From there I wrote as quickly as possible, not knowing what would happen next in the story, or what new character might show up. For me, writing felt almost like watching a movie as each story unfolded right in front of me. That process continues to this day.

The result has been thirty-five manuscripts of action-adventures and mysteries intended for readers eight years of age and up. At the present time, ten of those books are published, and ten more are currently under contract. Sometimes I sit back, shake my head, and wonder how I got here.

My work has been released by several publishers, I have an excellent agent, and there is no end to the additional stories I'd like to write. In addition, I've participated in several anthologies, write two monthly magazine columns about middle-grade readers, short stories for a children's magazine, along with countless other articles. All of this is something that would have been quite unthinkable to me years ago.

So what do my experiences mean to others? Is it possible to take such reversals in life and make something good out of them? I can't speak to every case, but think about it—I grew up hating to read, in the home of a father who authored a stack of books. My career path had taken me exclusively into the visual arts. Writing books wasn't simply the last thing on my mind; it wasn't in there at all. Yet, here I am, a multi-published author of books for kids. Just imagine what you can do. If one door closes—in my case it slammed shut—surely another will open, allowing you to make something good out of what seems like an impossible or desperate situation.

Today, young readers tell me that reading one of my books is like being in an exciting or scary movie—good scary, not dark. One of the titles, *Terror at Wolf Lake*, is even set in the place where I grew up. So you tell me, who would have thought?

~Max Elliot Anderson

A Year to Live

Life is short, so live it. Love is rare, so grab it. Fear controls you, so face it.
Memories are precious, so cherish them. We only get one life, so live it!
~Author Unknown

We needed a new phone installation for a dictating device in the word processing center under my supervision as Central Services Coordinator in our combined school districts. But an old, heavy wooden desk was in the way and the serviceman refused to move it. With disgust, I muttered, "I am woman, hear me roar," as I shoved the massive obstacle out of the way. I covered up the wince in my fifty-six-year-old back until he left. It soon increased from pain to agony when I had to leave work and go home to bed. After a few days, when I could hobble to the car, I had it X-rayed.

The call from my doctor was unnerving. "Your back is not seriously injured, but there seems to be a dark spot on your kidney which requires further investigation." A CAT scan revealed a cancerous kidney, which had to be removed. Fortunately the cancer did not appear to have spread, but unfortunately it was a type of cancer that would not respond to chemo or radiation.

"Either we got it all... or we didn't," the nephrologist intoned. "I would recommend that you take that cruise you told me about, and do anything else this year that you have been putting off."

"My God," I pleaded. "The doctor expects this to spread and take my life within a year! I won't even get to claim any of the Social

Security money I have contributed all these years. It isn't FAIR! Please help me!"

I hadn't intended to take an early retirement; my last child was still in college. But if I had only a year, I was going to make it count. A plea for volunteers at our local zoo appeared in the newspaper. I signed up for the twenty-three-week course to learn all about animals and how to handle them. The newsletter for my genealogy society arrived, hand printed, with genealogy misspelled and a plea for a volunteer editor. I had only a year, but I could surely do better than that! So I became an editor. I used the blessings of the new computers to resume writing and sold a few pieces.

I gave away many of my possessions, all my art supplies, and waited. As the year raced by and I was still around, I figured I still only had a few more years, maybe five. I marked off the years, filling them with everything I had procrastinated doing all my life. I took courses, Spanish and Russian; I taught night school courses in genealogy and family history. I savored every minute, soaking up visions of my new grandchildren I didn't expect to see grow up.

Now I've not only seen the first of the grandchildren grow up, but all ten of them and the first four great-grandchildren. I have been a zoo volunteer for over twenty-five years. After eighteen years as a genealogy society editor, I turned it over to another person and then walked into the editorship of a local historical society newsletter. I have had more articles and a couple of children's picture books published.

My "last year" of life continues to delight me, after a quarter century of making sure that every moment counts.

~Esther McNeil Griffin

22

Rediscovering Love and Balance

Follow your heart, but be quiet for a while first. Ask questions,
then feel the answer. Learn to trust your heart.
~Author Unknown

got my share of rejection throughout high school and college: the first dates that never called again; the positions I applied for but didn't get; the thin envelopes from editors at literary journals. My coping strategy included double-fudge brownies, a Nora Ephron movie or two, and my favorite mix CD on repeat. Then I would dust myself off and try again.

But in my senior year of college, rejection pummeled me flat. I poured hours into applications for fellowships and grad schools—revising essays, collecting letters of recommendation, practicing interviews. Four months later, my mailbox was filled with nothing but rejection letters.

A double batch of brownies didn't soften the blow. Neither did watching Harry and Sally finally get together at the New Year's Eve party. My roommate hid my favorite mix CD.

Friends and acquaintances announced their post-grad plans. I had nothing. The job market was worse than ever. All I wanted to do was write, but the writing market is famously volatile, and I knew I couldn't afford rent in Los Angeles without a steady job.

"Why don't you move back in with us?" my parents told me. "Save money on rent. Catch your breath a little."

My parents and I have always gotten along, and I knew it was a generous offer. But instead of being grateful, all I could focus on was how it would look to other people.

"And how is that?" my best friend asked.

"Like loserdom," I said.

She shook her head. Part of me knew she was right, but the other part of me muttered, "She doesn't understand." Her post-grad plans were all lined up: an AmeriCorps position as a reading tutor in St. Louis. Competitive, altruistic, impressive.

I feverishly applied for more jobs and internships. A month later, when college graduation spit me out into the Real World, I still had no prospects.

My friends scattered to all corners of the globe. I packed my belongings into my parents' minivan and moved from the heart of Los Angeles back into my childhood bedroom in the sleepy beach town where I grew up.

It was jarring to switch from a jam-packed schedule of due dates, exams, and social events to wide-open days with nothing on my plate. After a few days of sleeping till noon and eating dinner in my pajamas, I began to feel restless and bored. I had spent the past four years rushing from activity to activity, deadline to deadline, thinking about all the things I could be doing if I had more time. Well, my wish had been granted. I had time. I had more time than I knew what to do with.

At first, I boomeranged back to my comfort zone: busyness. I tried to fill the emptiness of my days with as much activity as possible: scouring freelance writing listings, sending out my résumé to magazine editors, writing articles for obscure blogs because at least it gave me something to tell people I was doing. I wrote long to-do lists and measured my days by checkmarks. Within a week I was back to my familiar frazzled, stressed-out state of mind. Yet the restless unease remained. I spent the whole day getting things done, but I wasn't really doing anything. At least, not anything that was meaningful to me.

One morning, as I hunkered down in front of my laptop, consumed by the black hole of my e-mail inbox, a new e-mail arrived from my dad sharing one of his favorite quotes: "The most important two words in the English language are love and balance."

Love and balance. I wasn't doing either very well.

That afternoon, I walked down the street to a local coffeehouse armed with nothing but my journal and pen. And I made lists. Instead of to-do lists waiting for checkmarks, these lists were dreamy, doodle-filled ramblings, notes from my inner self to a person who had been racing ahead on autopilot for way too long. What made me feel happy and energized? What did my "dream life" look like?

When I returned home that evening, I didn't feel like a loser. I felt grateful.

I began waking up early and running every morning. Afterwards, I stretched and practiced yoga moves in the cool morning air. I volunteered to pay "rent" by cooking dinner most nights, and I visited local farm stands and searched the Internet for healthy recipes. Nearly every day I visited my grandfather, who also lived in town, and soaked up his stories. I had lunch dates with my dad and gym dates with my mom.

And I wrote. Not for others, but for myself. I wrote what mattered to me, what I wanted to read: short stories, essays, plays. I established a writing routine. Some days, the words flowed easily. Other days, it was difficult to get words down on paper. But it was always time spent doing something that, to me, mattered.

Sometimes living at home gave me a strange sense of déjà vu. After a date with a new guy, it was a little bizarre to find myself back on the front step of my parents' house, porch light ablaze, saying goodnight like my teenage self used to after a school dance. Whenever I grabbed the car keys and headed out the door, my parents were still in the habit of asking where I was going and what time I would be home. I would talk to my friends about their new lives in Paris, D.C., St. Louis, New York, and sometimes I felt like I had nothing interesting to say. There were still moments when the word "loser" rushed around in my mind like water circling a drain. But I learned that I was the only one who could actually give that word power. If I didn't think I was a loser, then I wouldn't feel like one. Even living with my parents, I could still be independent. I could still live with purpose.

Looking back, moving home after graduation was the best thing I could have done. It forced me to stop, step back, and honestly evaluate my life and my dreams. And it taught me that expectations could become a prison. I thought my life would be "on pause" until I moved out of my parents' house and off to my new life in a new city, Miss Independent once again. But I learned there is no pause button on life. Waiting until your life conforms perfectly to your expectations—the right car, the right guy, the right job, the right house—means that you are missing all the opportunities right in front of you this moment, all the surprises and joys that are waiting for you to wake up and reach for them.

~Dallas Woodburn

23

Arising from the Ashes

Our passions are the true phoenixes; when the old one is burnt out,
a new one rises from its ashes.
~Johann Wolfgang von Goethe

As part of my early morning spiritual practices, I often trudge up the footpaths that wind around Glassy Mountain behind Carl Sandburg's house, a few blocks from my home in Flat Rock, North Carolina. On this morning, as I stop to catch my breath, my mind flashes to an ugly yet important time in the early 1980s. I was on the bathroom floor in my apartment in Greensboro during another period of contemplation. Sobbing and in a fetal position, I couldn't remember how I ended up there. I knew only that I was in great emotional pain and would do anything to make it stop. I imagined what I might do if I had a gun. Would I have the nerve to use it? If I did, would I screw it up like I'd screwed up the rest of my life? The more I thought about it, the more real the gun became, until finally I realized it wasn't my imagination but a real gun—which I held in my hand.

I felt the smooth wooden handle in my palm and the cold metal circle of the snub nose pressed against my temple. My finger began to tighten on the trigger. Just a little more pressure, a quick flash of pain, and the deeper pain would finally be over. Funny, I thought as I lay there, how many people would be surprised to learn of my suicide. To outward appearances, I had it made: my own veterinary practice, investments in real estate, a fancy car, a wallet full of credit cards—all the trimmings of a supposedly successful life. But beneath the well-crafted exterior was a hollow core of emptiness and suffering. My life felt worthless, without any real meaning. All the adornments of my good life didn't add up to true happiness or fulfillment. The truth is I felt alone in the world, with no one who truly cared about me or understood what I was going through.

You see, I had wanted to be a veterinarian since I was seven years old and I had stayed on that path until I graduated in 1974 from the University of Georgia. But after twelve years in practice, I didn't know if I could stand another day in the office. I was frustrated, tired and worn out by the constant stresses of my practice that included staffing headaches, client turnover, and financial strains. On top of it all, the stresses at work had a profoundly negative influence on my personal life. I felt disjointed and disconnected from those I most cared about. My life was out of balance and nearly out of control.

The pain of burnout had become so bad I started abusing alcohol and drugs in an effort to numb myself so I could get through another day. The downward spiral continued until I found myself on the bathroom floor in the worst pain of my life.

Thankfully, that day someone invaded my privacy. "Go away," I thought, and then realized I was shouting. "Go away! Leave me alone!"

But whoever it was didn't leave. A moment later I smelled the pleasant fragrance of a woman's perfume, then heard the voice of an angel. "It's okay, Brad. We're going to get you some help. It's okay." I recognized the voice of my friend Rebecca.

Now, as I sit watching the exquisite sunrise over the Blue Ridge Mountains, that day in Greensboro seems to be from a different person's life—and in many ways it is. I am no longer that confused, scared, lonely young man. I no longer practice veterinary medicine; instead, I'm the founder of the spiritually based Life on Purpose Institute. And today I can truthfully say my life is filled with purpose and meaning.

The journey of the last three decades has been a wild roller coaster ride filled with slow upward climbs and exciting, sometimes scary descents. It is what I affectionately term my Purposeful Path. Before my near-suicide I traveled the path mostly asleep, unaware that I was even on a journey. Then came ten years of awakening, with a few long naps mixed in. And for the last sixteen years, as I've continued my awakening process, I've done my best to assist others along their own Purposeful Path. It is possible to arise like the mythological phoenix from the ashes of a burned out life. With perseverance and patience, you can live a life on purpose.

~W. Bradford Swift

Target Practice

The rung of a ladder was never meant to rest upon, but only to hold a man's foot long enough to enable him to put the other somewhat higher.
~Thomas Henry Huxley

"It's too bad. When are they leaving?" Those were the whispered comments going around the office.

Later I found out that three staff members and I were being sent to another floor to work for another manager. Our current manager had told the people who weren't going to be affected but had neglected to tell those of us who were leaving. I was not terribly surprised when I heard the news, but I would have appreciated being told personally instead of via e-mail after I had already heard via the grapevine.

When I met my new manager, I immediately noticed a different approach. She invited me to sit down, formally introduced herself and asked me about my background with the agency. Then something unusual happened. She asked me where I envisioned myself in five years. I was like a deer caught in headlights. I searched my brain frantically and provided her with an answer. We chatted a few more moments and then I left.

As I walked back to my office, I was struck by a thought. I had not considered where I would be in the next five months, much less the next five years. In my supervisory position my days were spent in duck-and-cover mode to deal with staff shortages and irate customers.

What I said in response to her question was that I could see myself as an analyst or in some non-managerial role. I realized that I did not like being a supervisor, but that was how you got promoted at our place of employment. I didn't realize that I had given up on my career ambitions and settled into a rut.

I found that when I went to work for this new manager, she reignited my ability to envision a different career track—one I had not allowed myself to consider. What surprised me is that within a fifteen-month period I had interviewed and been selected for an analyst position. My new manager had helped me reorient my career and pick a new target. While everyone had felt sorry for us when we were transferred, and we were all a little apprehensive, the transfer turned out to be one of the best things that ever happened in my work life.

~M. Binion

The Side Effects of Cancer

Cancer is a word, not a sentence.
~John Diamond

When I was diagnosed with Stage 3 breast cancer in 2011, my first thought was, "Stage 3… that must mean 3 out of 10. That's not so bad. At least I am still in the early stages." Then I discovered that Stage 4 is as bad as it gets. Being a divorced, single parent of three children (with the youngest having autism), I had already taken on some tough challenges in my forty-four years. However this time I was in for the challenge of my life!

Over the next year, I endured: numerous uncomfortable and painful tests and procedures; three surgeries resulting in the loss of my left breast and associated lymph nodes; four months of chemotherapy; and twenty-five radiation treatments. In many ways, it was the worst year of my life. But in that same year: I met my soul mate and fell in love; I fulfilled a lifelong dream of being published; and I turned my passion for garden design into a new business venture. In many ways, it was the best year of my life!

As fate would have it, at almost exactly the same time that I found my lump, I also found my soul mate. Shawn and I were first introduced online. I immediately confided in him that I had found a lump in my breast, but at that time I was convinced that it was harmless. We spent the next few weeks e-mailing and talking on the phone, getting to know one another and planning to meet in person.

When I was officially diagnosed, already divorced and single for nearly ten years, my hopes of meeting the man of my dreams were dashed. Although we had not met in person, I really liked Shawn. He was funny, honest, hard working and handsome to boot! I thought that he could really be "the one." However, how could I possibly enter into a new relationship when my prognosis for survival was so uncertain?

Reluctantly, I called him in tears and said, "There is no point in us meeting. I just found out that I have breast cancer and I don't know what lies ahead for me."

To my surprise, he replied, "If you are trying to ditch me, it's not going to work. I am coming out there this weekend to take you to dinner."

As clichéd as it may sound, it was love at first sight and Shawn has been by my side ever since.

While cancer completely exhausted my physical body, most of the time my mind remained as alert as ever. I needed a positive outlet for my creative energy, and I found it through blogging. Just two months into my chemotherapy, I issued myself a challenge. I would find 100 perks of having cancer. Not only would this challenge help me to stay positive through difficult treatments, it would also provide a great distraction from thinking about the "big C." And so a blog was born (www.perksofcancer.com). I soon discovered that not only was my blog helping me through my cancer journey, but it was also providing inspiration and encouragement to the thousands of people who were following it. I cannot tell you how thrilled I was when I completed my blogging challenge of finding 100 perks, and soon after was offered a publishing contract with Basic Health Publications. Having a book published had been a lifelong dream for me.

In addition to writing my blog, I kept myself busy in my seventeen months away from work by completing an online garden design course. Gardening has been a passion of mine for most of my life. I had enrolled in the program a couple of years prior to my diagnosis, but could never seem to find the time to complete it. Whenever I did have time to spare, I preferred to spend it actually gardening, rather than writing papers about it. During my treatments, I did not have the physical stamina to do garden work, but I could still engage my mind in gardening through my courses. Just a few weeks after my last cancer treatment, I received my diploma in the mail. Shortly thereafter I accepted my first project as a professional garden designer, designing a sensory garden for children with autism. It was a true labor of love to design a garden that would stimulate and soothe the senses of children with autism. How rewarding to be able to supplement my income doing something I love so much! Even more rewarding was seeing my seven-year-old autistic son's delight as he interacted with this garden.

I did not have a choice in getting cancer. However, I did have a choice in how I was going to face it. By continuing to take on new challenges, follow my dreams, and allow myself to experience the magic of new love, I proved to myself that it is possible to live a full and rewarding life in the face of extreme health issues. The sensory garden, my new book, and my relationship with Shawn are reminders that not everything about my cancer experience has been horrible. It actually proved to have some rather pleasant side effects!

~Florence Strang

The Phone Call

Don't ask yourself what the world needs. Ask yourself what makes you come alive and then go do that. Because what the world needs is people who have come alive.

~Howard Thurman

t was never ending. One thing after another: strep throat, ear infection, sinus infection. I was sick of being sick. And I knew the exact reason for it too: job stress. To be more precise, it was boss stress. My boss—my principal—was making me sick!

How could things go downhill so fast? Here I was at my "dream" job. I had just switched to a new teaching position five minutes from home. Why, I could even ride my bike to work! Pure bliss. No more tedious traffic jams. No more icy roads. On snowy days I could even cross-country ski into work. I couldn't wait. No more stress!

No more stress?

I couldn't have been more wrong. "Go to Mary! Go to Mary!" It was a mantra I kept hearing over and over. "Go to Mary! She'll know just what to do," said the principal. Repeatedly. The trouble was that quite often I didn't know just what to do. As Special Education Resource teacher I was expected to handle all of the problems that came across the principal's desk. And, it seemed that I couldn't please anyone: the teachers complained, the principal complained, everybody complained. Everybody, that is, except my pupils. They never complained, well hardly ever, at any rate. They liked coming to my classes. Sometimes they even wanted to stay in and skip recess.

On that last day, the day before the phone call, we finished up the reading lesson: a puppet play using the new finger puppets we had crafted the week before. "The Hospital For Sick Sentences," a grammar game that they particularly liked, completed the program for that day. "Can my teacher borrow some of your reading games?" pleaded seven-year-old Whitney as she skipped merrily out the door. My miniature Sarah Bernhardt left in high spirits.

My spirits, however, weren't so high. Self-doubt gnawed at me. My normally cheery spirits had evaporated along with my self-esteem. What could I do?

And, to make things worse, I was swimming in an ocean of regret: I had just left the almost-ideal teaching job a few short months before. To come to this. Thinking: well, who can turn down a job that you can walk to?

What had I done?

Clearly, I needed a miracle. And, thanks to Whitney, an inkling of an idea began to grow. A germ of a possibility. I reminded myself that often teachers did want to borrow my learning games. What if I were to make patterns for the games that they could then make themselves?

Perhaps I could take out an ad in my teaching federation magazine?

The next day, after many false starts, I nervously phoned my teaching federation office and—gulp—asked to speak to the editor. I was going to mention the possibility of taking out an ad for the learning games. But I never got that far… A couple of minutes into the conversation the editor asked, with an intensity that surprised me, "Tell me more about what you do in your special education classes." I told her about the games and the puppet plays that I used to reinforce the 3 R's. "That's what my son needs!" she said. "He's only eight and he hates school. And he's not doing well. I'm at the end of my rope with him."

We talked for an hour. About education. About special education. About her son. Especially about her son. And how heartsick she was about his poor progress. We really hit it off. I felt I had known her all my life. At the end of the conversation she told me about the special education segment she was planning for the spring issue. "Would you consent to be interviewed for that issue?" she asked.

Would I?

She came. And my life was never the same again. The interview was a continuation of the phone conversation. Even better. In the middle of the interview she burst out: "Mary, you have to write a book about these ideas! If you do, we'll promote it for you!"

"A book? Me—write a book?"

Fast forward a few months: the result was *Joyful Learning*, a book of learning games for teachers and parents. My teaching federation did indeed promote the book. And one glorious thing led to another. It came to the attention of the press. And this led to a new job: The Federation of Women Teachers of Ontario hired me to present workshops to teachers around the province on how to encourage children to love learning. And off I went—by plane, by car, by bus, by train—to all corners of this vast and scenic province. A second book, a sequel, *A Whale in a Pail*, followed two years later.

And my former job? The one that was making me sick? As soon as I resigned, the infections, the colds, the viruses, all disappeared. And I never looked back.

~Mary Hansen

Second Chances

More than 10 million Americans are living with cancer, and they demon-
strate the ever-increasing possibility of living beyond cancer.
~Sheryl Crow

"What did I do wrong?" I cried out. The surgeon spoke in subdued tones, quoting statistics and survival rates, but I had stopped listening. Fear drowned out his words. This couldn't be happening to me! None of it seemed real.

He delivered the bad news and hung up—a dial tone filled the silence while panic seized my body. I was forty years old and in the best shape of my life—running three miles every day, working out at the gym, and eating tofu when no one else knew what it was. So what were the chances of me getting breast cancer?

One in eight!

There were a multitude of reasons for me to stick around—a husband of twenty years who was my lover, best friend, and father to our two boys, ages nine and fourteen, whom I desperately wanted to see through safe passage into adulthood. They were in the next room when I received the news.

Jon, my younger son, was terrified and immediately made a card from computer paper with two bunnies hugging each other. The words were simple, but came from the heart: "Mom, I love u, even though u have kancer!" Seeing the words "mom" and "cancer" in the same sentence created a surge of terror in me. What were they going to do if something happened to me? I hung the card on the refrigerator door as a reminder of what I was fighting for.

The following weeks were a blur of tests, more biopsies, and second opinions. At one point there were three doctors in the exam room—all delivering more bad news. I went from lumpectomy to double mastectomy within seconds. Laughter mixed with tears as I contemplated still more decisions.

Two weeks later, all the results were back and I only had "half" as much cancer as they originally thought. I would just need a lumpectomy—not a double mastectomy! I continued to work full-time through surgery, treatment, and finally radiation.

Working in the medical field, I simply knew too much. So in an effort to alleviate my anxiety, I would leave on my forty-five-minute lunch break for my radiation treatments and repeat the words: "Can't be late to radiate. Gotta go, gotta go, gotta go!"

Upon my arrival at the hospital, I would tap on the granite counter and say, "Excuse me, do you have my tanning bed ready?" The receptionist glanced up with her crinkling eyes and smiled. "I'll be sure to let them know you're here!" There's absolutely nothing funny about cancer, but making jokes was how I coped with my painful illness.

On the last day of treatment, which I know was a great relief to everyone on staff, I received the news I never wanted to hear—words regarding my survival rate. The metal door opened widely and the radiation oncologist entered, holding my now thickened chart in his hands. In a matter-of-fact tone, he announced, "I need to go over a few details before you leave. There are some long-term consequences of treatment that I need to discuss with you." As he enumerated the lengthy list, my mind wandered back to the pink brochure that was handed to me on the first day of treatment—the one I didn't want to read! As my feet dangled back and forth on the exam room table, I watched as the wall clock ticked off the seconds, and wondered just how much time I had left.

The doctor finished his discussion and ended with the word "death." What? Was that supposed to cheer me up? Obviously the doctor was oblivious to my fragile emotional state. Without a safety net to catch me—I "fell." I don't remember walking out into the dimly lit parking lot, how I drove home that evening, or how the dozen pink celebratory roses made it from the car to the kitchen table, but depression had replaced fear.

In an effort to get me "better," my husband sent me off to California to visit my folks. I'll never forget their expression when they saw me step off the plane. I was a mere skeleton with a zombie-like gaze—shuffling through the crowd of passengers. My parents tried to make small talk on the drive home, but they too fell silent.

I spent the following week staring out the window of the guest bedroom. One afternoon my dad sat on the edge of the bed—as tears rolled down his cheeks—while he choked out the words, "Connie, your mom and I have been praying for you, but we don't know what else to do. Please, tell us what to do." I grabbed my dad's trembling hand and whimpered, "But, Dad, I don't know what to do...."

Seven days later, in quiet desperation, my parents sent me back to Pennsylvania. When my husband, Mark, picked me up at the Baltimore Washington Airport, his face showed his shock and disbelief. I was in far worse shape than when I had left.

As we drove up the driveway to our home, I noticed the backyard had been perfectly landscaped. There were colorful flowerbeds where mounds of dirt had been. And in the center of the yard was a beautiful pink dogwood tree in full bloom. I pointed to the tree and asked, "What's this?"

Mark gazed into my eyes and said, "This is our tree of life—we're starting a new beginning. God hasn't brought us this far just to leave us." For the first time in weeks, I saw a glimmer of hope; it was brief, but it was there.

The next few weeks allowed me to build on that glimmer, and one afternoon, as I looked out at that beautiful pink dogwood tree, I asked myself the question. "What if I only had a year to live; what would I do differently?" I randomly wrote down twenty-seven things I wanted to do before I died. They included such things as: go back to Italy to visit friends, take a photography course, write a book, and #27—skydiving.

I laid the list down on the small oak table in the kitchen. Later that day, Mark picked up the list and read each one out loud. Afterwards he announced, "I'm going to help you accomplish every one of those goals and when that list is finished we'll write another one and another one… for the rest of your life."

That was seventeen years ago and today I've accomplished every one of those goals, except #27! I'm thankful for cancer in many ways—as crazy as that sounds. Not that I want to re-live the events of the past seventeen years, but I simply can't imagine my life without them.

On our twentieth wedding anniversary, we celebrated with a cruise to the Bahamas. Under moonlit skies, I whispered a silent prayer and thanked God for allowing me to experience life by facing my own mortality.

Life has become a series of celebrations—both big and small. But the greatest joy of all has been seeing my boys through safe passage into adulthood. They are now twenty-seven and thirty-two, pursuing passions of their own, which my bout with cancer taught them to do.

Now when I look in the mirror and see a "few" gray hairs and wrinkles (I call them laugh lines), I smile back and say, "What did I do right to deserve a second chance at this gift called life?"

~Connie K. Pombo

Overall Attire

Try not to become a man of success but rather try to become a man of value.
~Albert Einstein

I had just gotten my son to the bus stop when I noticed a run in my stockings. What a waste — on so many levels. Climbing the two flights back to my bedroom I pulled them off, scoured my drawers for an intact pair, and then struggled to get them on.

I forced my two-inch heels on one foot at a time, then fought with my skirt and blazer. I grabbed my briefcase and storyboards, along with my coffee, and stumbled out the door.

Going a tad over the speed limit, I made it to my meeting with minutes to spare. Working as a communications consultant, I prided myself on being incredibly organized, succinct and punctual. That morning I had a meeting with a major client with whom I had been working the last few years creating annual reviews, corporate videos and internal newsletters.

As a consultant, I met with my clients only once or twice a week. The balance of the time I worked from my home office. I loved the freedom that afforded me. When my children were very young I could help with their school and after-school events. But as they grew, one currently in middle school and the other in high school, I began to question why I was working for a company whose practices did not mesh with my own more environmentally friendly beliefs. (During one meeting, there had been an impromptu celebration in the hall as word spread that the company had won an asbestos suit brought against them.) With each conversation I started to feel less comfortable. Not to mention the stockings and suits.

This particular day, I felt reinvigorated. My husband and I had created boards for a new TV campaign that highlighted the efforts of a company that was working with clean energy. We were so excited about it and thought the entire campaign would help bring a new perspective to the company and its cause.

Juggling the boards, briefcase and now cold coffee, I entered the conference room. Instead of the normal in-house marketing team, there sat Bob, my main point person.

With a cold, even delivery, he explained that the company had just hired a Global Communications Manager who would be in charge of worldwide marketing. Long story short, she was bringing in her own people and my services would no longer be required.

But I was in the middle of planning the yearly review, an internal newsletter and a new spot. Wouldn't she at least meet with me and take a look at the work I'd done? What I'd been able to accomplish?

No. The newly appointed specialist would not speak with me or any other freelancer.

I gathered my work and made my way home. Immediately, I took off my stockings, put on my sweats, slipped on my boots and went for a walk in the nature preserve and farm behind my home. Step by step I struggled with the injustice. All those years organizing and updating their archaic ways. How ungrateful. How unfair.

I passed through the woods over the walkway to the city-subsidized farm and nature center where I volunteered weekly. As a volunteer I ran fundraisers and did a lot of hands-on work at the farm along with special events on the property. By the end of my stroll I was breathing again. I would just have to put my suit back on and reach out to new clients—communicating this time on my own behalf.

Instead, the next day I put on my overalls and went to the farm. It was getting close to Halloween and we were planning their big fall weekend with a scary hayride, pumpkins, apple cidering and a Boo Barn my son was creating for the little ones.

Weeks went by and I was spending more and more time stuffing scarecrows and planning special events for the farm. I was in heaven.

But I missed the paycheck. With two kids going to college in less than four years I needed to get back in the saddle (no pun intended) and find work.

One day I was a particular vision—dressed in my fashionable overalls caked in mud and who knows what—when a woman I had never met approached me.

"Good morning, I'm the new executive," she said. "You must be Jeanne. I've been talking to the staff and I was told that I had to hire you."

She explained how she had been working with the staff for the past few weeks and my name kept popping up. She was new to the area and needed someone tied in to the community and with marketing and communications skills. They needed someone to raise awareness and funds for the nature center. In short, they wanted me.

She asked me about myself—my background and what it was about the nature center that brought me there day after day. After forty-five minutes of non-stop talk, we were both exhausted.

I was hesitant to accept the position. I would be making considerably less than I did as a corporate consultant. On the other hand, I could wear whatever I wanted, walk to work and on occasion play with the goats. What more could a girl want?

I volunteered through the end of the year and then in January officially became part of the staff. In my new position I was able to create programming that tied the nature center to the community. Special events and activities flowed from me. I began to photograph and write human-interest articles for the paper. This gave me a new confidence to write less clinical essays. I started writing children's books and began my first novel.

The day I knew I had made the right decision came when I was in my office and heard cheering and celebration in the hallway. I popped my head out and saw the farm director in the hall with a box of ducklings that had gone missing. Someone had returned the ducks.

All were rejoicing! Especially me. I had found a new confidence and joy in working in an environment I loved with people I adored.

~Jeanne Blandford

Failing Up

The strongest principle of growth lies in human choice. Make wise decisions daily, follow through, and the results will be promising!
~Author Unknown

t was 1987. I was seventeen and had recently graduated from a small private high school. Anxious to expand my horizons and experience "more," I chose to attend the (very large) University of Florida.

Before going to college, I'd led a sheltered life under the watchful eyes of my parents and teachers. At UF, for the first time, I was on my own, and there was no one looking over my shoulder. Most of the classes were taught in large lecture halls and I soon realized my professors didn't know whether I was in class or not. I was expected to oversee my own life and make appropriate decisions—like attending class! But I was too young and immature to make good decisions without supervision. Suddenly, I could choose whether to go to class or hang out at the park listening to music and watching people make jewelry, tie-dyed T-shirts and candles. At the age of seventeen, music and fabulous homemade crafts were more appealing than academic lectures, and in blissful innocence (i.e. ignorance), I thought I'd pass my classes in spite of not attending them.

Despite my disappointing academic performance, my parents and I agreed that I'd go back to UF for my sophomore year. I promised to be more focused and attend classes. But when my parents received my next report card they were crushed to see my grades had not improved. There were tears as my mom rubbed her forehead saying, "I don't know what you're going to do, Becky. Clearly you cannot go back to UF. You're failing out."

The next morning my father tapped on my bedroom door and asked if he could talk with me. I dressed and came out, thinking I'd have to endure another lecture about my lack of discipline, but I was in for a surprise. We sat down at the oval dining table and he abruptly told me that if college wasn't right for me, then perhaps a career in the military would be. I was stunned, and started to protest, but he stood up, and in his quiet, firm way said, "Let's go."

The enlistment officer was named Sergeant Dutra, and from the moment I met this imposing figure, he called me "Hill" rather than "Rebecca." When I told him, "I would prefer to be called 'Rebecca,'" he was unresponsive and didn't care what I preferred.

After showing me a recruiting video, Sergeant Dutra gave me a written aptitude test. My parents and I sat in the lobby staring at the floor as he looked over the results. Returning, he informed me that I'd done well on my test and the army would like to have me.

"The position I have open right now is for a fry cook. Do you want to be a fry cook, Hill?"

"No," I whispered.

"No, what?" Sergeant Dutra asked as he stared sternly at me.

"No, I do not want to be a fry cook," I said with as much gusto as I could muster.

"'No, Sir.' When you answer me you say, 'No, Sir.' You got that, Hill?"

My knees felt weak as I walked out of Sergeant Dutra's office. I was silent on the ride home and grew thoughtful. I admire and respect military men and women but I am not cut out for the job. Had I enlisted I would've been a real live "Private Benjamin" and it would not have been a good thing for me, the army or the general security of our great nation.

I went to bed at seven that night. When I woke up the next morning my parents told me there was one other option, a small school called Georgia Southwestern College in Americus, Georgia. They said because it was a small school, the Dean of Students might be willing to take my good SAT scores into consideration and accept me as a transfer student despite my failing grades. As we pulled into the campus I yelled enthusiastically, "This is the most beautiful college I've ever seen. I know I will do well here!" I was right.

Dean Ritchie shepherded me through the process of becoming a transfer student at GSW. Under her guidance and the watchful eyes of my professors (who did, by the way, take roll call and know whether I was in class or not), I flourished. I partied much less, studied much more and felt good about myself when I made the Dean's List.

Of equal importance to my academic success was the fact that I blossomed within the tight-knit community of Americus and developed a sense of confidence that remains with me to this day. Sure, I had ferocious beauty pageant rivalries with some of my new South Georgia girlfriends, but the community as a whole accepted me and gave me opportunities that could only be found in a small college town. Competing in the Miss Americus pageant, I didn't win the coveted crown, but it did lead to being offered a job as a DJ at the local country music radio station, and to being invited to contribute as a freelance writer to the town's newspaper. These experiences awakened in me a lifelong passion for the art of interviewing others and communicating their experiences, and my own, through storytelling.

The other day, coming out of CVS pharmacy, I saw a young girl in a military uniform. She was coming out as I was going in. She looked happy and confident. It's interesting that what was wrong for me was right for her. I wondered what her story was? Did she end up on a direct path to destiny, or had she gone through a series of missteps, as I had, to find her footing?

I suspect that many successes are born from some sort of failure. I'm not proud of my terrible grades and wasted time at the University of Florida, but I'm convinced they have everything to do with my later successes at an out-of-the-way campus in a beautiful, sleepy South Georgia town.

~Rebecca Hill

Chapter
4

From Lemons to
Lemonade

From Adversity to
Acceptance

The Truth
that Healed Me

Seek truth and you will find a path.
~Frank Slaughter

"Great!" I muttered to myself, irritated, as I rolled over to get out of bed. "Don't I already have enough to deal with? Now I have to deal with this stupid shoulder blade pain again, too."

I knew what caused the pain. My rib popped out of alignment in the middle of the night. I remember halfway waking up from a bad stress-dream when it happened. I even remember thinking, "Oh, crud! Was that a good pop or a bad pop? (Did a bone go out of alignment or fall back into place?) I guess I'll know by morning."

As it turned out, it was a bad pop. By morning, the pain was excruciating. It felt like somebody plunged an ice pick into my shoulder blade while I was sleeping.

It was the third time it happened in two years. It usually happened when I was under exceptional stress.

Stress and back pain are related. Stress causes tense muscles, and tense muscles pull bones out of alignment. I'm a pain management specialist medical doctor, so I know these things.

I even knew what the emotional stress trigger was in this case. For a few months, my brothers and I had been fighting about how to care for our aging mother. Now in her eighties, Mom had begun to have nightly panic attacks. She also became physically unsteady and lost the ability to do complex tasks, like cooking.

If an Italian woman can't cook, you know she's on the decline.

Early in the course of my mom's illnesses, my brothers took up all the slack. They took off work to take her to doctor's appointments, they cared for her home and yard, and they paid her bills. They were the only ones who could help her, as they lived in the same town as she did.

I, on the other hand, lived 1,400 miles away, so I couldn't help at all, except for those few weeks a year that she visited me or I visited her.

Did that leave me feeling guilty? You bet. I was a "bad Italian daughter." At least, I would have thought that about me if I were in my brothers' shoes. Even though they didn't say anything to me about it, I just knew they were thinking, "She left us to do all the work."

My brothers and I weren't getting along, and I figured that was why—even though it was unspoken.

I guess none of us kids knew how to solve Mom's problems, so we just blamed each other and argued. It's understandable. All three of us are alpha dogs in our own packs. We all run businesses and we're all used to being in charge. However, in this situation, watching our mom decline, we all felt out of control and powerless to stop it—and that resulted in our feeling anxious, vulnerable, and irritable.

I guess I should speak only for myself, but I assume my brothers felt the same way. It would be understandable, don't you think?

As I said, my rib went out right at the height of this family conflict.

Deep down, I knew there was an emotional root cause that contributed to my alignment issues and my pain. I diagnose that kind of physical reaction to stress all the time in my pain management medical practice.

However, I also knew I needed physical therapy to fix the rib problem. So, I had my receptionist clear my schedule for that day, and I scheduled an appointment with my physical therapist friend, Holly.

As soon as Holly walked into the exam room and asked what happened to me, I started crying, almost uncontrollably. It was like the dam finally broke. "My brothers and I are fighting because of what's going on with my mother and I don't know what to do to fix the problem." I trusted Holly with this sensitive information because she was my friend.

As I continued to cry, and cry, and cry—actually, it was more like wailing—I felt something very, very weird begin to happen at the site of pain, near my shoulder blade. Even though Holly hadn't yet touched me, it felt like somebody grabbed hold of that knot and started squeezing it.

The squeezing pressure increased steadily, until it felt like that balled up knot of muscle in my back was nearly going to explode.

Right at the peak of the pain, I got a "word" from God. I didn't hear Him audibly. I just heard Him in my thoughts. But the message was clear: "It's not your fault."

"Not my fault?" I wondered. "What's not my fault?"

That's when it hit me. On some subconscious level, I believed the whole situation with my mom and my brothers was my fault—as if I could *cause* my mother's decline—or as if my staying in my hometown instead of moving away could have *prevented* it.

Obviously, that was an irrational thought, but I believed it, anyway, at the emotional level. It just goes to show that the heart and the head aren't necessarily connected.

It also occurred to me that I believed another lie, deep down. I believed that I should be able to "fix" my mother's situation (because I'm a doctor) and I should be able to make my mother happy (because I'm the only daughter), even though she was losing her independence. Thus, her decline was my failure, and her unhappiness with the situation was my fault.

In reality, I couldn't fix any of those problems for my mother, not even if I lived right next door to her. My mom's decline was a natural part of aging, and her happiness or unhappiness was entirely out of my control—not my fault and not possible for me to fix.

To put it another way, you could say I believed many lies about the situation, deep down. I was also "shouldering" a burden that didn't belong to me — hence the shoulder blade pain.

As soon as God revealed the lies that I believed, I was able to see how irrational they were. Almost immediately, they lost their emotional grip over me and I felt peace that surpassed all understanding. The truth really did set me free.

Not only did I feel free emotionally, I felt free physically, too. Even before Holly treated my alignment issues that day, my shoulder blade pain decreased substantially. It was at least three quarters better, just from my letting go of things that were (1) not my fault; and (2) out of my control.

The best part is the relief of my shoulder blade pain was permanent. See? As it turns out, going through conflicts and hardships can be good for you. You just have to look at those situations as opportunities. Through conflicts, you can learn a whole lot about yourself and move toward healing in your relationships as well as in your physical body.

~Rita Hancock, MD

Breaking Bald

Attitude is a little thing that makes a big difference.
~Winston Churchill

t's probably no surprise to hear that cancer instantly changes your world. Suddenly, your life has a dotted line, and two immediately identifiable halves—life before cancer, and life after.

It's a diagnosis with a lot of baggage. Even when you acclimate yourself to everything that follows—to the tests, surgeries, treatments, medications, fears and worries—it's sometimes the smaller things that can affect you the most.

Like the prospect of losing your hair.

It feels a little silly to admit it now, but the hair loss that typically accompanies chemo can be one of the hardest parts of those early days of life with cancer. It definitely was for me. It's not just a girl thing—it's tough for men too. Today's society puts a premium on thick hair that shines in the light and waves in the wind.

As a twenty-three-year-old woman at the time of my diagnosis, I bought into all of it. I loved my long hair. I had always been a tomboy, but I'd also had a girly-girl side. I'd modeled as a child, and dreamed of modeling again in the future, and I'd always loved to play with my hair, whether styling it or tossing it in a ponytail in order to pretend I was a superhero. The swing of my long hair made me feel pretty.

Then, of course, came the stunning diagnosis that I had pancreatic cancer, and the whirlwind days of treatment, tests, diagnosis, and more. I had the Whipple surgery within days of diagnosis—an incredibly dangerous twelve-hour operation that resects most of your digestive tract. In my case, the Whipple was completed in just nine hours and involved the removal of half of my pancreas, part of the bile duct, complete removal of gallbladder and duodenum, and part of the stomach.

However, that was just step one. After only a month or so of recovery (it normally takes a year), I faced an aggressive and grueling nine-month FOLFOX chemotherapy regimen (of leucovorin, fluorouracil, and oxaliplatin) that was either going to heal me or kill me. And while chemo doesn't always guarantee hair loss, in my case, the doctors told me right off the bat that with FOLFOX I'd lose my hair quickly.

I took a deep breath. I'd always dreamed of modeling, and when I began to face the coming year of chemo, I remember thinking, well, that dream was probably over.

Sure enough, it happened quickly. One week, I had hair. The next, it was falling away in clumps. So I got a referral from the hospital for a local hair academy that would shave it for free (and they even styled wigs for cancer patients). I marched in, and when I walked out, I was bald.

And then I cried.

Then I looked at myself in the mirror, really looked. I saw that my face was the same. My eyes were the same. I was still me. Possibly even more me than ever before, as there was something pure about my bald head in conjunction with my face, as if I had become my own guardian angel.

I straightened my shoulders and made myself smile at that reflection. I thought about how many other women or little girls out there lose their hair to chemo, facing it with courage. I would face baldness with courage too. It was just hair. So I put on a big chunky pair of earrings. I did my make-up with extra sparkle. And then I went proudly out on an errand without a hat or wig, my pale, newly bald head turning pink under the sun's rays.

Then I ran back inside and put on sunscreen.

Properly protected, I went back out again, and I never looked back.

This was my look now, and that was all there was to it! It took some getting used to, but I began to enjoy the freedom of my new look—no more blow dryers or hairspray—and to have more fun with make-up, especially around my eyes. My face was now the ultimate blank canvas! I stopped wincing at shampoo commercials, shrugging at them instead. Baldness was the ultimate hairstyle for a fast-paced life, and it was great to be able to shower and go. Soon, I was happily spending my hair-products budget on fabulous earrings.

My proud baldness eventually helped me achieve a dream. Not long after, and while I was still battling the worst chemo symptoms, my friend Shannon, a talented photographer, suggested an impromptu photo shoot to cheer me up. The pictures from that session built up my confidence. I began to take more photos, to track how I looked and how I was responding to the treatments, gaining further confidence. Eventually, I joyfully received news of my cancer's remission.

But the following year, the cancer came back.

I confronted myself. I could cry or I could tell cancer to kick rocks. This time, I knew what to expect and I didn't let go of my dreams. I began to pursue modeling in earnest, in spite of the newest grueling rounds of chemo, major surgery, and radiation. I wasn't going to let illness get me down for one more day.

And miraculously, it worked. I built up my portfolio and eventually achieved the notice of creative and exciting people like acclaimed make-up artist Paulina Perez, and photographer Steven Spoons, who gave me a huge start in networking within the industry.

Soon, I was walking the runway for fashion designer Erin Healy (who helped me get the right fierceness for my walk) and shooting a TV segment for Love Brigade's Alyssa Key. And I was thrilled to be able to walk two different looks for the FXSS event in Jacksonville, for famed designer Betsey Johnson, one of my favorite designers.

It didn't seem real to me. I wasn't supposed to be succeeding as a model right now. I was bald and scarred, undergoing chemo, radiation, and battling cancer yet again. And I was five-foot-two. I had given up on modeling without even realizing it.

Yet here I was.

I remember pausing at the end of the runway, posing in that beautiful Betsey Johnson dress in the pop of the flashbulbs, while an even brighter one went off in my head.

I realized that the thing I'd feared most, losing my hair, had actually resulted in making me unique and memorable. I had let go of my dreams, but oddly enough, cancer had given them back to me. It was a moment I never forgot.

Baldness is now my badge. Despite a third cancer occurrence, I've continued to model ever since, to run, sing, cycle, dance, and dream. I've never again let go of my dreams, and I spend every day trying to inspire others to do the same.

Never let someone tell you what you can't do.

They might tell you, for example, that nobody wants to look at a bald model. How silly is that?

~Alicia Bertine

A Lifetime of Stuttering

Awakening is the process of overcoming your false self and discovering your
True Self. It begins when you decide to grab the tiger by the tail and ends
with the tiger tenderly licking the sweat off your brow and face.
~Steve Baxter

For the first decade or so of my life, my older brother and I were the only two kids I knew who suffered from the speech disorder known as stuttering. Miraculously, around the age of twelve, my brother's stuttering stopped. I was very happy for him and equally excited for my future. I was thinking "two more years." Thirty years later, my stutter is still going strong and I wouldn't want it any other way.

If I had a nickel for every time I was made fun of, I could have potentially retired at twelve. It's not easy being a kid, and it's especially difficult when you're different.

The biggest fear for most Americans is public speaking, so imagine being a stuttering child having to read aloud a paragraph from *Charlotte's Web* as the entire class looks, listens, and laughs. It's not easy. Imagine sitting at your desk with your palms sweating, pulse racing, and heart pounding as if you're about to testify against the Mafia, when, in fact, you're simply sitting there waiting to read a paragraph from *Where the Red Fern Grows*.

That all changed for me in the eighth grade when I decided to ease my anxiety by volunteering to read each and every time. My hand was always the first to go up and stayed up for most of the class.

I chose to be in complete control of what and when to read. If kids laughed, they laughed. I'd usually have a witty one-liner to shoot back at them, which would ultimately shut them up. From that point on, I never again looked at my stuttering as a significant challenge.

Fast forward to 2012 and I'm a comic, a speaker, and a soldier with three tours of duty in Iraq. I currently hold the rank of Captain in the Alabama National Guard.

When I started out in comedy, my goal was simply to make the audience laugh. After each show or online video, I'd get feedback on how my comedy helped educate them with respect to their family and friends who also suffered from this speech disorder. I was blown away. Until seeing my routine, they'd never considered the challenges a person who stutters faces on a daily basis. Imagine the fear of talking on a telephone. Imagine the fear of ordering food at a restaurant. Imagine the fear of not being able to say your child's name.

I also get random messages from young men and women who aspire to serve in the military but feel they are not qualified due to their speech disorder. Being able to inspire them to follow their dreams might be the highlight of what I do. Stuttering is no joke but having the ability to inspire and create awareness of stuttering through humor has truly been a gift from God.

Stuttering is still one of the great unknowns. I've been stuttering for forty years and still can't explain it. I can probably do a better job of explaining the Pythagorean theorem. I do know, however, that four out of five people who stutter are male and that only around one percent of the world's population will ever know what it's like to get "stuck" on the simplest of sounds. I, just like any person who stutters, have my good days and bad days and everything in between. Additionally, we don't always get hung up on the same sounds, words, or sentences. And finally, the number one pet peeve for most of us is having people finish our words or sentences. We have something to say, so let us say it.

I've had the great fortune of attending the last two National Stuttering Association (NSA) annual conventions. The convention is not a pity party. It's a fun and inspiring celebration filled with education, awareness, acceptance and empowerment.

Because of my upbringing and military service, I've always been an adapt-and-overcome kind of guy, but attending the NSA convention has even opened my eyes to the difficulty many of my fellow stutterers face each and every day. I've even met people who stutter when they sing.

The NSA convention is a four-day conference. In 2011, we had the writer for the Academy Award winning film *The King's Speech* as the keynote speaker. I may be the only person who stutters who has not seen the film. Another great film featuring a person who stutters is *Star Wars*. James Earl Jones, the voice of Darth Vader, endured severe stuttering during his childhood but has gone on to have one of the greatest voices of our time. He truly beat the odds. Of course he did have one slight advantage; he was a Jedi.

There are days when I, too, wish I was a Jedi, but that has nothing to do with my speech.

Whether it's a big nose, ugly toes, or a run in your pantyhose, we all have perceived flaws that each of us should embrace, because if we don't embrace them ourselves, how can we possibly expect it from others?

~Jody Fuller

Why Me?

Attitudes are contagious. Are yours worth catching?
~Dennis and Wendy Mannering

"Why me?" That was all the teachers at our "newcomers table" seemed to talk about at lunch. This was back in the mid 1970s, when the Los Angeles School District decided to better integrate the faculties at its myriad of schools scattered around the city. White teachers in the school district's suburban schools were sent to the inner city. The minority teachers we replaced went to our mostly white former schools. Transfers were done by random selection and no one affected was happy with the situation.

Because misery loves company, we self-segregated by huddling together at one table to endlessly tell one another how stressful and wearing our long freeway commutes were and how much happier we had been in our former schools so much closer to home. It was so unfair. We had been doing so well where we were. Why did they move us and not someone else? Listening to the conversation day after day, I felt more and more unjustly treated and depressed.

Somewhere during the third or fourth week of school, Alan, the tall, white, redhead who had taught at this inner-city junior high school for most of his career, slipped into a chair at our table to welcome us to "his" school. He didn't get very far with his cheerful greetings before some members in our group began making it very clear they were not at all happy to be there. The last one to complain ended her long whine with the usual "why me?"

Alan looked into her eyes and said in a calm voice, "Why not you?" The table silenced. For me, it was an epiphany. He was right. Transfers had been done randomly. Why should any of us not have been in the mix? I realized how toxic our constant harping was. We were teachers, professionals who considered ourselves good at what we did. It was time we applied our skills and attention to teaching.

The bell ending lunch rang and I walked back to my classroom with Alan, whose class was across the hall from mine. As we reached our doorways, I turned to him and said, "Thank you." He grinned and nodded. I didn't have to explain. He understood what I meant.

I didn't return to the "newcomers table" for lunch the next day. Instead I sat with the teachers who were all old hands at the school. At first, I had nothing to contribute to their conversations about past events. But as time went on and conversations dealt with more current school events, or students I knew, I became one of the regulars.

The first weeks of that school year, my classes were totally out of control. My students were quick to accuse me of white prejudice if I asked them to stop talking or gave them poor grades on test papers. "You prejudiced!" was there firm response to any disagreements between us. I couldn't wait for the weekends to roll around and started counting off the days to Thanksgiving and the December winter break.

After Alan's comment at lunch that day, I began showing more interest in my students and working harder toward helping them improve. Slowly, the atmosphere in my classes became calmer, the dialogue less combative, the student participation more inclusive. By the end of the first semester, I found myself looking forward to Mondays, or counting the days until we returned to school after a break. I'd be eager to introduce a new lesson or technique I'd worked on in my free time, hoping it would be helpful for Chris, who had such trouble staying on task, or Maria, whose reading skills were practically nonexistent.

When Robbie got in trouble with the law and was transferred to juvenile detention, I worried about him. When Tony's family moved out of our school area, I missed him, in spite of the disruptions he often caused. Whenever I lost a student, I found myself thinking, "If I'd only had more time to work with him, or her, maybe we could have solved the problem." I regretted the lost chance.

By the spring break, learning was clearly taking place in my classroom. My students and I were getting along. We could joke together and share concerns. We liked each other. It took me some time to realize what had brought about the transformation. My initial resentment had brought a like response from my students. I didn't want to be there, so they didn't want me there either. I wasn't willing to make an effort, so neither were they. Once I committed to the hard work of teaching them, they responded by making the effort to learn.

Being transferred to the inner city was the best thing that ever happened to me, both professionally and personally. All of my experiences up to that point had come from living an upper middle class life in comfortable surroundings. The sights and sounds of my new environment were a shock to me. I had no real understanding of poverty or broken, dysfunctional families and neighborhoods. One by one, my middle class assumptions began to fall by the wayside as the school year progressed. By the last day of school, it was hard to say who had learned more—my students or me. They learned about proper use of the English language and became better readers and writers. I learned about life and became a better teacher—and person—for it.

~Marcia Rudoff

My New Job

Oh my friend, it's not what they take away from you that counts. It's what you do with what you have left.
~Hubert Humphrey

"I'm calling to tell you that you've been selected for the position of Technical Editor," the human resources specialist said. "The salary is $26,000, or would be if this were a full-time position. Of course, since this job is part-time, the salary will be half that."

I couldn't believe my ears. The salary range for the job was $26,000 to $60,000. With my PhD, I had assumed that my salary would be at the high end.

"Why is the salary so low?" I asked. Not the most effective bargaining move, but I was stunned.

"Management is not willing to negotiate on salary," she said, in a formal tone, which told me she was serious.

"But I'm earning more than that as a temp!" I protested. I had moved to Boulder, Colorado after earning my PhD in Linguistics, because I had decided to quit academia. I didn't want to be a professor—I wanted to live in a beautiful, exciting town and work as an editor. Editing jobs don't come along every day, so I had been doing temporary secretarial work for the past year, waiting for my break. "I won't be able to pay my bills."

"The job does include benefits," the HR woman reminded me.

And my temp job didn't. This job was with a research institute, exactly what I wanted. If they'd offered me a salary at the high end, I could have made it work. But this! The rent on my tiny apartment was $500 a month. I had student loans to pay, utilities, car insurance. I had to eat! "I'll have to think about it," I told the HR woman. She gave me three days.

There ensued a series of frantic phone calls to friends and family, asking for advice. "Could you do temp work the other half of the time?" my sister asked.

I didn't want to. I was so tired of secretarial work. But it seemed I had no choice. I went to my temp job supervisor and explained the situation. "Could you possibly keep me on part-time?"

"Of course! We don't want to lose you," Diana said. She was being kind. They had recently hired a permanent secretary and really didn't need me anymore. I often ended up doing impossibly low-level work, such as shredding documents. But, as mentioned before, I had to eat.

I called the HR woman back and told her I'd take the job, but I showed up for my first day of work in a bad mood. My new manager, Val, was friendly, but I kept thinking: this man thinks I am only worth $26,000—no, $13,000!—a year.

The first thing we had to do was set my schedule. Val wanted me there during the middle of the day, maybe ten to three.

"That's not going to work," I said, humiliated. "I've still got my temp job, so I'll have to be here either mornings or afternoons, not both."

"Oh! I didn't realize you were going to continue working elsewhere," Val said.

"I have to," I said. "I can't afford to pay my bills otherwise."

"Ah yes, well..." his voice trailed off.

I liked my new office, with its view of the mountains, but I noticed that the sign on my door had just my name, no title. I also noticed that some of the engineers in the lab did have "Dr." on their nameplates. I asked the secretary about it.

"Some of the technical staff that don't have doctorates are offended when others refer to themselves as Doctor," she told me. "We thought it would be better if you didn't use your title."

I was thunderstruck. My advanced degree had gotten me the job, but now I had to pretend I didn't have one? In the academic world, I was always called Doctor, but of course I'd wanted to get out of academia. In the "real world," apparently the rules were different.

Even without the offending title, I found that many of the engineers were hostile to me. One of my first jobs was to assemble the (very overdue) annual report. I couldn't believe how rudely the project leaders responded to my requests for information.

So, my salary was low, my degree was a dirty little secret, everyone hated me, and I still had to do temp work in the afternoons. Why exactly had I taken this job? Vacation time, I reminded myself. Health insurance. And maybe if I stuck it out, things would get better. I knew the job had potential, if I could just fix everything that was wrong with it.

A month after I started working, the director of the institute retired. Afterwards, one of my co-workers called me into her office to talk. Julie explained that it had been the director, not Val, who set my salary. "There were other well-qualified applicants, so he low-balled you. Don't blame Val. His hands were tied." I took her words to heart and started being nicer to my boss.

Through the grapevine I learned that the previous technical editor had not had a good relationship with the engineers. So I set out to repair the damage by demonstrating that I valued and respected their work. Gradually they began to warm up to me.

I remember once asking an engineer named Roger if I could read a paper he'd written. "Sure, I'll make you a copy," he said, getting up.

"I'll do it," I said quickly. "I don't want to waste your time."

Roger gave me a look, and walked down the hall to the copier. "They pay me the same, whatever I do," he said, feeding the pages into the machine.

I thought about his words later that day, as I stood in front of the shredder at my temp job. Roger and I both had doctorates, and undoubtedly our talents could be put to better use than photocopying and shredding. But someone had to do those jobs, and there's never enough support staff. It's like the dishes. Someone has to do them, and it won't kill you.

Within the year, Julie announced her retirement, and Val distributed her responsibilities among the remaining front office staff. My new extra duties were pretty strange: I would now be managing the institute's property, vehicles, and field site. But I didn't think twice about accepting them. I was willing to do almost anything to go full-time.

Over the years, this willingness paid off. Gradually I was given more interesting and appropriate assignments, as well as a promotion, and I even got my title back. When I left the job to move to California, many of the engineers told me how much they'd enjoyed working with me.

I'm job-hunting now, after staying home with my kids for a few years. I know I may have to do something menial in the beginning, and my starting salary may be low. But I also know that, given the chance, I can prove myself worthy of more.

~Margaret Luebs

The Negative Positive

Life holds so many simple blessings,
each day bringing its own individual wonder.
~John McLeod

I stared at the blue plus sign. Frozen in shock, I couldn't even move as my husband poked his head into the bathroom. It couldn't be real. It wasn't possible.

"Hey, if we don't get going, we're going to be late…." He trailed off. "What's that?" He grabbed the white stick. "Is this a pregnancy test?"

I nodded mutely. He gaped at the bright blue plus sign. "Does that mean…"

I nodded again. Bursting into nervous laughter, he wrapped his arms around me. One phone call later, and we had a doctor's appointment in two days. He whisked me to the store to buy prenatal vitamins and peanut butter, essentials he felt every pregnant woman should have. One week after my blood test I answered my phone, eager to hear the results. But as soon as the doctor spoke, a sinking feeling twisted my guts.

"I'm sorry, Mrs. Koerner." I slid to the floor, my cell phone dangling from my fingers as the nurse's voice squawked over the speaker. "The doctor wants you take your prenatals and start trying again…."

Her words jumbled together in meaningless condolences. But I wasn't crying for me. I was crying for my husband, crying for the gift I couldn't give him. As a woman, my biological purpose was to reproduce. And I'd already failed.

He came home with roses and kisses that night, wiping away my tears as he hid his own heartache. "We can try again," he assured me cheerfully as he whipped around the kitchen fixing dinner. "I bet we're pregnant again in a few months. Just wait!"

I did wait. And waited some more. A month went by, then two, then three. I wasn't having periods and I wasn't ovulating. Doctors either patted me on the head and told me to "give it a year and relax" or were eager to prick me with needles and brandish brochures with fertility treatments. I gained five pounds and traded Zumba for yoga and kickboxing for barre classes. Nothing. I ate salads with flaxseed and enough salmon to sprout fins. Every test was negative.

"I don't know what to do," I moaned to my best friend, burying my face in my hands. "I've tried everything. I've changed my diet, changed my exercise, slept more, everything. Nothing is working and no one knows what's wrong with me." I peeked through my fingers. "Maybe I should go see a *curandera*."

"A *curandera*?" She blinked at me.

"A Mexican medicine woman. I know one that I did an article on once…." I trailed off as she held up a single finger.

"What do you do?"

"When?" I asked, confused.

"For your job."

"Oh! I'm a writer." I looked at her like she'd grown another head.

"And what do you do for fun?"

"Paint, dance, hike…"

"So you're an artist."

"Right." I stuck my hand out with a smirk. "Nice to meet you."

She batted my hand away. "What do you do when a story or painting isn't working?"

"I take a walk or start another project." Her lips twitched and I sighed. "You're telling me to focus on something else, aren't you?"

"I'm not telling you to do anything." She raised her hands. "I'm just saying that this isn't a story where you can arrange the quotes neatly or make the characters do what you say. If you keep fighting this, you're just going to get frustrated."

"Everyone keeps telling me to relax, but they're not the ones that can't get pregnant!" I griped. "This wasn't what I had planned. I should have been pregnant a year ago." Tears dripped down my wrists, pouring through my clenched hands. "Everyone can have a baby but me. What if I never get pregnant? What if I can't have kids?"

"Then you focus on being a good wife and mother to your dogs. You write. You paint. You help others." My girlfriend touched my arm, her voice gentle. "Being a mother is about doing things for others, about touching lives and raising individuals into the world. You can do that without giving birth. You can adopt or volunteer or mentor." It was her next words that stopped my tears. "Instead of focusing on what you don't have, why not focus on what you do?"

I glanced up and wiped my eyes with the back of my hand. "You know, you're right." Sniffling, I shakily stood up. "Let me start by treating you to lunch at Twin Sisters."

Her eyes bugged out. "But that's expensive." Her stomach rumbled and we both pretended not to hear it. In this economy, lunches out were a treat.

"It's nothing for a friend." I smiled and hooked my elbow through hers. "So tell me more about your new story...."

I went home that night and threw away the ovulation tests and basal charts. I threw out the books screaming, *Take Charge of Your Fertility* and *The Impatient Woman's Guide to Getting Pregnant*. I cancelled my doctor's appointments and the appointments with the *curandera* and psychic.

Then I cleaned. I cooked dinner. I did laundry and scrubbed until the house gleamed. My husband came home to a turned down bed and hot meal. I hadn't seen him that happy since we were in college and *Grand Theft Auto IV* came out.

I called girlfriends I'd been too busy to chat with and donated paintings to the Humane Society auction. I started teaching a writing workshop for teens and mentoring girls who wanted to write. And every night when I took my two Chihuahuas for a walk, we stopped three houses down so the little girl could pet them and pretend she had a dog of her own.

I may not be able to give my husband a baby, but at least I can give those around me a happy life. And if children come, it will be even sweeter.

~Miranda P. Koerner

Fighting Back

A bend in the road is not the end of the road... unless you fail to make the turn.
~Author Unknown

Two weeks before my forty-ninth birthday, I was diagnosed with Type II diabetes. I woke up one morning with a sinus infection and decided to drop in at a nearby clinic. Most of the time, when I was sick, my sinuses would be the problem. Rather than make an appointment with my often-neglected internist, I usually just went to the clinic, got some medicine and a shot, and went on my way. It was the convenient thing to do.

On this particular visit, while I waited to see a doctor, I noticed a poster on the wall that advertised clinical trials for a new sinus medication. When the doctor came in, I asked him about it. He thought I would be a good candidate, so I signed up. A nurse came in to draw blood for the trial.

On my first visit, as part of the clinical trial, they gave me the results of my blood test. The doctor was quite concerned over my blood glucose level. He was so agitated, so insistent that I immediately see my internist, that I left his office terrified.

Sure, I had heard of diabetes. My grandmother had died in a diabetic coma; however, like millions of people, I did not realize how shockingly little I actually knew, or didn't know, about this disease. I immediately called my internist for the first available appointment. I hung up the phone, sat down and cried. I called my husband and gave him the news. Then I sat down and cried some more. I called a friend with the news. Then I sat down and cried again. I was a complete wreck. What was I to do?

I somehow felt that I needed to eat as little as possible until I could see the doctor. I ate baked potatoes, toast, and other bland foods, as if I were recovering from the stomach flu! These are the foods that diabetics need to minimize and I was making a diet of them. This was how little I knew. The only thing I knew about a diabetic diet is that it should be low in sugar. I had no idea that the body converted starches to sugar, or glucose, in the blood stream.

My doctor ran the tests that confirmed that I, indeed, was a Type II diabetic. He explained the differences between a Type II diabetic and a Type I diabetic. This was the first time I was actually aware that there was more than one kind of diabetes and how they were treated. He also explained how this put me in a high-risk group for other things, like heart disease. He prescribed some medicine for me and set me up for educational classes at a diabetic clinic. I attended them all and paid close attention.

I wondered how long the disease had gone undiagnosed. I did not want to hear that my weight gain, over the years, might have been a trigger for the disease. I did not want to hear that my life had become too sedentary. I was very defensive and very much in denial. I was still scared and frustrated. This was everyone's fault but mine!

But… I began to eat the way I was supposed to eat. I now knew what foods to avoid or minimize, and what foods to seek out. I searched the Internet and learned everything I could about healthy eating. I discovered the glycemic index, which measures the effects of a food on blood glucose levels.

I got on the treadmill every night. I never missed. At first I would walk and cry. If tears burned calories, I would have wasted away. I made up a song about diabetes and I sang it as I walked. It was a marching song, a war song. It was about not letting this disease beat me. I sang as if I were throwing down a challenge to a tangible opponent. I even shook my fist in the air from time to time.

Some unexpected things began to happen. I lost over thirty pounds. My bad cholesterol levels dropped. My good cholesterol levels went up. Even my blood pressure improved. My level of exercise had progressed to the point that I became interested in entering 5K runs, especially fundraisers. I was still a Type II diabetic, but I was much healthier than I had been before.

Most importantly, with the help of my doctor, I brought my blood glucose levels under control. I felt embarrassed and ashamed that I had neglected regular visits to my doctor. The truth was that I felt like I didn't need to see him. Things like early detection and preventative care were foreign to me. Why did I need to go to the doctor when I wasn't sick?

I started taking responsibility for my own health. I faithfully tested my blood and recorded my results. I did hours of research on diabetes. I wanted to know everything about the disease that had taken over my life. I wanted everyone around me to know. I did fasting glucose tests on my entire family. I didn't want them to be harboring this disease, unknown, as I had been. I also encouraged them to get their doctors to test them.

I see my doctor regularly. I am up to date on all my medical tests. I always ask for copies of my lab reports so that I can track changes. I make notes prior to going to my doctor so I won't forget what to tell him or what to ask him. He adjusts my medicine or gives me advice based on my tests and our discussions. We are partners in my health care.

It has been over ten years since my diagnosis. I still hate being a diabetic, but I am so thankful that I was diagnosed. I truly believe that it was divine intervention that led me to that clinical trial. It still surprises me how uneducated people are about diabetes, especially diabetics. I find that I am becoming more involved in spreading the word and helping fight diabetes.

We all have to live with some sort of adversity. Diabetes will always be a part of my life, and I have to deal with that, but it won't define me, and it happily led me to better health.

~Debbie Acklin

Teamwork

Act as if what you do makes a difference. It does.
~William James

I n early spring of my daughter's ninth year, her life's passion was to play soccer. She had been active and successful in softball, karate, ballet, and basketball in the past, so it was with enthusiasm that I took her to sign up for the recreational soccer league in town. However, when we arrived, we found out there were not enough coaches to start a new team and there was no room on any existing teams.

Since there were a couple of other girls awaiting a new team, the league director suggested that I coach. My daughter's confidence in my abilities outweighed my concern that I had never played the sport before, or even watched a game. I immediately ran to the library and got every book I could about the game and about coaching soccer. I had coached other teams before in the sports that I myself had played, so how hard could this be?

The coaches of the other teams were instructed to donate one of their players to our team so that we would have a full roster. Well, as you may have guessed, I did not get their star players; but I did have a group of ten girls who were excited about playing.

I wrote up drills and charts and team building activities and went to the first practice with only mild trepidation. The first activity was simply to familiarize the girls with the size of the field, so we all gently jogged the length of the field. It was then that I realized that I had some girls who could not jog the length of the field without taking a break.

During the next drill I positioned myself at different spots on the field with a stack of numbered cards. The girls were to walk with a soccer ball and gently kick it and then immediately look up and shout out the number of the card that I held up. I wanted the girls to get comfortable with looking down at the ball and then quickly looking up, as they would have to do that during a game. I quickly found out that I had a team of mixed capabilities, with some girls tripping over the ball and their feet, and others zigzagging down the field at great speeds.

I knew that what mattered most was for each girl to achieve her personal best and for the team to support each girl's efforts to do so. So we put all of the equipment away and sat on the field and talked. The rules for our "talk time" were to listen to each person and not make fun of what anyone said. I encouraged the girls to be honest, silly, and revealing by providing them a safe atmosphere to express their feelings. At the first "TT" (how we referred to talk time), each girl had to tell us her name, what school she went to, how many siblings she had, her favorite desserts, what she liked about soccer, and what she hoped to be able to do by the end of the season. It was a great way for the girls to start seeing each other as friends who wanted to work together.

We continued to practice twice a week, and we were really improving, except for one girl, Melissa, who was struggling with being overweight, uncoordinated, and discouraged. She would often hang her head and fight back tears. So, during the next TT, I had the girls go around the circle and tell each player something positive about her progress.

We lost our first game and the second, so during the next TT we sat and talked about what mattered most, with a focus on having fun, learning teamwork, and making friends. Those aspects were just as important as winning… even more important. It was exciting to win our third game and our fourth, but when we lost our fifth and sixth games, the girls needed a morale booster. So the theme of the next TT was "believe in yourself and work towards your goals." During this session I asked several parents to tell stories about their own personal experiences centered on that theme. The end result was we were building not only a team, but a family as well.

We ended up winning half our games and having a terrific time in the process. Since my daughter was recruited by a travel soccer team, I did not coach soccer the next season.

After my daughter started middle school, I stopped by the grocery store one day to pick up a few things for dinner and heard someone shout "Coach Judi." I turned and recognized that the woman behind the bakery counter was Melissa's mother. She came around the counter with her arms open wide and a huge smile on her face. We embraced and I asked how Melissa was doing, and she said that Melissa had made the middle school soccer team.

She told me an inspiring story. When Melissa went to the tryouts, the coach suggested that she might have better luck with another activity. (Melissa was still overweight.) But Melissa looked the coach right in the eye and said that she wanted a chance. Needless to say, the coach was taken aback but allowed Melissa to try out. When she was selected to be on the team, the coach asked her what motivated her to try out even when he initially discouraged her. She said, "When I first starting playing soccer, I could not even run the length of the field, let alone kick a ball and run. But my coach told me at the time that if I believed in myself and worked hard, I could achieve my goals. I figured if this person who barely knew me believed in me, then I needed to believe in myself as well."

Melissa's mom and I openly wept as she told me this story. After another big embrace, she said that she wanted to give me a gift. She went behind the counter of the bakery and returned with a pie. She said, "You always let the girls know that sometimes life would give them lemons, but you also taught them how to turn them into lemonade."

My throat was so filled with emotion that I could barely speak, but I smiled and choked out my reply, "Lemon meringue; my favorite."

~Judith Fitzsimmons

The Fruitful Life

Somebody should tell us, right at the start of our lives, that we are dying.
Then we might live life to the limit, every minute of every day. Do it! I say.
Whatever you want to do, do it now! There are only so many tomorrows.
~Pope Paul VI

Our friend Bob Faust had pancreatic cancer. He had been undergoing chemo for six months and was the sole surviving participant in an experimental test program at the local cancer center in Houston, Texas. But he knew... and we knew... that his time with us was limited.

Nevertheless, when my husband Art and I asked him if he wanted to take a driving trip to Mexico, he emphatically said, "Yes." Of course, his wife Debbie wanted to do whatever he wanted to do. His doctors felt the same way, and they removed his chemo port, taped it over and wished him a good trip.

So, after Christmas, with the ominous cloud of Bob's imminent death looming over us and the optimistic promise of a new year awaiting us, we headed off on a Mexican adventure.

Death rode with us and was the elephant in the car. We were outwardly, awkwardly jolly and wanted to make this time special, but it was Bob who managed to do that for us. When we crossed the Tropic of Cancer, I begged for a photo stop. Art braked, Debbie laughed, and Bob groaned out the words, "Cancer, oh, no." The car was silent and then we all began roaring at his joke.

The four of us were birdwatchers, and in the Mexican high

plains birds are sometimes few and far between. But Art had heard of a cemetery near the highway where people had spotted some special birds. As we pulled into the brilliantly flowered cemetery oasis, the screeching and cawing from the trees was deafening, loud enough to wake the dead. And when we got out of the car to get a better look, Bob raised his fist up to the buzzards circling in the brilliant blue sky. He took a Scarlet O'Hara stance, then screamed at them, "Go away! You can't have me yet!" Again, he brought down the house and we giggled at his black humor.

Our days were filled with laughter and fun, with Bob showing us the way it was. On another foray into birdwatching, while returning from a trip to Tamazunchale, Art spotted some darting color in an orange orchard and veered onto a private dirt road off the main highway. The birdwatching was incredible and we stayed for a half-hour, enjoying the winged world through our binoculars. It wasn't long, though, before we realized "we" were also being watched. A black truck slowly approached us as we eased back to our Suburban for the safety of numbers and the inside of our vehicle.

Sure enough, it was the landowner, with two of his workers, wanting to know our purpose for trespassing. Art pled our innocence to the stern-faced landowner/judge, while the non-Spanish-speakers among us awaited our fate in silent anxiety. Finally, after a second or two of uncertainty, a smile lit the man's face and he graciously welcomed us to Mexico and to his land. Spreading his arms, he announced, "*Mi huerto es su huerto*" ("My orchard is your orchard"). He invited us to continue with our avian pursuits and then instructed his men to bring us two buckets of "*naranjas*"—the most delicious oranges this side of Valencia. We overdosed on these juicy morsels, especially Bob, who savored every bite.

We celebrated New Year's Eve at a party with the locals, who soon became our friends, since Bob never met a stranger in his life. We stayed at the party until the eating of the grapes—downing one grape for each chime during the countdown to midnight. Afterwards, the fiesta continued in our room. Bob had bought and brought with him four bottles of expensive champagne! We did our best, but only managed to finish two bottles before we took to our beds.

We left the next day for home. It was at the border that we realized that we had more than twenty of the oranges left that we could not take back across the border due to customs' insistence on inspected fruit. Plus, though we had given it a good high school try, we were unable to finish the last two bottles of champagne the night before. The bottles had no tax stamp, so we weren't allowed to return with them either.

Art pulled off the highway, conceding our place in the long line through customs, and we held an impromptu memorial for our trip, reliving the experiences and laughter that had prevailed. We sat huddled in the car, with the heater running, toasting Bob at every gulp (since Art was our designated driver, he abstained from the champagne but toasted adequately with fresh-squeezed orange juice). When we finished we could finally carry the oranges and champagne across the border legally, albeit internally.

As the Suburban merged back into the line of traffic, glass in hand, Bob gleefully said, "When life hands you oranges, make mimosas!" And he had shown us how.

~Marilyn Zapata

Adventures in Staying

A father may turn his back on his child, brothers and sisters may become
inveterate enemies, husbands may desert their wives, wives their husbands.
But a mother's love endures through all.
~Washington Irving

Dad embodied adventure. Mom focused on the ordinary. He tickled me nightly on the living room floor, while she finished up in the kitchen. He took me on his rounds on the farm to water the fields of sprouting cotton crops, to jump in the trailers of freshly picked cotton, or to slide into the irrigation canals and ride the current. She made sure I made my bed.

I never lacked for excitement with Dad. He taught me how to catch and bridle my horse, and to snow ski at a young age. He would invent new ways to scare the daylights out of us every Halloween. And on after-dark hikes, he would eagerly recite his menacing "Headless Horseman" tale, as his dimly lit buddy skidded down a nearby mountain, supposedly without a head.

Dad was larger than life to me. I thrived on watching him in action—aiding the roadside birth of a new calf, rescuing the bloody neighbor who ran through the sliding glass door, or capturing the wounded coyote to mend in the empty chicken pen. I loved adventure and he was the adventurer.

Near the end of my third grade year, the action screeched to a halt. A closed-door discussion between Dad and Mom ended with

Dad making trips to his truck with all his personal belongings. I walked each painful load to the truck with Dad the night he left. I did not witness my siblings huddled around Mom, crying in the living room. I was so focused on the one who left that I didn't think of the one who remained. But in the years since that night, I have had the opportunity to discover who the true adventurer was—the one who stayed.

A single mom with four small daughters and no job—that, in itself, set the stage for disaster to come. Who would have guessed that, instead, life would evolve into one huge adventure?

It started small as we adjusted—watching the black-and-white Wizard of Oz with green sunglasses, pulling to the side of the road to gape at the special Christmas star, investigating a flood at the ranch from which we had moved.

Mom became creative. In an electrical outage, a flashlight at the player piano kept us busy for hours. Our not-so-intelligent dogs fighting through the glass sliding door served as simple and silly entertainment. And somehow, saltine crackers crumbled into a bowl, topped with milk and sugar, became a delicacy we begged for at suppertime.

Then the adventure grew. Simple outings transformed into explorations of unchartered territory, usually on the nearby Native American reservations. We escaped falling walls in dilapidated and crumbling Native American ruins. We appeased haunted spirits in Native American graveyards with the eye of the Kabbalah. We hunted for buried treasure in the old Cooley Civil War mansion. Each escapade left us with memories and scars to prove its worth.

Ordinary hikes became grand conquests of terrain, often leaving wisdom and safety back home. One ten-hour spree landed us above the snow and timberline with no supplies other than a picnic lunch and no more protection than an eight-inch tall dog.

Another day's jaunt led us high atop the nearby Hopi mesa. In the history of the Hopi Nation, they had allowed the public to view their ceremonial snake dances only twice. We were there, sitting cross-legged with the Native Americans and scampering panic-stricken when a rattler escaped into our ranks. Our interest level always seemed to outweigh the liabilities and risks.

We no longer vacationed, but set out on investigations into the fascinating. The boiling mud pots at Yellowstone National Park made us all feel unsteady, but no more than Mom's reading of *The Night of the Grizzly* in the tent—a poor choice in travel literature.

It never mattered that there was no father, uncle, brother, grandpa, male cousin, male anything around—we would bait, gut, and untangle at the toughest trout streams anyway. It never occurred to us that we should have experience. We naively assumed we could learn how to erect a tent on the first night of the two-week camping trip to Canada. And we did—a two-hour task, compared to the fifteen-minute job we whittled it down to by the end.

So adventure characterized Mom after all. But the adventure was not always easy. It required night classes to finish her college degree, and the after-work trip each week to the ranch, now over an hour away, to make payroll. It included not always having the money to pay all the bills. It involved de-skunking the ripe aroma from our over-friendly dog, picking up pieces of the glass sliding door I kicked in, and a lot of broom swinging to dislodge bats from the rafters. Yet she stayed.

It entailed the endless disciplining of four girls, who could easily find trouble. It also included raising us with no relative to pick up the slack. Mom lived with a constant fear of her four girls being separated into foster homes if something were to happen to her. So she stayed.

But in staying, Mom got to see her girls grow up. She whooped and hollered when we made the team. She scoured the racks with us for the perfect prom dress. She endured every concert and musical we performed. And she was there to plan each of our weddings. Hers was an adventure of family, of relationship, of love. And it produced a lifetime bond among five women.

Her adventurous spirit became so ingrained in me that it affected my choices on a regular basis. It influenced the way I raised my own kids, who, in turn, were fascinated by treasure hunts that never took

them beyond their own back yard, and amazed at what kind of crit-
ters they could find under a rock. I will never feel compelled to look
for adventure out there. Mom has proven there is great adventure in
staying.

~Ann Kronwald

Death Benefits

We must embrace pain and burn it as fuel for our journey.
~Kenji Miyazawa

I returned home from a shopping trip one Saturday to discover eight messages on my answering machine. They all said: "There's been a death in the family. Please call this number." I assumed that my eighty-two-year-old mother had passed, since she struggled with Alzheimer's and related illnesses.

But it wasn't until I heard the seventh message that I learned that my fifty-one-year-old brother Jerry had died from complications of a burst ulcer and internal bleeding.

Jerry had died one day before my birthday.

Stupefied by the horrific news, I quickly cancelled plans for my birthday celebration in Sonoma, California and purchased tickets to fly from San Francisco to Billings, Montana.

Jerry's son Stevie picked me up at the airport the next day and provided details of Jerry's unexpected death. For two hours he kept telling me: "Now I won't have Dad to hunt with." It was a somber 125-mile drive to the railroad town of Forsyth.

On our arrival, we joined legions of distraught relatives and friends at Jerry's house. I tried hard to process the enormous grief of Jerry's family, my brothers and sisters, Jerry's close friends, and most of the small town. I was perceived as the "Rock of Gibraltar" for many, many people.

I spent most of Monday at the wake, conducted at various taverns and homes. Everyone had a "Jerry" story to tell—resulting in much bittersweet laughter, enhanced by abundant liquid refreshments.

On Tuesday I delivered a eulogy at the mortuary chapel, which adjoined a furniture store. I was angered when the friendly-but-business-minded funeral director and storeowner tried to sell me a couch while I waited for the services to begin. I asked him: "How will purchasing a couch from you in any way help me assuage my sorrow?" It was just another stressful moment to complicate my situation.

After attending a formal church service, I served as pallbearer at Jerry's interment at Forsyth Cemetery. Since I'd been the shoulder-to-cry-on for every member of my family, I had no time to process my own grief at my beloved brother's passing. I was exhausted, having slept no more than three or four hours during the three-day period.

I flew back to California on Wednesday to begin the new school year at a Bay Area university.

Elizabeth, my department chair, told me: "You don't have to meet your first class tomorrow. Everyone will understand."

I replied: "Even under these circumstances, there's no way I'll miss that class meeting." I stubbornly elected to go ahead.

I'd never missed an opening day and the first class meeting was always a big event for me. I tried to pour all my energy into a fast-paced hour of information-sharing, storytelling, and inspirational messages.

Since cancelling the first class meeting was out of the question—even under my very special circumstances—I decided to meet my marketing class, despite exhaustion and lack of quality time to process my own grief.

Just five minutes into the first meeting of the class, I fell apart! Fifty befuddled students—mouths agape—watched as I stumbled for words and fought back tears. I was distraught and incoherent.

What could I do? Regaining some semblance of composure, I confessed to the class: "My brother died last week and I need your help! Please help me get through this class meeting." They were riveted—clinging to my every word and gesture and displaying a kind of empathy I'd never experienced—before or since. They were on my side, pulling for me to process my grief. It was the best opening-day class I ever conducted and probably the best course I ever taught. I was so grateful for their understanding and support that I poured my energy into every class meeting thereafter.

And when students, campus wide, voted for "Best Lecturer" the next spring, I won the honor, even though it was my first year teaching on that campus and there were many fine teachers who had larger classes and more history at the university. That recognition spurred me to work harder the next three years to become an even better teacher.

A few years later, I interviewed for a full-time teaching position at a small liberal arts college in Portland, Oregon. When a committee member asked me: "What was a very stressful time in your life and how did you handle it?" I told the story of my brother's funeral and my opening-day class. My heartfelt answer made a big impression. They hired me—that day.

The tragedy of a death in the family can sometimes enrich the living. Jerry left me more than great memories of growing up together and lots of entertaining moments we shared as adults. Besides protecting "little brother," filling me in on the "facts of life," and serving as a role model, Jerry inadvertently helped make me a better teacher over the next twenty-four years.

That funeral weekend—and how I dealt with it subsequently in the classroom—made me less of a sage-on-a-stage and more of a human being, a better listener, and a teacher who always made strong efforts to connect with his students.

Not quite so slick anymore, I now wear my heart on my sleeve. For that, I am eternally grateful to my brother Jerry.

~Robert J. Brake

Chapter

5

From Lemons to
Lemonade

From Problem to Purpose

Big Dreams

Wanting something is not enough. You must hunger for it.
Your motivation must be absolutely compelling in order to overcome the
obstacles that will invariably come your way.
~Les Brown

When I decided to apply to medical school, while in my first year of college at the University of Miami in South Florida, I realized my desire to be a physician had been influenced greatly by my childhood orthopedic surgeon. Dr. Steven Kopits had cared for me numerous times at Johns Hopkins Hospital in Baltimore, Maryland.

I never fully imagined what a challenge the application process would be. Up until that point, like many of my classmates, I had been used to working hard, making good grades, and achieving my goals. I never thought of myself as particularly smart or gifted, and I knew getting into one of the top ranked medical schools in the country, Johns Hopkins, was a long shot; but surely, my goal of becoming a doctor was not.

Even though I had physical limitations, I had learned that for most things, if I worked hard enough and wanted something badly enough I could make it happen. Well, my application process to medical school was an abrupt awakening that the world may not always be fair, and that sometimes hard work and good results may not be enough.

I submitted applications to thirty medical schools and only

received two requests for follow-up interviews. One was at my current undergraduate university: the University of Miami's Leonard M. Miller School of Medicine (UMMSM). The other was at my dream school where I had also been a patient so much of my childhood: Johns Hopkins University School of Medicine (JHUSOM). Even though my peers and I had similar Medical College Admission Test (MCAT) scores, high academic grades, along with well-rounded social and community activities, I was not as successful at getting many of these important and coveted interviews as they were.

It was during my first interview at the University of Miami when I realized for the first time that my stature was influencing the med school application process. I am a little person with a somewhat rare and random genetic mutation known as spondyloepiphyseal dysplasia. At twenty-three years of age then, I was three feet tall and had endured over twenty-seven orthopedic surgeries on my legs and spine since a very early age so that I could stand straight and lead a productive life.

During what seemed like an all too long interview, I felt as if I was being interrogated about a crime by two interviewers assuming a role of tough cop and nice cop. First a trauma surgeon severely questioned my ability to crack open the chest of an adult motor vehicle accident (MVA) victim. Then, an internist accepted my response that I never planned to crack open the chest of an adult MVA victim, but instead I believed with just the use of a stepstool I could perform very well in many other fields of medicine.

When the "tough cop" (the surgeon) went on to ask me how I could possibly resuscitate a person in cardiac arrest, I answered, "Well, I am an avid watcher of ER and apparently there is no one person who resuscitates a patient by themselves. However I believe I could do any one role with the aid of a stepstool and an education." The "nice cop" generously gave a small laugh to my response. The "tough cop" remained emotionless. I left the interview feeling as if I'd just had to defend my perceived inabilities instead of recounting my already well-demonstrated determination and results.

Although this was really the first time I became aware that my stature and "disability" could limit me, I decided I would keep going until someone else or something else told me I couldn't and I had exhausted any and all options. If it wasn't meant to be then it wouldn't happen, but I wasn't going to let a lack of effort on my part be the reason why I didn't become a doctor.

My second interview, at my dream school, Johns Hopkins, was very different. Here the pediatrician who interviewed me never mentioned or challenged me about my abilities or lack thereof as a short-statured individual. Moreover we discussed my interest in medicine and my academic path thus far. By the end of the interview, I was so worried that he hadn't asked me about my stature, that for a moment I actually wondered, "Did he even notice I am a Little Person?"

After that seemingly too easy interview, I thought I had no chance of getting into medical school. One school doubted my capabilities and the other never acknowledged my limitations. Even though others might not believe I could be a physician, I still knew I could. Of course, I was very aware of my limitations and capabilities, and I knew that being a trauma surgeon would not be practical as I would never want to put a person's life at risk due to a physical limitation. What I hoped for was to specialize in pediatrics, psychiatry or even ophthalmology. So I started to prepare myself for rejection.

To my great joy, two weeks after my interview at Johns Hopkins, I received a call from the Dean of Admissions that I had been accepted! I was going to realize my long-held dream of becoming a physician and helping others, after all those years of having been a patient myself.

The next four years at Johns Hopkins were unquestionably some of the hardest years of my life. I learned as much about myself as a person as I did the field of medicine. Ultimately after medical school, I decided to go into the field of neonatology, a field where I would never have to worry about any of my patients being bigger than me because I would be working with newborn babies!

I learned that success in life and career is not solely about achieving your goals, but is also about knowing one's true capabilities and limitations and then striving to overreach those every day. Today,

I'm happily immersed in meaningful work. Yes, it's hard, and yes it's demanding, but it's also invigorating and fulfilling. On occasion, I give pause and consider that of all the obstacles, of all of the reasons not to, I stayed determined!

As a practicing neonatologist, with each new miracle I help into this world I reaffirm my own blessings and I consider what great individuals these little ones can amount to. And my big dreams are not over, as I now continue down another important path as a wife and mother as well.

~Jennifer Arnold, M.D., MSc

Lost and Lonely

I wondered why somebody didn't do something.
Then I realized, I am somebody.
~Author Unknown

The first day I transferred to a new college was heartbreaking. Why did I leave my friends? Why did I choose a school that was farther from my family? I didn't know anyone on campus and I didn't know how to find the buildings for my classes. The world had just celebrated another New Year's holiday and I was sitting alone in a dorm room, surrounded by painted white brick walls and with an unknown roommate. What had I done?

I wandered around campus, consulting my flimsy paper class schedule and the buildings that I passed. I bumped into shoulders and backpacks. Bikes whizzed by me, clipping my heels as my eyes welled up with tears. I was late to chemistry class twice. I felt very lost and alone.

As a runner on the school's cross country and track teams, I looked forward to practice each afternoon. It was a chance to be part of a group, to escape the loneliness. It was a chance to be me. The pounding of my footsteps on the city sidewalks gave me a chance to discover myself. I began to think that feeling lost and alone might sometimes be a good thing. If we never felt lost then why would we search for the deeper meaning of life?

When an injury kept me from practice, I found myself with numbing amounts of free time. I had nothing to do but sit in my small dorm room. I began to swim laps in the campus pool, but I still felt trapped. I needed something more.

Having grown up with pets in our family home that I had rescued, I missed having a pet around. When I found the address for the local animal shelter in the phone book, I invited a running teammate to visit the shelter with me.

"Can you believe this place?" Amy asked in awe on our first day. The dark building looked like something from a horror movie, surrounded by a barbed wire fence. A small sign covered in dust hung sideways on the latch of the tall gate.

"It says they're open right now." I shrugged, thinking we must have the wrong place. The building had only one small window and not a shred of green grass.

A few minutes later a man emerged from the dark building wearing a red flannel shirt and blue jean overalls. "What do ya need?"

"We were hoping to volunteer, to spend time with the animals...." I stuttered, wanting to run back to the car and drive away quickly.

"Come on in," he muttered as he shuffled towards the door, cigarette pressed tightly between his lips.

Our first day of volunteering led us to the cat room. The cat room was a small 4x10 area with wire crates stacked one on top of the other, filling the entire room from floor to ceiling. Most of the food and water bowls were empty, some filled with dust, which told me the cats must have been hungry. Many of the cats were ill, and all were starved for attention. They were clearly lonely and they were scared. I could relate and they instantly won my heart. Cats of every age, size and color lined the walls. Their paws reached forward through the rusty steel bars of the cages, begging for help, pleading for attention. They meowed with force, letting us know that they needed help. Amy and I stayed at the shelter until they closed that day.

We went back to the animal shelter every Sunday. We walked the dogs, we provided food and water to every cage, we let cats out of their cages one by one to stretch their legs and feel the sunshine that poured through the tiny window in the next room. We brought pet treats and we made toys. The following year we organized a volunteer day where more than fifty track team members came to walk the dogs and spend time with the lonely pets. Before I knew it, I wasn't lonely anymore; I wasn't sitting quietly in a silent dorm room. I was in the city, I was giving back to lives that were in need and I was living life. I was learning not only about a great need of our society, but a great need in myself—the need to give back to those who can use a helping hand.

The animal shelter was changing my life as much as we were changing the lives we intended to help. Adoptions were increasing, the quality of care had risen by leaps and bounds, the shelter euthanasia rate was dropping and more people were signing up to volunteer. I was ecstatic! I was in awe that one person could really make a difference. I began to learn that we each have the power within us to make miracles happen. It takes three elements: effort, persistence and a positive attitude. With those three qualities, I learned that anyone could make a difference.

A few short years later, Amy Beatty and I co-founded Advocates 4 Animals, Inc., a non-profit animal welfare organization helping to save the lives of death row shelter pets in need. I had turned my loneliness and fear into positive action and change. I had learned to live outside the confines of the comfortable walls that I once called home. And most of all, I had learned to use what I had already possessed to create something that so desperately needed to exist. Through my desire to discover the world, I created a no-kill animal rescue, rehabilitation and adoption group that continues to help thousands of homeless animals annually. Feeling lost and lonely sure led to some amazing miracles for thousands of lost and lonely pets.

~Stacey Ritz

Frequent Survivor

When the world says "give up" Hope whispers "try it one more time."
~Author Unknown

For nine years, the company I worked for as an engineer went through the nerve-wracking process of layoffs, forced early retirements, restructuring, and other trendy corporate buzzwords. Somehow I survived, but many of those who were dismissed were personal friends I'd known for years. Each time someone disappeared from my department, I grieved silently. I felt thankful it was someone else, yet I felt guilty. Why them and not me? Why was I a frequent survivor?

When the company sold off one-third of the organization, it meant downsizing our engineering department. Most employees were warned their jobs were in jeopardy and were told to consider taking an early retirement package or face forced retirement. Since I hadn't been warned I thought I was safe. Besides, I'd just turned fifty and retirement was not on my list of goals.

Then the day of reckoning arrived. By lunchtime, the grapevine was buzzing about who would be evicted from our department. Before lunch all but one person was accounted for. When I returned to my desk after lunch, a voice message from my director awaited. "Tom, call me as soon as you get back."

Soon after, I was in his office. "Today is a bad day," he exclaimed, looking down at his desk. "I regret to inform you that your position has been eliminated." With a brief, cold handshake he ushered me out of his office, mumbling something like, "Good luck, Tom."

Dazed, I went back to my office. Then I called my wife, Laura, to give her the news. She tried to comfort me. Oddly, I felt excited about my newfound freedom and the prospect of trying something new.

Reality set in as I searched for a new career. After thirty-two years in engineering, I didn't know anything else. Four months later I accepted an engineering position that I had turned down months before.

The new job was awkward. I felt like a new college graduate and hated going to work. After six weeks, I spoke to my boss. "Every morning I ask myself, 'Am I doing what I want to do? Am I going where I want to go? And am I becoming what I want to become?' You know what my answer is? No! I want to quit!"

"Since you're having such a hard time, let me offer you a different opportunity at our secondary location, not far from here. Hope it works out for you, Tom." The new job worked out for a while but in my heart of hearts I knew I was destined for something else.

During the latter part of my engineering career, I co-authored a technical book with a dozen other men and women across North America. As chair of that committee, I spoke at conferences in the U.S. and Europe, explaining the purpose of our upcoming publication. Although I never had a passion for public speaking, I soon discovered I enjoyed it.

As a professional engineer, I attended technical seminars and thrived on some of the softer skills. Sometimes I would ask the instructor, "What is it like to be a seminar leader?"

I learned that to qualify, I'd need to provide a video of me conducting a seminar to a real audience. That year, my New Year's resolution was to send out résumés and videotapes by February first.

Six packets went out and responses trickled in, mostly thanking me for my interest. I was elated when one company responded. They wanted me to fly out to Kansas City for a "training the trainer" session, at my own expense.

After intense auditioning with twenty other applicants the first day, I headed back to my hotel room to rest and prepare for the next day. As soon as I unlocked the door the phone rang. Our trainer said, "Not everyone will be returning tomorrow. Unfortunately, Tom, you are one of them." I was stunned.

I changed my airline ticket and called my wife. Once again I was devastated. I pleaded with God. "Dear Lord, please give me a sign of what I'm supposed to do with the rest of my life." I went home and tried to make the most of my engineering job.

A few months later, a different seminar company called. I thought they had rejected me. "We'd like you to come out to Kansas City for an audition." I thought, "Not another expensive trip for nothing."

The gentleman on the phone continued. "We'll fly you out, pick you up, cover your hotel expenses, and the next day you'll audition. You'll know whether or not we've accepted you almost immediately. Then we'll drive you to the airport."

After passing the audition I began my first training assignment about a month later in Buffalo, New York. Soon my engineering job became half time. I conducted seminars one week and, on alternate weeks, I donned my engineer's hat. The schedule was challenging, but my family made it work. My new life was finally taking shape.

For many years I've found fulfillment through various projects, including volunteering at our local prison. One afternoon, in the midst of juggling my two half-time jobs, the warden asked me to conduct a special life skills training session for a group of 100 men who were not enrolled in any programs.

I willingly accept any challenge, but I found trying to motivate an audience forced to be in attendance torture. My previous work as a prison volunteer with inmates who chose to be there was gratifying, but after that first horrific session I knew I had to take a different approach.

I went to the local bookstore and, as I browsed through the self-help section, I found some interesting options. In the mix were several titles in the *Chicken Soup for the Soul* series.

"What if I started collecting stories written by and about inmates?"

I thought. "If they can do it, so can I." I began asking everyone I met at the prison if they had a story—inmates, staff, volunteers, anyone.

As a trainer, I sold resources in the back of the room. Two of the books we offered were *Chicken Soup for the Soul* and *Chicken Soup for the Woman's Soul*. Each month, the combined sales of all trainers were about 10,000 copies of the "Soup" books. Jack Canfield, delighted with our company's sales, offered the trainers a special discount to attend his Facilitation Skills Seminar in Santa Barbara, California. Only a handful of trainers took advantage of the opportunity, and I was one of them. A fellow trainer asked, "So, Tom, why are you going, and what are you going to do for eight days?"

My answer was simple. "I don't know, but a little voice inside me is saying I need to be there." I was never so certain about anything before. My wife went to California with me for what turned out to be a life-changing experience for both of us.

Expecting Jack Canfield to be involved in the training for only a few hours, I was surprised when he conducted the training throughout most of the first day. Amazingly enough, Jack was available during the breaks, chatting with many of the 270 attendees.

On day two, I walked up to him and shook his hand. "Hi Jack, my name is Tom Lagana and I work with prison inmates." During our brief conversation I asked Jack some questions about how some of the experiential exercises at his seminar might be applied to prisoners. Then I thought, "Should I tell him about the book I'm working on?" He seemed interested so I continued. "I'm also working on a book, like a *Chicken Soup for the Soul* book for inmates."

Jack paused for a moment, his eyes fixed on mine. "I want to do a *Chicken Soup for the Prisoner's Soul*, but I don't have anyone willing to 'own' the project."

A little voice inside my head asked, "I wonder what 'owning' the project means?" Then my other little voice chimed in, "Just say, 'Yes!'" I told Jack, "I'll do it. Just let me know what I need to do."

Smiling, he shook my hand. "Jot down a note and give it to me to remind me of our conversation."

The next day before the seminar, I handed Jack a piece of paper.

The note referred to our conversation, and stated I would co-author *Chicken Soup for the Prisoner's Soul*.

A week after returning from California, I received a letter on Chicken Soup for the Soul stationery confirming our agreement. I began announcing a call for stories on a grand scale.

After three years of hard work, we put the book in the hands of prisoners. It has been the most rewarding work of my life. The bumpy journey from engineering to co-authoring *Chicken Soup for the Prisoner's Soul* took many twists and turns, but I know it was God's way of answering my prayer.

~Tom Lagana

Public Assistance

*Men are made stronger on realization that the helping hand they need
is at the end of their own arm.*

- Sidney J. Phillips

t was the coldest of December days. The frigid temperature outside was no match for the icy breeze that came across the telephone line, the words that made me lose my breath and left me sitting on the side of my bed, frozen. "I have to let you go. I can no longer afford to pay you."

I had barely recovered from the events of the December past, a month in which I was robbed at knifepoint and almost suffocated by my assailant, the same month that my marriage of twenty-two years officially came to an end. That December ended on somewhat of a high note however, with my children and me moving into our new home ready to make a new start.

Now a year later, the day before New Year's Eve in fact, I received the bone chilling news that I was unemployed. I spent the next three days in a state of depression. Then something inside me began to stir. The spirit that saw me through difficulties, trials and tribulations in the past demanded that I get up and stop feeling sorry for myself.

I had a little bit of money stashed away, an excellent credit history, and a line of credit, so I figured we would be okay until I could find another job. How long could that take? After all, I have a master's degree. I searched for a job, but to no avail. All the interviews led to the same response — overqualified.

I managed to secure a few freelance jobs in film production and editing. Yet, it was not enough. I swallowed the bitter pill called pride and applied for public assistance.

Though the food stamps helped tremendously, the cash assistance offered was nowhere near enough to sustain a family of six. In addition, in order to receive cash assistance, you had to dedicate thirty hours per week to the EARN Center, a place where you could receive training and assistance in securing a job. I did manage to obtain a position at a newly opened production company through a Pennsylvania work subsidy program, which was supposed to pay my whole salary for the first six months and fifty percent of my salary for the next six months. Unfortunately, this opportunity came at a time when Pennsylvania was experiencing its state budget crisis. My new employer was never reimbursed and ended up letting me go after only one month.

I continued to receive the food stamps, but I could not see the value in devoting thirty hours a week to the EARN program in order to get cash assistance that was not enough to meet my family's needs, so I did not reapply. I decided to try to go it on my own one more time.

I took out cash advances in an attempt to keep up with my bills, and I even received a generous gift of fifteen hundred dollars from my dear friend Angelique. But just like the ground that eventually becomes parched for a lack of nourishing rain, everything began to dry up—my resources, my opportunities, and my hope. Over two years later, I found myself facing a fate that was far worse than losing a job; I was about to lose my home.

I knew about a program that offered rental assistance to people who were having trouble paying their rent, so I applied, only to find out that they were out of funds. I was told, however, that there was another program in the city I could look into and given the number to call. I called and was told to come into the office immediately, which I did.

I arrived with my hope soaring. I sat for four hours. When my number was called, I was informed that there were no housing counselors available and that I would have to come back Monday morning.

I stomped down the street full of fury. They could have told me on the phone that there were no counselors! I vowed that I would not return to that place. Then, from the recesses of my mind, images of my children's faces appeared, as if to remind me that this was not about me. I had to do this for them. In a moment of epiphany, I was reminded that sometimes life doesn't give you what you want or need immediately. So on Monday morning, I returned as instructed.

This time, when my number was called, I was greeted by the program manager for the City's Homeless Prevention and Rapid Re-Housing Program. She explained that she was filling in for an intake worker who had called out sick. During my intake interview, she was having trouble navigating through the screens on the computer, so I began to help her. At the end of my intake, she informed me that I was eligible to receive the assistance. Then she asked me a question that rang in my ears like the sweetest melody I had ever heard: Do you have a résumé?

I e-mailed her my résumé as soon as I get home that afternoon. I interviewed two weeks later. Then, on August 9, 2010, I began working for the City of Philadelphia's Homeless Prevention and Rapid Re-Housing Program.

It is two years later. I am still here, and I am so grateful. Grateful that I am able to lend my gifts and talents to a program that continues to help people in the position that I once found myself in. Grateful I was able to overcome another obstacle in this journey called life.

~Nancy Gilliam

Growth Through Giving

The deepest principle in human nature is the craving to be appreciated.
~William James

Last night I found a yellowed, crumpled piece of paper in a drawer of my battered desk. I have a habit of putting away small snippets of poems, stories and sayings that move and inspire me. The author was unknown but the words affected me. They are one of the reasons why I volunteer and why I work with children.

Four years ago, I helped start a Blessing in a Backpack program in my school district. It is a neighbor-helping-neighbor program designed to supplement the nutritional needs of children and their families. Each week we distributed backpacks filled with a weekend's worth of non-perishable food for at-risk students in our district.

Our packing area was located in the district's charter high school, made up of students who could not make it in a traditional classroom, or who had academic issues that would keep them from graduating. We had to pack 400 backpacks every week, so it was important to have help. The principal of the academy assigned us a young man who was having classroom and personal issues. Andrew was a polite, handsome young man, tall and lean. He had a ready smile, but his eyes showed hurt and he seemed fearful of adults. You could see the toll the "hard knocks" had taken on him.

During the packing, he did what we asked but we could tell his heart was not in it. But after a few weeks, our young volunteer started to warm up to us and the job. After a month, Andrew was very involved and recruiting other young people to help us. At the end of summer, we said our goodbyes. Andrew promised to be back in September so he could help us organize. We could see he reveled in being given a leadership role.

We came to rely on Andrew more and more. He blossomed in his leadership role as our liaison to the school. Then he goofed up and was expelled for three days. He begged the principal to allow him to pack during that time, but the principal said no. The following week my co-chair and I talked to our young friend, letting him know how important he was to the organization and how he had disappointed us with his behavior. You could see the tears in his eyes during our talk. He was embarrassed that he had let us down.

As the months passed, we could see a change in Andrew. He became focused and positive about his future. A few months before June, he informed us with a huge toothy grin that he was going to graduate. I think that might have been one of his proudest moments. This young man had no family unit to live with or care about him. Now as he bragged about his grades, he was a new, confident young man who looked at his future with happiness. The principal later told us that had we not stepped in and given him support, encouragement and guidance, he was sure Andrew would have been dead from gang violence.

As graduation approached, students talked about who they were inviting and how proud they would be to have their families there. Everyone, that is, but Andrew. Not wanting to embarrass him, I asked the principal who Andrew was inviting. He had no one who would come. No one cared. Those words cut deep into my heart. I knew that I could not let him down, not after all his growth and improvement. I would be there for him.

As the proud graduates proceeded down the aisle to sit on stage, I made sure that Andrew would have to pass by me. I could see a light in his eyes as he approached. When he reached me, he touched my hand, as if to say thank you. Tears welled up in both of our eyes.

I learned that my dear friend Andrew turned his life around.

He had earned a scholarship and was going to major in mechanical engineering. He is now in his second year and doing very well. Not only had we fed him meals on weekends through his own Blessing in a Backpack, we had fed his soul.

~Kessie Kaltsounis

Zeal for Teal

The willingness to share does not make one charitable; it makes one free.
~Robert Brault

had two choices. Wallow in self-pity or put on my big girl sneakers and start walking. One part of me opted for self-pity — it was easier. After all a cancer diagnosis does knock the wind out of a person's sails. It was easy to justify defeatism given the nature of the verdict. Others would understand.

But during my journey through the valley of cancer I had a thorn in my side and she was determined not to let me wallow in self-pity. My daughter Amanda responded to my ovarian cancer diagnosis by stepping into a new role — sergeant major!

While my body battled the bittersweet chemotherapy poison, Amanda got busy finding ways to help and encourage me. She contacted Ovarian Cancer Canada and learned there was a Walk of Hope taking place in Barrie. She signed us up, and before I knew it we were fundraising with fury in preparation for the five-mile trek the following September.

Chemotherapy exhausted me, so it was important that I rest, but I found myself occasionally wanting to withdraw and cut myself off from others. I did not want people feeling sorry for me. Out of sight, out of mind. But the more I tried to keep out of sight, the more Amanda was determined to keep me active and involved.

"Mom, I have an idea," Amanda said one day between treatments. "What if we did a special fundraising event that would help raise both funds for the Walk of Hope and awareness for women in the community?"

My daughter, an avid scrapbooker, wanted to invite women to get together for a day of scrapbooking and crafting for the cause. I did a lot of thinking and praying and enjoyed some pensive moments. But I found myself loving her idea and before I knew it I jumped on the bandwagon.

Teal was the awareness ribbon color for ovarian cancer and Amanda's zeal was contagious. Zeal for Teal seemed a perfect moniker. I started to love our new name. I also started to realize the importance of focusing on the positive and using any excess energy to be a light to others.

The more I helped plan and prepare for the first Zeal for Teal event, the more I found myself thinking less about my cancer journey and more about how I might just be able to help other sisters not yet diagnosed. The idea of doing my part to find an early detection test motivated me.

The first Zeal for Teal event started out in the fellowship hall of our church. Our theme for the inaugural occasion — Pajama Day — was a big hit. So we decided to create a theme for each year. The second year we had a beach theme. The following year was The 50s; last year was The Wild West and this year we are doing Alice in Wonderland. A group of very cool people have been helping, and because our committee has grown so large, we meet at the local hockey arena.

Soon, we will be celebrating our fifth anniversary. Our themed Zeal for Teal event draws women from near and far, with ladies returning year after year and bringing their friends.

Every so often, in between the busyness of the moments, I sit back and reflect. Never would I choose to be diagnosed with cancer. The rigors of chemotherapy and the toll it took on my mind and body were far from pleasant. Yet I am glad that, with a little help from my darling daughter, who really is more a beautiful rose than a thorn, I was able to use my experience to help inform other women. And, with all the money we raise from Zeal for Teal, Amanda and I participate each year in the annual Ovarian Cancer Canada Walk of Hope.

Zeal for Teal helped me see the good in the not so good, find hope in the hopeless, and experience a great deal of love from family, friends, and my community. We have created some mighty sweet lemonade from some very bitter lemons.

~Glynis M. Belec

Fire, Fire, Fire

... and a little child shall lead them.
~Isaiah 11:16

Bang, bang, bang... Someone pounded like machine gun fire on my front door... Ding-dong, Ding-dong... I glanced at the clock: 10:17 p.m. on a Sunday night.

"Karen, David, open the door! My house is on fire!"

I recognized my neighbor's voice and raced to open the door. Frazzled and in her pajamas, Kathy pushed her two preschoolers into my arms.

"Smoke's everywhere. I can't find the fire." Kathy turned and ran back to her house. My husband, David, took off after her.

"Mommy, what's going on?" Five-year-old Lori's little voice quivered as she leaned out of her bedroom door.

"Hold on," I called out, distracted. I fumbled a bit, rearranging Kathy's kids in my arms. Then, I stumbled to the den and propped them both on the couch.

"What's wrong with Kathy?" Lori asked again.

I rounded the corner in time to see Lori carefully pulling her left foot back to keep her toes inside the invisible line. A month ago, Daddy had drawn a line and instituted The Law—all good little girls stay in their rooms, no matter what, after nighty-night. In their rooms meant behind the invisible line.

Sleepy-eyed, with mussed hair, Monica crept out into the hall. Being four, Dad's Laws didn't mean much. Neither did the concept of an invisible line. Dad tried. He even stretched a piece of yellow yarn across her bedroom door opening but Monica got Lori to tie it in her hair.

Now both girls stood in their long, flannel nightgowns, confused and a little frightened, waiting for an answer.

Stressed and worried, I tried to answer in a light and breezy manner. "Kathy brought over Josh and Anna. We're going to have a party... a movie night. Ya'll come. We'll find *Cinderella* and put her on."

The kids settled down in front of the TV.

"Lori, you're in charge. I'm going next door to see if everything's okay. I'll be right back."

She nodded, asking, "Mommy, is Kathy's house on fire?"

I hesitated, weighing the pros and cons. "Yes, Lori. But Daddy's there. I'm sure he's got things under control." Then, before she could ask anything else, I dashed out the door.

Smoke bellowed out of Kathy's front door. I rushed in. "David... Kathy... Where are you?"

"I'm here." David's voice sounded from afar.

A layer of smoke filled the three feet below the ceiling. Below it, the air seemed reasonably clean, breathable at least. I ducked down and moved forward in searched of David, calling out, "Have you found the fire?"

"No." David grabbed me. "Let's get out. Kathy, let's go. It's too late."

Kathy came whirling out of a bedroom. The three of us ran into the front yard to the sound of screaming sirens. Help was on the way.

Firemen, dressed head to toe in yellow, with gas masks and oxygen tanks, rushed into the house. Seconds later the fire was out.

"Fire in the outside air-conditioner unit ma'am. Sucked all the smoke right into your home," the head fireman said, as the others walked back to the fire truck and put their equipment away.

As I left to check on the kids, Kathy was making the rounds. Saying "thank you" and shaking each man's hand.

Ten minutes later, David entered our house. Firemen followed. The neighborhood crowded in after that.

With a shrug, David said, "The firemen would like to meet Lori."

"Lori?" I asked.

"Yes." The head fireman came forward with a smile. He looked me straight in the eye. "If that's alright with you ma'am?"

"Sure." I shrugged and led him into our family room where Cinderella sang and danced with the birds. Everyone followed.

"Lori, honey, this fireman would like to meet you," I said, wondering why.

Lori popped up and peered at us over the back of the couch.

"Hi," she said. "Are you a real fireman?"

"Yes, I am." He walked over and took her hand.

"Wow, that's cool," she said, awe filling her voice. "Did you save Kathy's house?"

The room filled with people. David grabbed my hand, pulled it up to his lips and kissed it. We smiled, proud parents, watching magic.

"Yes, we did." The fireman smiled down at her. "That's why I'm here. To thank you for calling us and letting us know that Kathy's house was on fire. You were the only one who did."

I froze. David's hand stiffened in mine. Everyone stared at us.

"Oh, I thought…" I stammered.

"Happens all the time. Everyone thinks someone else called and nobody does. Not until it's too late." The fireman turned back to Lori and shook her hand. "That's why I wanted to meet Lori and thank her for calling. Because of her, the dispatcher was able to pinpoint Lori's location and then, through the city tax records, we found a 'Ken and Kathy' who lived one house north from her. And, that's how we came to fight the fire."

He let go of Lori's hand. "How did you know to call 911?"

"My teacher, Mrs. Williams, taught us last week…" Lori's excitement changed to concern, "but I'm not big enough." She pointed across the room.

Everyone turned and saw a kitchen chair pushed against the wall, right underneath the wall-mounted phone.

The fireman looked hard at the chair, and then back at Lori. "Impressive." He began to clap. Everyone, including David and I, joined in. The sound filled the room.

Beaming, Lori stood tall, on the middle cushion of couch, bewildered, but proud.

A month later, the city gave her a commendation for "being smart enough to call the fire department." They gave her a plaque. And, once again, we stood there like the fools we were, while the world applauded Lori... for being the only one "smart enough" to call the fire department.

Then some reporter picked up the story and ran it in the local paper—quotes and all.

~Karen Ekstrom

A Dance with Destiny

Dancing is like dreaming with your feet!
~Constanze

My mother was a drug addict. She was deemed unfit to care for me, so my single grandmother raised me from birth. My father was incarcerated during most of my childhood, like a lot of kids I knew. I grew up in the projects in East Harlem, New York. Drugs, gangs, violence, it was a dangerous place to be a kid, especially a small kid. But I was strong, I was fast, and I was motivated—so pretty early on I learned to be as big and bad as I had to be. My life depended on it. We were church-going people, but I have to admit that antisocial behavior, belligerence, and fighting occupied much of my early years.

Church was the one peaceful place I knew. I always loved the music. My cousin Journee was in the praise dance group, and when watching her dance I felt something beautiful bloom inside me.

But back outside on the street, in the "'hood," it was same ol', same ol'. I spent time mouthing off and fighting other boys to gain respect. Of course I was a difficult student—although I was intelligent, teachers had a hard time with me. I made sure of that. The school principal got tired of telling me to shape up. I had no purpose and I was going nowhere. I pretended I didn't care.

A school field trip to see the Dance Theatre of Harlem saved my life. Those dancers on the stage seemed superhuman. Their every movement thrilled me to the core. I wanted to do that. I wanted to be that. My first experience with classical ballet moved me to make a deal with my principal: if I promised to stop fighting, behave myself, and pull my grades up, she would contact the dance company and arrange an audition for me. Within a year, I had a full scholarship to the Dance Theatre of Harlem School. Dance became my safe place, my secret place, a place where I didn't feel the need to prove how big and bad I was.

I was focused and disciplined, and the teachers at DTH noticed. I progressed quickly. I had a talent for remembering choreography and could jump very high. From my years on the streets I had developed strength and agility beyond that of most of the other young dancers. After additional training at Ballet Academy East, Boston Ballet and Jacob's Pillow, after graduating with good grades from high school at age seventeen, I signed my first professional contract—with the Dance Theatre of Harlem ensemble. My dream had become reality. I began performing immediately on the DTH 40th Anniversary Tour.

The tour mission was to bring dance to communities that might have never seen ballet before. We were bringing a message of hope and inspiration to damaged youth in those communities, and I felt a personal responsibility to be on that stage. I wanted to inspire someone—one kid—the way I had been inspired. I felt I was representing something much larger than myself. I had a purpose.

I received a mandate from my hero, the legendary Arthur Mitchell, at Dance Theatre of Harlem. According to him, it's my mission and destiny to live "in service to the art form"—and, to me, that means a lifetime commitment to giving back, in any way I can.

Now I am in my third season with the Los Angeles Ballet. It has been my privilege to perform solo parts in both *The Nutcracker* and *Swan Lake* throughout Los Angeles County. And it's also my privilege to work with disadvantaged youth in low-income neighborhoods around Southern California as a part of Los Angeles Ballet's Power of Performance! (POP!) program, which brings hundreds of underprivileged children to performances, free of charge, through a network of community service organizations.

Sometimes when I injure my knee or sprain an ankle—it comes

with the job—I feel like I want to cancel a performance. But I think of those kids from the "hood" who are coming to the show, and I have to be on that stage. I want them to see their own reflection, to see themselves up there. The house lights go down, the curtain rises, and as I dance I know that there is someone out there in the dark, from one of those neighborhoods, needing a little inspiration. I'll be there to give it to them.

~Christopher Charles McDaniel

Stewie to the Rescue

To err is human, to forgive, canine.
~Author Unknown

The funny thing was, I didn't even want the dog. I didn't have one growing up, and I didn't see any reason to become a pet owner in my thirties. I tried to convince my girlfriend that it wasn't a good idea. We both worked full-time, and I wasn't missing something that I'd never had or wanted.

"Please?" she beseeched.

I stood my ground.

She batted her baby blues.

I held firm.

Sometime during the second month of her pleading, while not thinking clearly, I made a tactical mistake.

I asked, "If we were to get a dog, what kind of dog would you want?"

And that was that. We bought a dog and named him Stewie.

For story arc purposes, I should say how at first I didn't take too kindly to Stewie's intrusion in my life, how my normal day-to-day schedule was turned upside down, how I viewed Stewie's very existence as an inconvenience, until slowly but surely, I came to love him and how the very things about Stewie that irritated me were now enchanting. But that's not what happened.

Stewie owned me from Day One. I didn't mind when he peed on the carpet. I didn't mind when he used my socks as chew toys. I didn't mind when he ate a twenty-dollar bill that had fallen to the floor. (Okay, I did mind that a little.)

Things went incredibly well for the next two years. I even stopped going away as I used up all my vacation time (and sick days—shhh!) to stay home and play with Stewie. We'd go to the park, where he would play with the other dogs or fetch his favorite ball for hours. And then we'd go home where he'd bring me his indoor (i.e. non-squeaky) ball, and we would play fetch. For hours.

Though my girlfriend loved him too, she didn't have the time to spend with Stewie that I did. While my accounting job was strictly nine to five weekdays (and sometimes I'd even sneak out earlier), she worked as a hairstylist, which meant long days and some weekends as well. That's probably why Stewie followed me, and not her, from room to room like a two-foot stalker.

Unfortunately, things started to change. What was cute and lovable at the beginning grew tiresome. Though I had loved making sacrifices, I became less apt to compromise. Our relationship was strained, to the point where I didn't see any point in continuing. So my girlfriend and I broke up. (You didn't think I was talking about Stewie and me, did you?)

There wasn't even a discussion about who was going to take Stewie. He was my dog.

Eventually, I met my wife, Josie, and we became a family of three. On the morning of November 26th, a month after our wedding and one day after my birthday, I was walking Stewie off-leash in Riverside Park, as I had mostly done, whether it was legal or not. But on this day, he was straying a little far from me....

"Stewie!" I called out, and he froze, staring at me but not moving at all. It was almost as if he heard his name but couldn't see me. I took off the black knit hat I was wearing.

"Stewie, get over here!"

This time, instead of staring or coming to me, he took off, running south towards the entrance to the park. I took off as well, following, but soon lost sight of him. Someone near the entrance saw me running and asked if I was chasing a small dog.

"Yes!"

"He ran out that way," she said, pointing to the entrance.

"Shoot!" I thought, and climbed the stone stairs.

When I reached the street, I immediately spotted him, lying on Riverside Drive, lifeless, with blood everywhere. Stewie was four years old. The car that hit him didn't even stop.

For the next six months, I walked around like a zombie, not caring about anything. I agreed to go to therapy, but it wasn't really doing anything for my grief or me. Eventually, I decided that for my own wellbeing I had to do something. Stewie's death couldn't be for nothing.

We decided to adopt a homeless dog. We were looking for a senior dog, as we couldn't afford a dog walker and with a day gig and a comedy career, I didn't have the time to give a younger dog the attention it'd need. I also knew that it was tougher to find homes for seniors. Online, I found a post by a woman advocating for a nine-year-old great-on-the-leash Pit Bull mix named Kilo who was scheduled to be euthanized in the morning.

I decided right then and there… this dog was not going to die. I wrote to her immediately.

We met outside the animal shelter, known as (NYC) Animal Care & Control. From the outside, it is a depressing building, located on a depressing block in East Harlem. Walking in was no better. I felt like I was entering a prison (which, in one respect, I was), and a smelly prison at that.

We walked back to where the dogs were kept. The barking was loud and constant.

When she took Kilo out of his cage, Josie and I looked at each other, as if to say, "Are you sure this is the same dog described in the ad?"

He was a maniac. We thought he might be a little hyper from being in the cage, so we took him for a walk. After twenty minutes of him literally dragging me around Harlem, we asked, "Are you sure this is Kilo?"

Yes, he was insane, but like I said, this dog was not going to die.

I owed it to Stewie. We took Kilo home and loved him, in spite of his high energy (or maybe because of it).

But that wasn't enough to ease my pain. Thankfully, Josie came up with an idea....

"Why don't you start your own rescue, and name it after Stewie?"

That sounded great! Not only would I be memorializing Stewie in a more public manner, but, being the founder and president, I could focus on what I felt was important, and direct my energy where it was needed the most.

In July of 2010, Stewie to the Rescue was founded.

In the two years we've been around, Stewie has helped save the lives of more than 100 animals. We have raised over $100,000 for our rescue and others by producing comedy fundraisers (I am a also stand-up comedian). We have partnered with more than thirty other animal rescues to lend our time and fundraising talents to their efforts. Personally, I have become a leading animal advocate in New York, and I no longer eat meat or chicken, and was even recently named cable channel NY1's "New Yorker of the Week" for my work in animal rescue.

And to think, I didn't even want a dog.

~Harris Bloom

Going to Full Lengths

*Only those who will risk going too far can possibly find out
how far one can go.*
~T.S. Eliot

The State of California has offices throughout the state. I worked in one of them. It was a cubicle maze with many of the attributes of a *Dilbert* cartoon, and it contained just as many absurdities. And none of them were about to change due to our dismal budget.

I had enough when, for the third day in a row, a woman in my office walked back from the ladies room with her skirt tucked inside her pantyhose. Of course, she didn't know she was flashing her derriere to the rest of the office until someone told her.

As I sent yet another e-mail to management requesting a full length mirror, I wondered what I could possibly do to correct the situation.

Our newly remodeled ladies room was indeed beautiful. It was much closer than our prior one. It sported a handicapped stall and a partial handicapped stall along with many additional stalls. We no longer had to wait in long lines. But the only mirrors were placed above the sinks.

My e-mails had progressed from merely requesting a mirror, to offering to pay for it myself, to now stating that the women in the office were willing to go in together to purchase a full-length mirror.

Management replied negatively to all my requests if they replied at all.

I was ready to take on the world. A co-worker stopped by my desk; Ray was known as the local union steward. He had a way of asking just the right question. He asked me one that day. His question completely changed my life.

As I explained the situation to him, he listened politely and then asked, "You have a very valid issue. What are you going to do about it?"

As I turned back to my work, my mind replayed the question. It was a turning point. I realized that if anything was going to happen I was going to have to make it happen. But how could I do that?

Perhaps management would give more weight to my requests for a mirror if I provided a valid reason. Was that possible?

The handicapped stalls in the ladies room seemed somewhat out of proportion. I started my investigation right after work on the Internet. After several nights I found the solution I was looking for.

Federal American Disability Act (ADA) regulations stated that the door to the handicapped stall could not swing out into the path of another door. If it was located at the end of a row of stalls, that door was supposed to swing inward.

I had found my first valid legal issue!

I kept searching. ADA regulations stated that the sink actually had minimum and maximum height requirements if there was a handicapped stall. The next day I measured and found my second valid issue. Our sinks were too high and so were the soap dispensers!

On the third night of reading federal regulations I found the small print I needed. If there was a handicapped stall, a full-length mirror was required.

My next e-mail to management outlined the three infractions. I provided the Federal Regulations number and the website so they could read it for themselves. I asked for a meeting to discuss these items.

I did not get a response to this e-mail.

However, about three days later, the ladies room was closed for repairs.

The door to the handicapped stall was reversed so that it swung into the stall.

The entire row of sinks was reinstalled and lowered along with the mirror above it.

There was a full-length mirror placed on a wall so that a person would get a full view of herself as she exited.

I thought the problem was solved. I was finished. I could rest and get back to work. But that isn't quite what happened.

A few weeks later a visitor in a wheelchair came to my cubicle. I had seen this lady exiting the paratransit bus as she arrived at work each morning.

"Are you Linda?" she asked.

"Yes."

"I want to thank you," she began. "I've worked here for seven years and I have never been able to wash my hands in the ladies room. I understand you are responsible for that." She had tears in her eyes and she reached a tentative hand out to me.

I then thought about the other people I had seen in the office in wheelchairs.

"Oh my!" I replied as I grasped her hand in mine. "I am so glad I was able to help."

Sometimes we see only ourselves in the mirror. My tenacity in fighting for a mirror opened the door to many ladies rooms. When I retired from my job working for the State of California I went on to fight for ADA requirements in other state offices.

The question Ray asked changed my life.

The mirror changed how I looked at things.

~Linda Lohman

The Adventures of a Middle-Aged College Student

You are never too old to set another goal or to dream a new dream.
~C.S. Lewis

I was staring into the abyss. A month earlier, my supervisor Ana had called me into her office. She had been fighting to keep me on amid massive budget cuts in the city of Reno, Nevada, but seniority trumped skill, so I was laid off.

A layoff is never good, but this was worse. It was the end of 2008 and, with the highest unemployment rate in the nation, Reno was the worst place to look for work.

In Hollywood, they call it the inciting incident. In 2006 I was a stay-at-home husband, living a mundane life of cooking, cleaning and taking kids to school. Then one day, my world ended when my wife left. This incident changed my life for the good, although I didn't see it that way at the time.

I lost more than 100 pounds, my health improved, I got my driver's license and I filed for divorce. I worked at Walmart for about a year, looking for a job in accounting, my specialty.

When Ana called me, telling me I got the job at the city, I was thrilled. The pay was low, but I didn't care. I wanted to work, to prove to myself what I could do. After a few months, however, I began to realize something: I hated working in accounting. But that is what I was trained to do.

And that's when Ana dropped the hammer and I went home. A month later, after sending out hundreds of résumés and applications, no one called. I was out of money and slipping back to my old complacent self. I felt like I had gotten in shape, physically, emotionally and spiritually, to run the race of life, only to trip at the firing of the starting gun. It was then that I wrote this in my personal journal:

It is the last day of the year and, in a way, the final day of my previous life. I turned forty this year, to no fanfare whatsoever. As I reflect on the past year and take stock of my current condition, I can't help but come to the conclusion that I've accomplished nothing in this life. ~December 31, 2008.

Robyn, a friend of mine I had met working for the city, had just graduated from the University of Nevada, Reno (UNR). I went to her commencement and, while a bit bored with the event, noticed that some of the graduates received degrees in journalism. A seed was planted—deep in my subconscious—that people made money writing, something I did happily for free.

Robyn and I kept in touch. She commented frequently that she had written and read hundreds of essays while in school and I wrote better than many of the professional writers she was exposed to in school.

But I wasn't really listening, my hearing dulled by whispers in the darkness. I was at that abyss, wondering why I should go on. My myopic vision only saw blackness ahead.

One day she called me. "Hey, are you dressed? No? Well get dressed. I'm on my way. We are going somewhere."

Trusting her, and pretty sure she wasn't taking me to a vet to get fixed, I got dressed, ran downstairs and got in her car. We chatted about the usual day-to-day stuff, but she refused to tell me where she was taking me.

We ended up at Truckee Meadows Community College. She said she started there before transferring to UNR and she just wanted to show me around.

Within an hour, before I could even absorb the surroundings, I had registered for classes at the community college. She had tricked me!

Classes started just a few weeks later, so I was nervous. Not only had it been more than twenty years since I had gone to school, I had dropped out of school at the beginning of my sophomore year because of a previously held religious ideology. I took the GED exam a few years later, getting a ninety-three percent. Leaving school had been a long-held regret, something I had nightmares about.

After the first day of school, I saw the light. I moved away from that abyss. Sitting in class, older than everyone but my professor, I felt, not like a non-traditional student, the politically correct term for old geezer, but like a real student, ready to learn and work toward becoming a journalist.

Still, a voice in my head kept saying I should give it all up. My ex-wife, upon hearing I was going to school, laughed and told my kids that I would give it up in a few weeks. My father used to tell my mother that I was "inept at everything." Those voices started growing louder and I thought that maybe this old dog should just roll over and die.

Then I began to reap what I was sowing. My first English essay came back: ninety-eight percent. Soon the second essay came back to me with a 100 percent. My professor told me I was the first student she ever gave a perfect score to on an English essay. An extra credit project I submitted to my journalism professor got published in the school's paper.

I may have felt like a failure, but the feedback told me I was lying to myself. And I started to feel, for the first time in decades, happy.

Four years later, on the verge of graduating from UNR with a degree in journalism, the voices still rise at times, but I know now that these ghosts of the past do not have my best interests at heart. I have work to do and things to learn. Learning at an older age is not that hard. An older student may need to clear a few cobwebs from the mind, but learning is about desire and open-mindedness, not age.

I started learning when I trusted a friend to take me for a ride.

She knew I wouldn't listen to her, but believed that, once set free, I would thrive in college.

The lesson is that I have the ability to change my future. It may not be easy and it requires a willingness to be open to change, but it is so much better than living in the immutable past.

One of the oldest proverbial sayings in the English language is "you can't teach an old dog new tricks."

My commentary on the proverb: It's a lie. Don't believe it.

~Paul George

From Lemons to Lemonade

From Sickness to Success

I Own It

A successful person is one who can lay a firm foundation with the bricks that others throw at him or her.
~David Brinkley

y mother used to say "I would give you all of my hair if I could." She used to try on my wigs, turning her face from left to right, and back again. Angling her chin, fluffing the synthetic bangs with three fingers. I would watch her from behind her vanity table, silently taking everything in. Alone there, in her room, I never felt ashamed, or different because of my alopecia. Would I ever be like her, so confident, brave and strong, brimming with sureness and beauty? But this was my alopecia, my hair loss, not hers. When she took my wig off, her golden curls bounced around her face, and perhaps she never gave it another thought. My cold hands absentmindedly rubbed my bald head.

I will never forget the day I lost my hair. Not because it affected me so, but because my mother acted as if the world had ended, collecting waist-length locks into plastic bags and storing them in the china cabinet in the dining room "just in case anything could ever be done."

At four years old, I had no sense of worry about losing my hair. On the contrary it was painful for my mother and sister to vice grip me between their knees, hushing me as they brushed out my tomboy snarls. I would cry and wriggle and beg for them to just cut it off.

Then overnight, against my cool cotton pillowcase, out it came, lying all around me in clumps as if a ghostly hairdresser had come in the night and razored most of it off.

Even amidst all of the doctor's appointments, the cortisone treatments and the pull tests, still I did not feel any differently. Pictures of me in horrid 80s clothing, dashing across the cameras frame, bald head wild and free, I never even stopped to consider that I was different.

Because alopecia had touched my life so early, none of the children in my elementary school minded. Girls with silky, thick pigtails used to line up in the bathroom for a peak under my hats. They would ask month after month if there'd been any change, any growth. I was everyone's personal peep show, but it was also harmless, and I was accepted. Things were okay.

There was nothing more beautiful, and I never had a closer sense of self, than when I was young, before I was made aware of my physical differences. Alopecia felt good. It was light, and airy and it was just me.

Junior high was the year when everything changed. School went from being a place where I was loved and accepted, to a place where I was bullied and tormented. I went to a junior high that had an open enrollment program. That meant kids would be bussed from Detroit to the suburbs surrounding Detroit. That meant there were new children who didn't know about my alopecia. It was an abrupt change, one that no one had prepared me for. When I accidentally singed the bangs of my new wig in seventh grade, there was nothing my father could do; he could not afford to buy me a new one.

It became apparent that I wore a wig, and now, instead of my differences making me popular and loved, they made me a target to children who were unaware and angry. One girl in particular bullied me for what felt like the longest year of my life. She and her friends would play football with my wigs. They would walk up behind me and with the slightest of hand movements pull my hair from my head, earning me the nickname of "snatches." Teachers and lunch ladies, friends and janitors would watch in horror, but no one said a thing. It made me feel as though I was not worth anything, since no one, not even the adults, would stand up for me. And I was too ashamed to stand up for myself.

Somehow I made it through to high school but then we moved. I would have start a new school and face telling everyone about my alopecia, a condition that was now something I tried my best to hide.

I reinvented myself. I told people I was sick and was dying. Cancer was much more glamorous than simply having no hair. When other students would question me, I would panic and spend that class period in the bathroom, hiding, from them, from myself, breathing hard, internalizing my anxiety, and hoping to just disappear. The next day, and the day after that, I would stay home sick. I just couldn't bear the possibility of going through what I went through before. Yet still, I made it through, just as I had before.

Something happens the older and older you get. Women with alopecia bloom. Maybe it's the experiences we endure, tucked under our belts like weapons, like armor. I can't tell you the specific day or time my alopecia no longer shamed me, but empowered me. With each person I told about my hair (or lack thereof), it became easier and easier to do so. Slowly, I started to have fun buying wigs, enjoyed being different from all of the other girls. I had knowledge, and I had gone through things no one else I knew had ever experienced. The stronger I became about my alopecia, the less people cared, and the more they supported me.

Even if adults behaved the way those junior high kids did, I would still be proud to be who I am—a strikingly beautiful twenty-eight-year-old writer with alopecia totalis.

Now I spend a lot of time in front of the bathroom mirror, wig off, lights burning bright, admiring the things about myself that are enhanced by my alopecia. I have amazingly high cheekbones. Because my hair does not grow, I have the softest skin of anyone I have ever met. I can change my hairstyle, color, and length in an instant, and then change it back if it suits me. I will never have a bad hair day. I have experienced swimming bald, and nothing will ever compare to that. When I go to sleep at night, my pillow comes up soft and cool to meet my warm head. I am beautiful and desirable, and I stand out, with or without my wig on.

I gained that confidence I watched my mother have for me. Except it is mine. It is stronger than hers, more wild and sincere than hers. It is mine. Because I earned it. I understood that being proud of having alopecia was a dream my mother had for me, but I ran with it and made it my own.

~Kate White

A Joyful Life

In the end, it's not the years in your life that count.
It's the life in your years.
~Abraham Lincoln

When I was first diagnosed with cancer in my right breast in 2007, I figured I probably had about five years left. After healing from my mastectomy, I set about accomplishing everything I thought I might want to do, so when my time came, I would have no regrets. I didn't want to waste a single minute being sad or angry—those would be minutes that I couldn't get back.

In 2011, when cancer showed up in the left breast, I felt I was right on track with my original prediction. I continued my quest to be grateful for every day I woke up, and tried to squeeze the most joy I could out of every one.

My disease made me realize how precious our time here really is, and that I'd better get busy and make mine count! It gave me the courage to get out there and do things I never thought I could.

I taught classes on interior decorating, wedding planning, and self-publishing for the Adult Continuing Education Department at my local community college. I didn't have a college degree, but that didn't matter to me. I still thought I had something worthwhile to share with others, and enjoyed every minute of it.

I wrote and self-published more than twenty books on various topics, including how-to books on interior decorating, crafting, and wedding and party planning, plus a variety of cookbooks and humorous short story collections. I've never had so much fun in my life, seeing those books go from notes on a page to a finished product I could hold in my hand.

I started writing a newsletter for my subdivision, which forced me to get out and learn more about my neighbors and the issues we all faced. After learning about my neighborhood newsletter, the Chief of Police in our small town asked me to write one for all of the Community Watch groups in the city. Both those experiences allowed me to meet so many wonderful people who are now my closest friends.

Since writing seemed to be my new passion, I began crafting stories about my life experiences and submitting them to the *Chicken Soup for the Soul* series. So far, I've had five accepted and four published. I was thrilled!

My breast cancer has proven to be a powerful motivator for me. Would I have been brave enough to attempt all those projects if I hadn't felt my time was running out? I'm afraid I can't answer that question. But my life has been so much more joyful and fulfilling because I did.

And now I'm facing the final leg of my cancer journey. A recent bone scan showed signs of cancer in my bones, with a prognosis of about two years. Since I'm now an old hand at squeezing joy out of every day, I've started a brand new "bucket list."

The first item on my list was a new car, so I can spend many happy hours driving across this great country (with my favorite traveling companions) to see lots of amazing things and meet many more wonderful people. I plan to share those special memories (including photos, of course) with all my beloved friends and family members through e-mails and a blog.

I've also asked my group to send me their suggestions for fun activities and travel destinations to add to my bucket list, and invited each one to join me on my journey.

I have had a fabulous life, and consider myself to be truly

blessed, but, in spite of my disease, it's not over yet—more exciting adventures are on the way!

~Gloria Hander Lyons

Heart Surgery

We have all a better guide in ourselves, if we would attend to it,
than any other person can be.
~Jane Austen

"Tere is something wrong with your heart," the surgeon said. "Your arteries are clogged, and if we don't get blood to your heart you will die." The whole thing seemed surreal, as if they were talking about someone else.

Those words regarding my heart sounded all too familiar, only in the past they had not come from a surgeon but rather from someplace deep within my soul. I had felt for years that there was something wrong with my heart, but I never thought it was cholesterol. I sensed it was something more, something within the depths of my being that had been lost and was screaming out for life.

While lying there in the hospital bed and listening to the conversation, I asked God if there was something more that I could learn from this. Millions of people had gone through what I was now going through, but was there a deeper lesson to all of this? Was there something else?

My thoughts drifted back to my youth, when my heart was filled with awe and joy for life. Back then, each day was a new adventure; but over the years, disappointments, failures and relationships seemed to have sucked the life right out of me. I used to believe, I used to trust, I used to care, but now it was enough just to get up every morning and face a new day. Something was missing and I did not know what it was. Maybe I could use this challenge as a way to examine some deeper issues.

Just as no one ever knew the condition of my physical heart by looking at me from the outside, it was also true with my inner heart, as I had hid my malaise pretty well. If someone got too close I would simply move away to a safer distance and hide behind a mask of jokes and business. At times when I was alone and my mind would quiet down, a small voice would gently give me a nudge and ask me if I wanted to talk about it. "Not tonight," I would answer. "Maybe another time when I am not so tired." Unfortunately, the other time never came. So now here I was, hooked up to an EKG with an entire room full of strangers looking at the very heart that I had tried to hide for so long.

They were talking about my physical heart but I was thinking about my spiritual one. "So what caused this in the first place?" I asked. "Probably from your lifestyle and diet," the surgeon replied. "Whatever you put into your body as well as the stress you experience will sooner or later affect your heart."

Was that a true statement! If I allow anger, bitterness, fear and worry into my life, it will in turn cause internal distress that will sooner or later affect my physical heart as well as my spiritual heart.

As I lay there before the operation began, I released all the things that had stolen my very life from me. I set them free. I made peace with God and myself and let go of all the things that over the years had clogged my heart. That day, to my amazement, I had not one, but two, major heart surgeries.

It has taken me a lot longer than I thought to recover from the surgery, and at times I can still feel a slight pain as I go through this process of healing. At those times, when I grow discouraged and concerned, I sit quietly, clear my mind and trust the surgeon who said that everything would be fine.

Come to think of it, I have learned to do the same thing when I feel a slight pain deep within my soul. I relax and let those old thoughts pass. Then, I focus on those things that make me grateful for my new heart and this precious gift called life, and trust my divine surgeon with the rest.

~Ken Freebairn

Your Marriage Is Killing You

Life's problems wouldn't be called "hurdles" if there weren't
a way to get over them.
~Author Unknown

n April 2000 I became very sick. I thought I had the flu, but there were other symptoms that led me to believe it was something more. I wasn't one to visit the doctor. While my three children had health insurance, my husband and I did not. Besides, I was super mom and could conquer any illness that came my way.

I was thirty-two at the time, working a full-time job and going to school at night. To say I was doing it all was an understatement. I was the breadwinner for our family.

After a battery of tests the doctors diagnosed me with Crohn's disease. When I went to the doctor's office for the test results he looked me square in the eyes and said, "You need to make some major lifestyle changes."

I nodded, waiting for him to tell me what needed to be changed.

"Your diet will have to change. You need to stay away from fried food, spicy food and chocolate, to name a few."

"Okay," I said. "It'll be difficult, but I can learn to eat better."

"It's really important, Tina. Your health requires the change."

I sat on the edge of the chair, worried about what else was going to change for me.

"And the other things?" I asked.

"Stress. You need to get your stress levels under control. I realize you want to go to school, work and care for your children, but something has to give. You can't do it all."

"Do you really think I have to give up school?" I'd finally just gotten to go back after having children at a young age.

"Yes, and I need to know how your marriage is."

I shrugged. "It's like all marriages. We have our good and bad times."

I refused to tell him that my husband was abusive and we fought all the time.

"Just try to keep the fights to a minimum please. Low-key is your goal."

"I understand." I wasn't sure how I could manage that, but I'd tell my husband what the doctor said.

I left the doctor's office in shock. My life really had to change.

It didn't. By July I was in the hospital. I needed intense treatment, blood transfusions and pain meds. What I also needed was rest and relaxation, but that wasn't to be. My husband called and harassed me every day. He said I would lose my children because I was sick and in the hospital. He didn't like having to take care of the children even if I was at death's door.

His calls would last five hours at a time. Nurses would come in and check on me, only to leave shaking their heads.

"Please, I need rest and I want to see my children," I'd beg. He refused to bring my children to see me. It was his way of punishing me for being sick.

Twenty days passed and I felt Crohn's was a death sentence. My health was terrible and I feared losing my children and my home. On the twentieth day, my doctor walked in and looked down at me lying there weak and worn. He touched my hand and I could see he was pensive.

"I don't normally stick my nose in something that isn't my

business, but I feel I must. Your marriage is killing you and if you don't get out of it, it will."

I was stunned. At first I didn't know how to respond.

"Thank you," I said. "It's something to think about."

Think about it was all I did. It was the doctor's words that made me change. I fought to get better. I spent twenty-seven days in the hospital that time, and once I got out it took another four months to get back on my feet and back to work.

When I went back to work I had a plan. I was going to sock away cash in a secret savings account and when it was time I'd leave my husband.

It took almost a year, but one day while in the middle of a fight I'd had enough. I ran and ran and I didn't look back.

I left my marriage that day. To this day I still recall that conversation with my doctor. Most people would find a disease like Crohn's a life sentence. There is no cure, just ways to control it. I see it as a lifesaver. If I hadn't been diagnosed I probably would still be stuck in an abusive marriage. Instead I'm now married to a wonderful man who would never dream of harming me. For that I'm truly blessed.

I took a potential death sentence and turned my life around for the better.

~Tina O'Reilly

The Unwanted Guest

The gem cannot be polished without friction,
nor man be perfected without trials.
~Danish Proverb

I came from a family where food was always at the center of our lives. It was how we celebrated life and survived whatever ills prevailed. Then food became a big part of our daughter's life, too, though not in a celebratory way. She came home from her eighth grade science class one day and informed us that she was no longer going to eat red meat. The following Thanksgiving, she informed us that due to inhumane treatment she would no longer be eating turkey or chicken. However, she remained a healthy eater, seeking recipes that fit her vegetarian lifestyle.

As the years progressed, she spent a great deal of time talking about food, the nutritional value, her likes and dislikes, and she began eating less and less. She often stated that she "felt fat." Her vision of herself was becoming skewed.

By tenth grade, Francesca and I were in what we call "the food wars." The more I tried to reason with her, the more she restricted. No matter what I said or did, it was to no avail. Needless to say, lots of tears were shed by both of us.

In college she joined the crew team. There were two-hour practices before and after classes each day. Because of the intensity of the practices and her minimal eating, she passed out after a crew practice and her coach told her she would have to increase her protein intake if she were to remain on the team. She did just that, and we were relieved.

Francesca loved rowing. She worked hard and excelled, but in the process tore her meniscus. The pain was excruciating. She was told to strengthen the muscles around the knee. That summer she exercised twice a day to strengthen her muscles. However, the injury did not heal enough and her coach moved her to the coxswain position — the person in the boat who sets the pace and directs the boat. She hated it and it wasn't long before she dropped off the team. It was then that the eating disorder took over our daughter's life.

During this time she pushed us away, wanting as little contact with us as possible — mostly to avoid confrontation. Since she was no longer putting in four hours of crew practice, her workouts at the gym became longer and more intense, and her eating was greatly reduced. During the week she would starve herself and then on weekends overindulge in sweets and alcohol. She was five foot five and weighed less than 100 pounds. Worse, she was suffering from exhaustion, dizziness, low blood pressure, collapsed veins, thinning hair, and severe depression. It culminated in a car accident and a desperate phone call for help. Could she come home? Yes, we told her, but only if she agreed to seek professional help for her eating disorder.

Francesca entered The Renfrew Center for women with eating disorders as an outpatient. The first week she came home and begged us not to make her go back. "I am not one of them: I am not that bad." She had been witness to patients who were cutters, survivors of abuse, alcohol and drug addiction, and suffered with various eating disorders as well. The routine, the strict food requirements and the prohibition of exercise were difficult for her. A battle was raging between our daughter and this disease. She called it "Ralph" — an entity with a huge head, small body and wild hair!

We held her, cried with her, and sent her back. By the second week, she began to connect with her peers and realized that though their lives were different, she shared many of the same feelings. She began to meditate, and sought spirituality by finding a church and a college-age Bible study group. She threw herself into getting healthy, both physical and mentally.

But it was not easy. Even though Renfrew provided her with the tools to overcome her eating disorder, she elected not to take medication and did not continue with outside counseling or support groups. She felt she could do it herself. She returned to college, graduated with honors, and married a wonderful man.

But the war was not over. She continued to struggle with her eating and our relationship continued to deteriorate. There was nothing we could do that we had not already done. "Ralph" set out to destroy not only our daughter and our relationship but now her marriage. While she continued to keep us at arm's length, she began to distance herself from her husband as well. His frustration was growing as his wife was disappearing. We shared with him that he was her husband, her lover, her friend, but that he could not choose her food, nor make her eat. We were left to watch. We realized we were not in control and had never been. We told her that we would love her unconditionally and would love her "where she was at."

Our prayers were answered in the form of a second breakdown. The loss of her job and the possibility of losing her husband finally broke the hold "Ralph" had on her. She sought care and elected to take medication. It made all the difference. Slowly, ever so slowly, she became healthy. We began to heal our relationship. We learned not to dictate her eating, her behavior, and her feelings. We learned to trust her ability to acknowledge her body's signal for nourishment, her desire to seek out healthy eating practices and faith that she would overcome "Ralph's" voice in her head telling her to restrict. In turn, she learned to trust those who loved her to be honest with her when she was in a battle with this disease, and to accept that sometimes her vision of herself might be skewed.

Today "Ralph" is unrecognizable and although she is aware of him in the background of her life, he is on mute! Francesca still has days when she "feels fat" and knows it may be a life-long battle. She utilizes her knowledge to help others through her work as a fitness instructor for the YMCA and through her church—where she combines her love of health and faith to administer to others. She is a happy and healthy wife, mother, and daughter.

I am so proud of the woman my daughter is. It was a difficult journey and one I wished she never had to take. I did not like the journey myself. There are some battle scars for both of us. There is the saying that "What doesn't kill you, makes you stronger." I believe that because of "Ralph" we both have grown and have a close, personal and open relationship. Together we have built a relationship far better than we could have ever wished and prayed for. Today, we are each other's best friend.

Thanks, "Ralph"!

~Loretta Schoen

Broken Heart

Exercise should be regarded as tribute to the heart.
~Gene Tunney

One of the valves in my heart is too small, giving me a heart murmur and occasional blood flow in the wrong direction. I am very comfortable with doctors, as they have been examining me from the day I was born. My small valve and I got along well during my childhood. I had no restrictions and could climb trees, play baseball and ride bikes with the best of the boys on my street, being the tomboy that I was.

When I was eighteen, my valve began to express unhappiness. Any stress I felt led to chest pain. It was as if I was cutting off the oxygen supply to the valve and in return, the small flap was screaming at me to relax. According to the doctors, the only solution was medication, which I soon learned I would be on for the rest of my life.

At eighteen, the "rest of my life" sounded like 100 hundred years. I had to find an alternative to reduce stress and increase blood flow to my heart. I found myself in an aerobic exercise class — good for mood boosting, relaxation and cardiovascular health.

The instructor "saw something" in me. She said I was always smiling and moved to the beat. Then, she asked if I would like to be an instructor.

My response was, "Sure, but you'll have to teach me." God bless her, she did. Donna spent the entire summer showing me how to be a fitness instructor and then hired me to teach classes for her business.

That same fall, I entered college not knowing what degree I was pursuing. Once there, I learned I could get a degree in exercise science. How perfect. My fitness-instructing career led me to a desire to learn about the body and the body's response to an exercise program. I could not get enough. I wanted to know everything about the heart, muscles, bones and the brain.

During this time, I experienced a reduction in chest pains and would exercise or walk whenever I felt an episode approaching. I studied biology, physiology and my favorite, the heart. During my class on EKGs, which are electrocardiograph tests for the heart, I learned more information about the medication I was taking and the effect of my body's response to exercise. I did not like the side effects, so with the doctor's guidance, I weaned myself from the drug.

If it weren't for my "broken" heart, I would not be where I am today. Twenty-three years have passed, and when I occasionally experience chest pains, movement is my solution. I am passionate about exercise and look forward to work every day. My career in the fitness industry has taken me many places. I owned a gym, competed in a fitness competition, worked in cardiac rehab, wrote six fitness books, filmed a workout video, instructed others on land and in the water, taught new instructors, and have trained many personal clients.

~Lisa M. Wolfe

The Choice

You're a winner. The tests of life are not meant to break you,
but to make you.
~Dr. Norman Vincent Peale

"From now on, I want to be called Tess, not Tessie. Oh, and Tess is going to be spelled with one s, not two." So declared my preadolescent daughter one day after school.

I smiled. "T-e-s, that's very modern. It will take me a while to remember to call you that, since you've been Tessie since the day you were born." She hugged me.

"I know, Mom."

A few years later, thirteen-year-old Tes with one "s" and I were on our way to yet another doctor's appointment. We both sat quietly during our drive. Today we'd get answers. Tes had endured eight weeks of robotic doctors and technicians, injecting, poking and prodding her through a myriad of tests, without really showing her any respect as a human being.

Tes lay on the cold metal table for an assessment by a grandfatherly doctor we had never met before. His manner was gentle and respectful. She chatted quietly with him, as he examined her abdomen and inner thigh one more time. Now why couldn't he have been one of the doctors testing her during these past weeks?

The examination finished, Tes dressed quickly and a nurse directed us to the doctor's office. I sat opposite her, squeezed into the small room. The doctor sat between us. The tiny room shrank as if the walls pushed inward. The doctor started to speak; I couldn't take a breath.

"You'll need to find a special oncologist; Teresa has lymphoblastic non-Hodgkin's lymphoma." When he said it, my eyes locked with Tes's. Time froze. We stared at each other. My mind screamed. I needed the sound of his voice to stop. But like a machine running through a cycle, he kept slamming us. "She'll need a regimen of chemotherapy and radiation," the doctor said, looking at me. Then turning to Tes, "As you consider the radiation your oncologist will prescribe, Teresa, prepare yourself for the long term that you will probably not be able to have children. Radiation treatment will cover your entire abdomen. You have a decision to make." Tes didn't say a word; we just stayed frozen.

The doctor explained what I needed to do to locate a child oncologist. I kept thinking, you're repeating yourself. I just wanted to leave, to be alone with Tes.

As we got in the car, I asked her if she'd like to go out for something to eat.

"No," she said. "I just want to go home."

After that, we rode along silently. I didn't want to wait until we got home to talk. I quickly found a shady place to park, slamming the brakes and stopping abruptly. "Okay, sweetie; I can't imagine what you're feeling." When I heard the nervousness in my voice, my anxiousness was apparent even to me. "I know my fear level is obvious and yet you're the one going through this." I reached over and touched her hair.

Looking thoughtfully at me, she surprised me with her first words. "Mom, I guess I'm not going to have children if I choose to have radiation."

I hesitated while I thought about what she said. "Well, sweetheart, if you choose not to have radiation, the treatments may not be enough to cure you, according to what the doctor said. Is there truly a choice? We're talking about your life. If you don't have the radiation, there may be a possibility you won't be here to have a child. Do you understand?"

I couldn't hold back the tears any longer; I couldn't believe I was telling my sweet child she had to choose infertility. I reached out to hug her. We held tight to each other.

"I guess you're right, Mom." She sounded pensive and lost in thought.

"It's decided then. You're going to be okay, sweetheart. I'll find you the best doctor; I promise! Do you still want to go straight home?"

"Yes, Mom, it will feel good to be at home. I'm very tired."

"I'll begin searching for your new doctor right away."

Tes was quiet again as I drove. I held her hand most of the way home, and she held on tight.

At least we said the words out loud. This was the only choice — the choice for Tes to live.

I made call after call, looking for the right oncologist. I researched doctors and recommendations from friends and checked through lists of doctors from several clinics. One name showed up in about six places. I finally knew whom to contact to help Tes.

He was everything I hoped he'd be. His rapport with Tes was immediate. He listened as she spoke and he spoke directly to her. I was there just to sign papers. I knew she trusted him the first time they were together. I was so relieved. Their relationship was a major step. The next week, while in the hospital, Tes's days were a whirlwind of appointments, more blood tests, a spinal tap, and multiple scans.

Two full weeks of radiation, two and a half years of chemotherapy every two weeks, and about twenty spinal taps finally brought Tes's treatment to completion. After that, her yearly exam included a scan for monitoring the illness, which appeared to be gone from her body! After six years, she was pronounced cured! The important choice made that day in the park gave Tes the chance to live.

During these years Tes enjoyed the luxury of time to graduate from high school and move on to get educated at a local community college, eventually meeting a young man. They became serious in their relationship; she loved him. When he joined the Marines, she followed him to live in North Carolina near the military base.

Tes lived happily, experiencing joy in the everyday, in the life that she had been given by choosing radiation years before. Then one day my phone rang. I heard Tes's melodic voice. "Hi Mom, I have news. I'm going to have a baby!"

~Amy E. Zajac

One Tough Chick

There is no education like adversity.
~Disraeli

I crossed my arms over the skimpy towel and shivered as my shoulder blades pressed into the tiles on the bathroom wall. Someone knocked twice, insistently, on the door. The nurse opened the door just wide enough to slip in, and pushed her glasses further up on the bridge of her nose.

"I need to examine your body surfaces for marks, scratches and scars," she intoned, without looking up from her clipboard. "Step forward, please, and face me, feet slightly apart, arms at your sides."

I did as she asked, pressing the towel with my elbows to keep it there. Her pen broke the silence as it shuffled across the paper, making notations here and there. I wondered what she was writing. I hated this feeling—not being able to look her in the eyes.

"Drop the towel, please."

I released my grip slightly on the thin fabric, already expecting her response.

"All the way." She blinked at me through her bifocals. I wondered if all the nurses in the psychiatric unit hid their opinions behind emotionless eyes.

I reluctantly let the towel slip from around my waist. The rush of cold air raised bumps on my flesh and set my teeth chattering. I stared at the floor as the nurse made notations on her chart. A flush of embarrassed heat rushed through me, but I refused to cry.

After the examination, another nurse led me to one of the empty rooms.

"Dinner will be served at 5:45," she said. "We'll announce it over the intercom so you'll know when you need to come out and join us. Take all the time you need to settle in."

When she left, I got up to close the door behind her. I didn't want anyone walking past and gawking at me. I lay curled on the crinkly plastic mattress, a fraction of the person I used to be. Memories of the bright, animated young scholar who entered college eager to tackle the world had taunted me without respite.

Now, there was no remembrance and no expectation. The motivated student disappeared, replaced by this strange shell of a person who cared nothing about education. It hurt to think of what I had been compared to what I had become.

I had entered college two years before with a declared major in biology, determined to become a medical examiner and bring justice to those who could no longer speak for themselves. I focused on my studies to the exclusion of all else. As a result, I didn't make much of an effort to establish relationships. When my parents advised me to relax and spend time with friends, I laughed. I was too busy.

I ended up spending most of my time alone and isolating myself from social situations. What I didn't know was that during the first two years of college, I was actually struggling with obsessive-compulsive disorder.

By the end of the spring semester, suicidal thoughts brought me peace rather than tension, which scared me enough to check into a behavioral health facility, leaving my classes incomplete. I made progress with a new medication and returned to school, but by the following November I was back in the facility.

This time, when I entered the hospital, I decided that I would not return to school. The events of the previous spring semester combined with the crushing disappointment of a repeat visit to the facility caused me to think that I didn't belong in school. It wasn't fair to me or to my professors, who would have to give me incomplete grades until I managed to pull it together and finish the course.

My psychiatrist, a gentle woman with clear, sympathetic eyes, told me that she would try a new medication. "It won't be like this forever," she assured me. My eyes stung with unshed tears, and she placed one hand over mine. "You're one of the toughest people I know," she said. "You are one tough chick."

I looked up in surprise. Tough? Me? No way. Not in comparison to the rest of the population. She herself had recently given birth to extremely premature twin daughters and stood at the window of the neonatal intensive care unit, powerless to do anything but watch their tiny chests tremble and twitch with each borrowed breath. And I was the tough chick?

Still, her words stayed with me as I worked through the new medication and spent my Christmas break finishing my incomplete college courses and taking long walks on the backcountry roads. One tough chick, I thought as I declared a new major in history and signed the registration form for two spring classes.

Five months later, the exchange flashed briefly through my mind as I sat at a round table in one of the university's multipurpose rooms for the annual history banquet, wearing the nicest dress I owned and a borrowed strand of my mother's pearls. I felt a little nervous in the formal atmosphere, but the faculty worked diligently to put us at ease.

One of my professors cracked jokes about his own quirks while we enjoyed chicken Monterey, mandarin orange salad, and generous slices of turtle cheesecake. After the meal was over, the waiters served coffee while another professor took the lectern in order to present the departmental scholarships.

Before the banquet even occurred, my mother asked me if I would get a scholarship. I said no, of course, since I'd only just become a history major. These awards went to students who had worked hard in the history department for a long time. God had already blessed me with a miraculous recovery, and I could not have asked for more.

That was why I nearly knocked my coffee mug over when my name was called along with two other recipients for a memorial-endowed scholarship. I remember wondering for a brief moment whether he meant a different Emily Raymond, but my friend Nikki gave me a gentle shove out of the chair toward the platform where the two other recipients were already standing.

"Congratulations, Miss Raymond," Dr. Beasley said, and smiled as he handed me a white envelope. I turned red as the banquet attendees clapped. I picked my way back to the table, praying I wouldn't trip over something.

Later that month, when I visited my psychiatrist for a checkup, I told her all about the scholarship and how I'd already begun work on my senior thesis, and that I intended to enroll in graduate school. She just smiled as I rattled on.

"Like I said, you're one of the toughest people I know," she laughed. "You'll do all of that and more." And this time, I believed her.

My parents supported me through the treatment process and encouraged me as I adjusted to the new medications. On days when I thought I could feel myself slipping back to that void, they reminded me that I'd faced those problems before, and I could do it again.

One of the best things that grew out of the adversity was a friendship with my college advisor. I trusted her enough to share my experiences, and she listened without criticizing or treating me as though I was fragile. She celebrated each new accomplishment with me and encouraged me to be honest with others about how I felt.

Eventually I became comfortable enough to share my story with others. To this day, just hearing the relief in someone's voice when they say, "I'm glad I'm not the only one" is to me the sweetest reward of all.

~Emily Raymond

The Hat

The only courage that matters is the kind that gets you
from one moment to the next.
~Mignon McLaughlin

t started as a typical first class of the new semester at Wright
College in Chicago. Twenty-five faces were staring at me with
the fear of college students who would prefer to be anywhere in
the world other than in a communication class. As I looked back
at them with all the empathy I could express, I asked that everyone
wearing hats please remove them. They looked at me with the confusion of a generation unfamiliar with such etiquette.

The hats were removed except for one young man's. When I
asked him directly, he answered "no." I was shocked but did not
show it. Not ten minutes into the session and in front of new students
whom I was meeting for the first time, I was being challenged. How I
handled this moment could determine how I survived the semester.

The students were intently watching me and waiting. It was
my move. I decided not to deal publicly with this challenge to my
authority so I asked to see the young man after class. His name was
Mark and he looked like the most unlikely of all the students to
demonstrate insubordination. He was slight in build, clean cut with a
pleasant face. He was not someone who stood out among the others.
Yet he had said "no" to a directive from his new professor in front of
new classmates on the first day of the new semester. I had to convince
him to take off his hat. He would have to back down.

After class, alone in my classroom, Mark and I faced one another. He would not look at me as I spoke. His hat, the symbol of his defiance, still sat securely on his head.

"Mark," I said softly, "you must follow the rules of this class. Removing your hat demonstrates respect. Is there a reason you feel you must wear your hat? I am willing to listen."

Mark lifted his eyes and looked into mine. "No," he answered. His look was empty. His tone was flat.

"Then you must remove it," I answered in my most professorial voice. He did as I asked.

At that moment I recognized my challenge with this young man. He complied in removing his hat but I had not reached him. I had forced him but I had not persuaded him.

Slowly throughout the semester, I felt a bond growing between Mark and me. Sometimes he would even smile at my jokes and ask thoughtful questions in class. When I saw him in the hall, he would tip his hat. I would not let him see me smile at that obvious gesture.

The final week of the semester Mark asked me to stay after class. He had something to tell me which he had kept secret.

I had come to know him as a gifted poet and hard working writer and speaker. Harder than most perhaps, because Mark suffered from MS, which had affected his coordination and vocal cords. Some days the class and I understood him better than others.

"Do you remember the first day of class when I refused to remove my hat?" he asked.

"Oh yes I do," I answered.

"Well, now I would like to tell you why I did that. About a year ago I went to an open mic forum to read my poetry. They laughed at me."

"They what?" I asked, not wanting to believe what I was hearing.

"They laughed."

His speech was labored and painfully slow. "I was humiliated."

Once again, like that first day of class, we were alone in my classroom. We looked at one another through our tears.

"The first day of class when I refused to remove my hat I was trying to get you to throw me out of your class. The course was required but I did not want to ever stand before an audience again and perform my writing. But you would not give up on me. You would not let me leave."

"You chose to stay, Mark," I answered softly. We stood there for a moment looking at one another.

For his final persuasive speech, Mark spoke on stem cell research funding. He passionately argued for his classmates to vote for legislators who favored stem cell research. Would it be soon enough for him?

After offering an articulate and informed argument, with great difficulty Mark walked to his visual aid, which was an empty white poster board. He asked his audience to give him one thing. Only one thing. He picked up a marker and with a shaking hand, he painstakingly wrote, one letter at a time, "Hope."

A year after he had completed my course, Mark came to my office to say hello. He proudly told me that students from our class would stop him in the hall and tell him that they would never forget his last speech. The MS was progressing and he was suffering. Yet he looked happy and at peace with himself. He had formed a team in his name for the MS Walk and was trying to raise money for research.

Three years later I received an e-mail from him. He wanted me to know that he was writing again, and that for the first time since he had been traumatized by the experience, he again performed his poetry in an open mic at a Chicago club. He said he could have never done it without my course and my friendship. In his last line he told me that he always wore his cherished hat.

~Elynne Chaplik-Aleskow

From Lemons to
Lemonade

From Heartbreak to
Healing

Wisdom at the Water's Edge

Sometimes you have to let go to see if there was anything worth holding on to.
~Author Unknown

The summer I turned twelve had every indication of becoming the lowest point in my young life. However, thanks to the wisdom of a dear aunt, and the beauty of a natural wonder, that particular summer provided me with a deep strength that I have drawn upon throughout my life.

Earlier that year, my parents had decided to end their fifteen-year marriage. The only home I had ever known would be sold, life with my father would be reduced to a weekend experience, and I would begin seventh grade in a new school. While all of these changes were terrifying to me, somehow that June, they didn't seem to matter that much. What had disturbed me the most was foregoing our annual vacation to the mountains. Instead of spending the summer tucked away in the cool, verdant forest, I was going to spend the next ten weeks with my elderly aunt, who lived in a quiet seashore community. From what little I knew, the only friends I could expect to make were seagulls.

Needless to say, I did not want to go. I had never been a fan of gritty sand and salty surf, and though I did love my aunt, I hadn't seen her in nine years. I barely remembered her, and I sincerely doubted she would be much of a companion to me. But I had no choice in the matter. My parents were breaking up, not only with each other, but also our home. The only thing they agreed upon that summer was removing me from the battlefield.

So despite my misgivings and protests, the very day school closed I found myself on a train heading south. Beside me were two canvas bags that held my summer clothes, my books and a daily journal I had been keeping since learning of my parents' impending divorce. Traveling with me, too, was a heart so heavy with resentment, bitterness and loss I found it difficult to breathe.

When the train pulled into the station, I was the last passenger to leave my seat. The conductor must have sensed how desperate I was, because he patted my shoulder as if to offer assurances that things would somehow sort themselves out. But I knew better, for my life would never be the same.

Waiting for me on the platform was Aunt Olivia, who was actually my grandmother's eldest sister. Demure, slender, and almost shy, she smiled at me and then hesitantly patted my shoulder in much the same manner as the conductor. I supposed I must have looked as forlorn to her as I had to him.

Poor Olivia, I thought. She was as much a victim in this desperate situation. Her summer plans had not included a ten-week visit from a grandniece. I tried to force a smile for her, and I remember thinking how out of place she seemed at the station, almost like a young girl dressed up in her mother's clothes. I was suddenly reminded of an old *Highlights* magazine from my childhood. Its theme was "what doesn't belong," and even to the most casual observer, Aunt Olivia seemed almost foreign standing in that station.

Hauling my canvas bags in the direction of the taxi stand, I trudged after Aunt Olivia, who moved with surprising grace and speed for an older woman. Fortunately, the line was a short one, and Aunt Olivia and I were soon seated in an old-fashioned checkered cab heading east toward the shoreline. In no time at all, the landscape started to change. With my face pressed against the window, I noticed the city's tall buildings, traffic and people soon receded. Within a half hour, I sensed a hint of salty air, and viewed a series of ramshackle bungalows bearing signs like "Bait and Tackle," "The Chowder Shack," and "Boating Supplies."

Three blocks from the ocean, Aunt Olivia directed the driver to stop in front of a small, pink cottage. As I dragged my bags up the seashell path to the front door, I remember thinking that the house looked like Cinderella's coach, a transformed pumpkin. I tried to swallow the lump that was forming in my throat as I thought "this will be my home for the next ten weeks."

Settling in with Aunt Olivia was much easier than I had anticipated. To her credit, she respected my privacy and sensed my need to be left alone. She didn't try to distract me with useless activity or engage me in meaningless chatter. Because the cottage was so tiny, my aunt had adopted a very simple lifestyle, which was precisely what I had needed at the time. Since the dwelling was so small, I slept in an open loft, tucked in the eaves. Every night, as I climbed the ladder to my bedroom in the stars, I felt like Heidi. But unlike my storybook heroine, I had a view of the ocean, not the mountains which were familiar to me.

During the day, I used a rusty bicycle that had once belonged to my mother to get around. For the first few days, I purposely avoided the ocean and beach, preferring to exhaust myself pedaling alone into the town. At the time, I didn't think that much about it, but in retrospect, I think there was so much anger in me, I was unable to even see, much less appreciate, the beauty of the shoreline.

By the fourth morning, I somehow found myself pedaling to the beach. It was a beautiful clear sunrise, and while I had always been partial to the mountains, the seascape before me held a unique beauty. When I arrived at the beach, it was virtually empty but for two lone silhouettes—one feeding the seagulls, the other fortifying a sand castle against the approaching tide.

Leaving my bike on the boardwalk, I ventured toward the sea. As I walked, I studied the figure feeding the gulls. There was something vaguely familiar about the stance. A natural grace, the fluid movements, almost an affinity with the sea. Then it hit me—it was Aunt Olivia. Dressed in worn jeans, a faded T-shirt, and a baseball cap, she resembled a young teenager from a distance. I recalled the dichotomy of seeing her in the train station, stressed, strained and out of place. Here, against the backdrop of the sea, pounding surf and beach, she looked at home.

Though she did not turn toward me, she sensed my presence. "Have some bread," she said softly, handing me some crusts without taking her eyes off the pair of gulls she was feeding. As I crumbled the crusts, the sound of the gulls overhead, the scent of the salty air, and the sight of the young boy defending his sand castle effected a calmness within me. I had not felt such peace since learning of my parents' impending divorce.

Long after the last of the bread was gone, Aunt Olivia and I continued to watch the boy. Finally, she spoke. "You have to admire the persistence in that boy," she said softly. "He's trying so hard to defend that castle. He's decorated it with beautiful shells; he's put his heart and soul into that project. But no matter how high the walls or how deep the moat he builds, the ocean is stronger and more powerful."

As she spoke, I watched the boy. The closer the waves came, the more frenzied he became. His digging became manic; his face was marked with apprehension at each wave. Finally, Aunt Olivia extended her hand to me, and together we walked down to the water's edge.

The boy looked up at us. At first, he seemed confused, but then I saw him smile. Aunt Olivia must have extended her other hand because the boy left his sand castle, stood up, and took her hand. As the three of us watched, a final wave crashed upon the castle, leveling it, destroying the walls, and flooding the moat.

As the seashells that had decorated the castle scattered, Aunt Olivia released our hands. "Let's collect as many of these beautiful shells as we can," she said. "These shells were actually the best part of that castle. Let's gather them together. We'll use them to build a new castle in a more protected area." And that's just what we did.

Throughout my life, Aunt Olivia's words would guide me on more occasions than I cared to remember. That day on the beach would help me countless times as I fought to rebuild my life after forces beyond my control sent me into a tailspin. Years later, as I struggled to survive my own divorce, a corporate downsizing, and the death of a best friend, Aunt Olivia's soft words would quiet my heart. And while attempting to rebuild my life, I tried to follow Aunt Olivia's example by taking the best of my previous existence with me, to ensure that each new castle I erected was a little bit better, a little bit richer, and a little bit stronger than the one before.

~Barbara A. Davey

Refurbished Me

Being deeply loved by someone gives you strength,
while loving someone deeply gives you courage.
~Lao Tzu

I followed my husband Joey outside, all the while protesting to no avail. He was insistent, and as we made our way around the house to the workshop I spotted what he had been so eager to show me. A makeshift workbench sat in the middle of the driveway. Extension cords, a sander, paint cans, brushes, and several pieces of long forgotten, dilapidated furniture were arranged in a big, neat, "do it yourself" display. A lone chair sat nearby.

Joey put his hand on the chair and motioned for me to take a seat while he cheerfully explained that we were going to refinish some of my furniture, my rescued "project pieces" that had been sitting in our garage the last few years. I looked at him in disbelief. Had he really made me leave the safety of my bed for this? Could he possibly think that I cared about fixing up some old furniture?

Our sixteen-year-old daughter Kyley had been gone two years. She had died in a car accident just down the street from our home. I had not made peace with my loss. I looked at Joey and silently turned to leave.

"Stop, Melissa. Just sit here with me. You don't have to do anything. Just sit here and make sure I'm doing this right." Joey's voice was soft, pleading.

I turned towards him and grabbed the back of the chair, dragged it from the sunshine into the shadow of a nearby tree, and sat down. He seemed satisfied and began the task of selecting the first piece of furniture, a small table. He repaired and sanded it quickly.

"What color should we paint this?" Joey asked enthusiastically.

"I don't care," I answered flatly.

Joey grabbed some black paint and soon the little table was as good as new. His project was complete.

Good, I thought. We were done with this and I could go back to hiding out under the covers. Joey had a different idea, though. When he arrived home from work the next day, he pulled back the blankets that hid me away from the world and once again had me follow him outside where he proceeded to transform yet another piece of old furniture. We did this day after day; Joey would lead me outside, he'd select a piece, do the prep work, and then ask me what color he should paint it. I always answered the same, "I don't care."

It was several weeks into our now familiar routine when Joey asked me his usual question, "So, what color would you like to see this?" It was obvious the old chest he was working on had seen better days. The deep scars in the wood were evidence that this piece had a story. It was damaged and no amount of paint was going to hide it.

"Turquoise, let's paint it turquoise." I'm not sure who was more surprised by my response, Joey or me. He hurried to the garage in search of paint and returned with an armful of supplies.

We sat there examining the perfectly painted, finished product.

I impulsively got up from my seat under the tree and walked towards the chest. I grabbed a nearby brush, dipped it into one of the cans, and brushed the dark liquid onto the pristine paint. Joey quickly grabbed a towel and began wiping it away, protesting while he worked. I watched as the tinted mixture found its ways into the pronounced battle scars and laugh lines of this old chest, enhancing every imperfection in a strangely beautiful way. I watched, fascinated, as a story emerged from its wounds. The battered old chest had been reborn. It had been given new life and it was even more stunning for what it had suffered.

I threw myself at my startled husband. "It's beautiful!" I collapsed sobbing in his arms. I could no longer deny the healing taking place in my own heart. I knew, now, that this was all for me. Joey cared nothing about refinishing projects. He wasn't a "DIY" enthusiast. This was all about transforming me… healing me.

We had amassed quite the collection of painted furniture, and as the weeks went on the colors, chosen by yours truly, became bolder and brighter.

Joey walked by our home office one day to discover me on the computer, absorbed in my task.

"What are you doing?"

I explained to him that I was creating an online page to showcase our furniture creations, complete with pictures and stories about how they came to be. He seemed impressed.

ChIC vInTiQuE was born on Facebook and immediately grew beyond our expectations. The response to our furniture was amazing and we were inundated with requests to purchase the pieces. Something rather unexpected happened, though. As I shared tales of furniture transformations, the story of how and why ChIC vInTiQuE came to be, people, total strangers, immediately wanted to know more. I shared true, candid, stories of my own personal journey. I bared my scars, those deep wounds that had begun to heal but had definitely left their mark with our followers. The feedback I received from those touched by our story did even more to feed my soul and help heal my grieving heart. My spirit was becoming beautiful again. With a paintbrush in one hand and a pen in the other, I underwent my own transformation.

We still have much the same routine as we did when Joey first dragged me out to the driveway, although I now go willingly and have a lot more to say about how each piece is refinished. Bold, vibrant colors have become our signature, miles away from those first black and white pieces Joey painted. My chair has long been dragged from the shadows and now has a permanent spot out in the sunshine. That's where you'll find me most afternoons, creating "Inspiration for the Heart and Home" with the man who helped transform me.

~Melissa Wootan

A Boulder in My Path

You are my sonshine.
~Author Unknown

I knew he was gone. Before the policemen ever knocked on my door, I already knew. They say when you are really connected to someone you can feel it if something happens to them. I had known for hours. The police were surprised by my reaction to their visit when I answered the door and said, "I know. My husband is dead."

From that night on, I knew my life would never be the same again. I knew as I held my two-and-a-half-year-old son that he was destined to feel a loss for the rest of his life.

I was totally in love with my husband and always said that I knew as long as I was married to Eric, life would be good. There was nothing he wouldn't do to make sure that Jackson and I were happy and taken care of. Yet, here I was, two weeks before my thirty-fifth birthday, a widow with a toddler, at three thirty in the morning, listening as two strangers in uniform recounted the painful details of my husband's car accident.

The days following are still a blur… people coming and going, a constant flurry of activity, an endless stream of family and food, an endless supply of gifts for Jackson and kind words for me. I do remember sitting on the floor of our sunroom going through an old box and finding a CD my husband had recorded for me to play to Jackson while he was still in my belly—sun-filled choruses of Jimmy

Buffett, classic Beatles, Van Morrison and a half dozen children's stories he had read aloud so that Jackson would get used to the sound of his voice before he was born. I jumped up, screaming with excitement, so thrilled that Jackson would never have to forget Eric's voice, so grateful that something that had once seemed a cute gesture from my traveling husband now meant the world to a toddler too young to understand what he'd lost.

My friends and family stared at me in disbelief as I danced around the house with joy at the treasure I had uncovered. A voice in the crowd said, "Wow, I can't believe you are handling this so well, that you can even smile about anything." In that moment something inside me clicked and I said out loud, as much to myself as anyone else, "My son lost his father, and he sure as hell isn't going to lose his mother." From that moment on, I resolved to be the most extraordinary mother I could possibly be, making sure that I never wasted an opportunity to make my son feel loved, connected, confident and blessed—regardless of what happened around him.

Today, I look at my confident, brilliant, funny, wise, spiritual, amazing thirteen-year-old son and I am so proud. I am proud of the young man he is becoming, and I am proud of the mother I am to him. I know that losing Eric forced me to step up in ways I could have never imagined. Jackson and I have cried thousands of tears, but for every tear, there has been so much more laughter and understanding and genuine closeness and friendship.

Jackson is an exceptional boy, and I am so privileged to be his mother. I would have given anything for him to not lose his father, and for me not to lose the most amazing man I have ever known, yet I can still see the gift in the loss. Jackson and I are closer and understand each other in a way most mothers and sons could never imagine. His spiritual side is so rich, so real and authentic. He is comfortable in his own skin and can find a way to fit into any situation. I know that he will always be okay, because everything he needs is inside him and he is amazingly resilient.

Ever since Jackson was two years old, almost every day I have repeated the same ritual with him:

"How much do I love you?"
"More than the sun and the moon and the stars."
"What's the best thing that ever happened to me?"
"Me."
"What makes me happiest in the whole world?"
"Me."
"What am I most proud of?"
"Me."
"What can you be when you grow up?"
"Anything except a bad guy!"
"That's right!"

Even though my little man is now thirteen, I still do it, and I mean every word.

There have been other ways that this experience has enabled me to grow and to give more than I could have ever imagined. I have learned compassion in a whole new way, and have been able to support other women who have lost their husbands when they have become members of this strange sorority. I have also learned to not sweat the small stuff and to find joy, beauty and happiness in every day.

I always say the world is full of people who are thrown into a tailspin by a pebble — what are they going to do when life puts a boulder in their path? I have learned to barely notice the pebbles, to climb the boulders, and sometimes to even go around them by focusing my energy on something else. I am grateful every day for the gifts in my life, my amazing son, and for having had the privilege of being married to an extraordinary man like Eric. I have learned how precious life is, and that it can be short. I have learned to appreciate the love I have, not spend my life mourning the love I've lost, but to keep it alive — through Jackson, through talking about my husband, and by being the kind of mother and woman that would make Eric proud.

~Joelle Jarvis

Let It Go

Everybody's got a past. The past does not equal the future
unless you live there.
~Tony Robbins

have been a freelance writer for eight years. Well, eight years with
a two-year hiatus. You see, I can only write when I'm happy. Not
deliriously, goofy-grin-on-my-face happy, but even-keel happy.

Several years ago, my husband walked out on our two
young children and me. Within three months time, I had to sell the
only home my children had ever known because I could no longer
afford it on my teaching salary. We moved more than 200 miles to my
hometown, so that we could be closer to my parents. I couldn't eat or
sleep and my weight dipped dangerously low.

For several months, I felt like a zombie. I took care of my children, but not of myself. I was sick almost constantly. I felt as though
I had lost everything: my marriage, my home, my job, and, most of
all, my dreams. I felt like nothing would ever be okay again. I hated
my ex-husband for taking everything from me, for causing my life to
fall apart.

But gradually, a little bit every day, I began to feel better. I started
to smile again, and then even laugh. When I went to bed at night, I
was pleasantly surprised that I had actually had a good day.

I began to realize that the things I had lost were not gone forever... just for the time being. I knew that I would eventually own
another home, get a better job, and maybe, just maybe, a better man

too. I started to see that I had a lot going for me. I had a supportive family, great kids, and a strong, positive outlook on my future. And I was skinny.

I landed a job teaching kindergarten in our new town, and I loved it. My kids and I rented a little house across the street from a park. It was far from my dream house, but it was ours. It was clean and comfortable, and it felt like home. I gained a few pounds and I even began dating.

Life seemed to be getting back to normal—whatever that was in this alternate realm, the divorced single mother world. It was a world I never wanted to be a part of, but here I was, making the best of this new reality.

I felt mostly like my old self, except for one very important thing: I couldn't write. Not one word. Not an essay for publication, an article for a magazine, not even a journal entry for my eyes only. I had been writing since I was a kid and I had been doing it for publication for several years. But now, I couldn't formulate a single sentence. My passion was dead and my ideas were all dried up.

One day I bought a pretty notebook and a package of multi-colored gel pens. I had always preferred typing on my laptop to writing longhand, but at that point, I was willing to try anything to get myself writing again. That night, after my children were asleep, I sat on my secondhand couch and tried to write.

Nothing came. Absolutely nothing. I had always had more ideas than I knew what to do with, but for almost two years now, I hadn't written a word that wasn't required for my teaching position. Writing had always been so therapeutic for me, almost a catharsis, but now, when I truly needed the therapy, my gift was gone.

I sat on that couch, holding my new purple pen, and cried. My ex-husband had taken my house and most of my other possessions from me. How could I let him take my writing too?

Those other things were our things, and by law, he was entitled to half of them. But my writing? Well, that was mine alone, and I couldn't let him take that too. But it seemed that it was already gone.

I glanced down at my new notebook, and there, written in my own script, were three little words: Let it go.

I wasn't aware that I had written the words, yet there they were. Those words were as close to an essay as I had gotten in years.

As their truth sank in, I realized the reason I was unable to write. I was still holding anger and resentment against my ex-husband. I knew that I wouldn't be emotionally free until I forgave him. In order to write again, I was going to have to do what my purple pen said. I was going to have to let it go.

While it didn't happen overnight, it did happen. I began to appreciate the freedom of my new life. When my children were with their father, I could eat microwave popcorn for dinner and watch any movie I wanted. I could wear my pajamas all day long if I felt like it. For two weekends a month, I got to be me, not just my children's mother. It was a small thing, but as time went on, I began to embrace my new life. It wasn't what I had dreamed of, nor was it where I thought I'd end up, but it's where I was, and in truth, it wasn't such an awful place to be.

And when my kids came home from their father's house, I made an effort to view their dad through their eyes. I tried to see him as they saw him, as a fun guy who acts goofy and makes mistakes, just like the rest of us. For months, I tried to picture him as my kids did, and one day, I realized that I was no longer angry with him. I went from seeing him as the villain who robbed me of my perfect life to seeing him simply as the guy who was no longer perfect for me.

I let it go, and I began to write again. Just like that.

~Diane Stark

Taking Life Back

Hope begins in the dark, the stubborn hope that if you just show up and try to do the right thing, the dawn will come.
~Anne Lamott

On a cold December morning, I sat in the kitchen of my sister's apartment with a handful of pills a few inches from my mouth. All my life, I grew up knowing that the holiday season was supposed to be a time for happiness and joy, yet here I was alone in the kitchen, about to try and take my life for the fourth time since the summer. The stress of my first semester of college had taken its toll on me. All-nighters and getting adjusted to living in a room with two other people wasn't as easy as I thought. Being a homebody, going to a proclaimed "party school" was also a huge culture shock. It was the first week of winter break and I was already dreading the day when I had to walk back through the front entrance of my dorm.

Yet at that time, college was just one of the many issues at hand. I knew that as soon as January approached, I would be entering the fifth year of my on-and-off struggle with depression. Since my symptoms had heightened in the recent months, I had been trying different prescription antidepressants, none of which seemed to improve my symptoms. I even started self-harming as a way of relief. It felt like nothing was working and there was no way out. I thought I would be stuck in the pit of depression for as long as I lived, and for the fourth time, I decided that I no longer wanted to continue with life.

I brought my hand even closer to my mouth, but instead of dropping the pills in, I walked across the room and threw them in the garbage. A question popped into my head that I'll never forget: "If I think my life is so bad that I want it to end, why not fix it?" After I came to that conclusion, I spent the rest of my day completing tasks that I had left on the back burner. I sent messages to old friends, read my Bible, and created my own blog. Each day I search the Internet for motivational quotes to post. I wanted to share my new way of thinking with others so that they could be inspired to power through hard times and depression, simply by believing in themselves.

No matter what, I promised myself that suicide wouldn't be an option. The first quote I posted on my blog read "I will do my best to live." As a constant reminder, I set it as the background on my tablet. Every time I felt like quitting again, I turned on my tablet and told myself to keep going.

The next step in my journey to regain my life was something I'd been working on for almost three years. All the people around me had been driving since they turned sixteen. I was going to be nineteen in a few short months and I still had my learner's permit. After two years of trying to learn the ways of the road, I just couldn't get over my overwhelming fear of driving. Not having my license was one of the main factors contributing to my severe anxiety and many sleepless nights. With only three weeks left of break, I knew it would be a tight stretch to conquer my fear of the Florida roads and get my license. The next time I got behind the wheel, I forced myself not to panic. Everyone else could drive. So could I. Three days before heading back to school, I was holding my driver's license.

Going back to school, I felt like a changed person. As I put my anxiety inside, I reached out and began socializing instead of hiding in my room. Getting a job was the next thing on my list, so I sought one on campus and received an interview soon after submitting my application. Even though I didn't get the job, I remained positive and moved on. Right away, my friends and roommates noticed how much I'd changed in just a few short weeks. I went from moping around to being a smiling social butterfly. I never thought that trying out positive thinking could make such a huge impact on my life. All I had to do was remove the restraints depression had on me.

~Jess Forte

Hello, My Name Is Claire and I'm an Alcoholic

A desire to be in charge of our own lives, a need for control, is born in each of us. It is essential to our mental health, and our success, that we take control.
~Robert F. Bennett

am an alcoholic. It took half my lifetime to admit it. I kept thinking that if I did, it would give me a label I wasn't ready to wear. I am so many other things first: a wife, a writer, a ballet teacher, a child of God.

I have no blatant, dramatic war stories, I didn't suffer any losses and I never hit rock bottom, which is typically the thing that leads to the undeniable admission of alcoholism. What I had instead was suspicion and a psychological dependency that grew until it took over completely.

Alcohol is in the very fabric of the culture in which I was raised. In the Deep South, very little is done without it. It stands sentry at the center of every social gathering from the cradle to the grave, and I never questioned it or considered it unusual in the least because it was always just there. Outside of the house I grew up in, alcohol was everywhere, and within the walls of the house, varying bottles held pride of place on a large, silver serving tray upon a marble console in the living room. Every night, when the grandfather clock in the entrance hall approached five o'clock, I could find my mother in the living room, seated elegantly across from my father, holding what would be the first of three Scotch and sodas. This was how my parents reviewed the happenings of the day and it left me with an implied template of civility, which I carried outside of my childhood, and into the life I would create.

Because alcohol was in my life, because I was someone who used it socially, I formed many friendships with women who did the same. It gave us a reason to get together after work; it dictated the venue and gave us something to bond over. We'd talk about our work, our relationships and our lives expansively, and boy, we had some good times. The men we were attracted to did the same, so suffice it to say, alcohol was also at the heart of our romantic relationships. The two-year courtship I had with my husband was fueled by champagne, and our wedding wasn't any different. When the honeymoon was over, we settled into the rhythm of our lives. After we set up home and hearth, I had my own silver serving tray of liquor bottles on a marble console.

And, I was indiscriminate. I drank when I felt celebratory and I drank when I was stressed or sad. I had many different justifications. I was indiscriminate in the blind way that one foot unthinkingly follows the other, until a distance has been covered and you turn around and recognize how you arrived at the very place you are standing. When I finally turned and looked behind me, it was three in the morning, I was holding a wine glass in my hand, and my husband had retreated to the master bedroom in anger hours before. I was outside on the patio praying to God for my life to change.

"Please, God," I begged. "I'll do anything you want, just please, please, change my life."

I had this vision that one day I was going to be whole, one day I was going to be fulfilled, one day I was going to be the person I always suspected I could be. I could almost feel the best-case scenario of myself living and breathing but I couldn't fathom what it would take to usher in the change until a thought occurred to me: "Why don't you start by putting down that glass you're holding?"

When I did put down the wine glass, I woke up my husband with these words, "I need to go to treatment and I need to go today."

I pressed pause on my life and went to treatment for thirty days. While there, I became a voracious student of the disease of alcoholism. I wanted to know everything there is to know about it. I became the focus of my own case study, sponging up all the information until I was saturated. Admitting that I am an alcoholic wasn't enough for me; I wanted to know why I am one. I wanted to know what got me there. I wanted to know why I was anesthetizing myself.

If you're reading this and saying to yourself that you can relate to any point within whatsoever; if there is a nagging similarity to your relationship with alcohol and mine, then there is a good chance that you have someone in your bloodline who can say the same. That's what I learned in treatment. It didn't take the onus off me but it did help alleviate my self-judgment. I am after all, a nice girl from a nice background; it's just that I had this genetic time bomb that lay dormant until I set it off like an atom blast whose fallout will go on forever. It doesn't make me a bad person; it just makes me an alcoholic.

The hardest part of all of this was admitting that I have a problem with alcohol. But now that I have, the self-exploratory work that has ensued has been liberating and my life has turned drastically in a positive direction. It must have something to do with the adage of when you see your enemy, call it by name and the truth is, I can't hear myself say it often enough:

"Hello, my name is Claire and I am an alcoholic."

~Claire Fullerton

Loving Liam

When you are a mother, you are never really alone in your thoughts. A
mother always has to think twice, once for herself and once for her child.
~Sophia Loren

I suppose the homogenous world I grew up in contributed to the motherhood fantasies I created for myself. I was raised by my reserved British parents in a quiet household as one of two exceedingly well-behaved girls. The street I lived on in suburbia looked like the set for a family sitcom. Each morning I ceremoniously dressed in my plaid uniform as a reminder to be just like everyone else. I mastered how to be the perfect Catholic schoolgirl when the nuns and adults were watching. I conversely knew how to be cool enough to fit in with the "it" girls. I became adept at being who I was expected to be in any given situation.

This was the canvas on which I created the dreams for my own future. For as long as I can remember, the biggest part of those dreams was to be a mother. I had a vision of what that world would look like someday. The handsome husband and the well-behaved children in perfect outfits. The everyday fun and the picture-perfect family vacations we would take together. Me doing it all, while looking fabulous. My children would be smart, kind, talented and loved by all.

I do have a beautiful family that includes a handsome husband and four wonderful children. There are moments when I look fabulous. My children are smart, kind, and very talented. But they are also frequently misunderstood by the world. Their days are filled with moments that would have thrown the nuns who taught me into a tizzy. My kids' eccentric behavior would have the popular girls in my class cringing in embarrassment. I am the mother of three boys with autism.

I remember the simultaneous rush of panic and excitement when I felt the first pangs of contractions. I was pregnant with my first son and my due date was weeks away. When we arrived at the hospital, the doctor told us that he couldn't be sure how long it would be, but that "this baby's birthday will be today!" When he left the room, I remember gazing out the window and thinking in amazement that I was about to become someone's mother.

That someone, my oldest son Liam, was born hours later. I was in awe of him. I felt such peace with him in my arms. I couldn't stop smiling or looking at him. The brush of his velvety skin against my cheek was pure heaven. When he was in someone else's arms I counted the seconds until they gave him back to me. I was blissfully happy.

Weeks later, the picture was not so perfect. Liam started to cry. A lot. He couldn't be held tight enough or long enough. He screamed when others held him. He barely slept. I was inundated with expert parenting advice from family, friends, and strangers on how to "fix him." Nothing worked. At his one-month checkup, my pediatrician's exact words were, "Wow, you're a pretty intense little guy, aren't you?" Oh, he had no idea. When Liam learned to crawl, he became inten-sity on the move. When he learned to walk he was running days later. I watched other children playing in the park while my child ran in circles and was literally drawn like a magnet to whatever he should not be near.

The dirty looks and disapproval quickly followed. Clearly, I was not doing something right. I felt the stares of other mothers at the play-ground burning through my back as I struggled to help him through one of his frequent and explosive meltdowns. He acted like the chil-dren around him did not exist. Once, in a split second, he dumped sand all over a child as I helplessly tried to reach him and intercept. My profuse apologies were no match for the mother's understandable anger. I left quickly in shame with a kicking and screaming Liam. I sat in the car and cried while Liam repeatedly banged his head on the car seat.

I knew in my gut something was not right. His doctor said he was just an active little boy. My in-laws said I was overprotective some days and not tough enough other days. Maybe I was just a horrible mother. I felt as though I was failing miserably at the only job I ever really wanted in life.

During the summer when Liam was two we spent a beautiful breezy summer day at a friend's cookout. All the children were playing together in the grass. All of them except Liam. He was fascinated with the tools in the garage and everything else he was not supposed to touch. When my husband took a turn on Liam duty, I headed towards the food to quickly eat something before I would be called back into action.

As I was making a plate for myself, I heard Liam's screams first and the comment second. The so-called friend behind the grill muttered to his company, "If that was my kid, I'd put a boot in his behind." I looked up and his eyes met mine. I put my plate down. I rushed over to Liam and announced to my husband that we were leaving. I heard no one else and saw no one else as we marched straight out of that party to our car in the street, with my husband chasing behind in confusion.

I sat in the back seat on the way home trying to console Liam, who was distraught over our early exit. I showed him a magazine to distract him. He started to look through it on his own and quieted. I put my head back, closed my eyes, and tried to cool the rage inside me. The calm lasted all of about thirty seconds.

"Look Momma! Look Momma," Liam repeated over and over while jabbing me in the arm.

"What, Liam!" I exploded. I opened my eyes to the page in front of him. It was a mother and her little boy walking on the beach holding hands.

"It's just like you and me!" He beamed from ear to ear. I started to cry and smile.

"That's right," I said, "just like you and me." I kissed his sweaty head and whispered into his hair. "No more, Liam. I am done listening to all of them. From now on I am listening to you, and I am listening to myself. I hear you. I see you." That was the day I truly became someone's mother.

The next day I call my pediatrician and demanded to see a specialist. Months later, Liam was diagnosed with Asperger's syndrome, an autism spectrum disorder. I have battled schools, insurance companies, and others' opinions every day since then. It has been a tough road but a true gift. Liam has taught me that so many of the rules we have for ourselves we have made for ourselves. He has taught me to enjoy every inch of life and to see beauty and humor where I hadn't looked before. I live and love more fully because of him. The truth is that real love shows itself in the moments that wouldn't make it onto the front of your Christmas card but should. Real love is not about expecting perfection, but appreciating one's rarity.

Today Liam is ten years old. The busy toddler who ran circles in the playground just finished his first 5K road race this summer. The rambunctious preschooler who didn't notice anyone else in the sandbox has a best friend and volunteers at church. The little boy who always said the wrong thing now writes beautiful poetry. He is still quirky and marches to the beat of his own drum. I love that about him. He is braver than I am.

When Liam was five, he and I were having a special afternoon out together during which we stopped at a local carousel. We paid for our ticket and he was off to find the perfect horse.

"This one!" he announced in excitement as he clambered up the saddle and tightened himself into position. "Oookaayyyy, we are ready to go!" he pronounced with the full intensity of a space mission. I chuckled and climbed atop the horse next to him.

The carousel began to spin slowly and then faster as we passed the same faces in the crowd watching us over and over. Liam started to lift his arms up in the air and alternated loud and enthusiastic cheers of "Woohoo!" and "Yee-hah!" and "Ride-em cowboy!"

I saw the blurry faces start to whisper and stare. I began to tell him to quiet down but then I stopped myself. I turned my gaze away from the faces circling around us and looked instead at the pure joy in the face of my son. I lifted up my arms, hesitantly at first, and then with more purpose. "Woohoo!" I cheered. Liam's face lit up.

We circled around and around, hooting and hollering and waving our arms in the air as the world watched. This was our ride together. We only had one ticket. We should ride it our way.

~Mary Hickey

Getting My Bling Back

Love yourself first and everything else falls into line. You really have to love yourself to get anything done in this world.
~Lucille Ball

didn't think the word "bling" applied to me. I'm far from wealthy and my only diamond ring sits in a box. I know it is a commonly used word in the entertainment and fashion world and it comes from the imaginary sound produced when light reflects off a diamond. But for me, bling was a thing of the past, the victim of a debilitating disease.

I was the kind of person who counted her blessings. I read *The Power of Positive Thinking*, by Norman Vincent Peale, a hundred times. I believed the words of the Bible when it said, "I can do all things through Christ who gives me strength." So, when my doctor diagnosed my low-grade fever, joint pain, and fatigue as rheumatoid arthritis (RA), all my defenses came to attention. No way was I going to let it get me down like it had my grandfather and uncle. They had suffered until their will to live had vanished. With that in mind, I got busy looking for answers.

First, I found a rheumatologist whom I could trust. He put me on a combination of medications proven to reduce inflammation and improve mobility. He also recommended keeping a record of my pain to see if we were making progress or needed to make changes. Some drugs helped, but many that had helped thousands of other people didn't help me. RA had dealt me a hefty blow.

Still, I wasn't one to give up. I did my best to stay active and keep a positive attitude. RA wouldn't kill me, but I had seen for myself how it could diminish one's quality of life. I fought back with all my being. I had too much living to do.

Despite that, as time went on, the disease progressed and I became unable to work. Without an income, I faced a dim future. That's when my self-esteem began to crumble.

The decline started with little things. When a cheap pair of earrings hurt my ears, instead of buying better quality earrings, I made the decision to do without them altogether and let the holes close. Also, I got tired of asking my husband to fasten my necklace. It just wasn't worth it. And, when all my rings had to be removed because my fingers were so swollen, I gave up on jewelry for good. The bling was gone from my life.

The downward spiral continued as I cut out activities such as shopping and yard sales. They were no fun with my ankles and knees hurting with every step. Besides, what good would it do to buy cute clothes and shoes when the disease persisted? I was too self-conscious to wear dresses any more. Pantyhose were impossible to pull on. Tennis shoes with jeans or slacks would have to do for any occasion—even for church.

I had always enjoyed my hair at shoulder length and my husband liked it too. The problem began when I couldn't raise my arms over my head. Once again, I had to lean on him. Always the optimist, he never lost his sense of humor. "I never thought I'd become a beautician," he said.

When my hair was showing more and more gray, I opted to let it go. Never mind that all the women, and some of the men, in my family had colored their hair for generations to look younger. To me, nothing could be more aging than RA.

Since my teens, I had worn hard contact lenses. Now, I decided they were too much trouble, especially with my dry eyes. My eye doctor said my medicine was to blame and wanted me to consider soft contacts, but I passed up that offer too. With my crippled hands,

I wasn't sure I could put them in or get them out. Glasses would have to do. I was in a tailspin.

Then, just when I needed it most, a good friend stepped in. "Why don't we re-pierce your ears?" Julia Ann asked. If anyone could inspire me, she could. Despite chronic back pain, she always managed to look great.

I couldn't see what difference it would make. "No. That's okay. I'm getting by just fine," I said.

"I'll bring my kit next time I come over," she said, unwilling to take no for an answer.

In a few days, she came back determined to get the job done. I was reluctant, but since she was so sweet and I didn't want to seem unappreciative, I agreed.

After she was gone, I looked in the mirror at the gleam coming from the tiny cubic zirconium earrings. Was it possible that I could actually be attractive again, in spite of my condition? Had I been letting my illness stand in the way of my appearance? Maybe if I did things to be more beautiful on the outside, I might feel it on the inside too. It was worth a try.

One thing led to another. I started looking for necklaces that would go on over my head and I added extenders or easy clasps to a few of my other favorite pieces; my friends took me shopping to find easy-on, comfortable, yet stylish tops and elastic-waist pants in stretchable fabrics; my husband ignored my argument that New Balance shoes were too expensive, so I ended up with several pairs of them in different colors; I found out I could handle soft contact lenses; and, my hair would soon have highlights and a much needed trim. At last, I realized what had happened over the years. Every time I had given something up, I had given up more of myself to the disease.

Today, thanks to Julia's persistence and the encouragement of many other friends, I'm getting my "bling" back. The changes wouldn't be noticeable to most people, but for my friends and family they are significant. Only, in my case, they won't see the light reflecting off a diamond. It will be coming from the sparkle in my eyes.

~Linda C. Defew

An Unexpected Blessing

Even hundredfold grief is divisible by love.
~Terri Guillemets

I f someone had predicted that my husband and I would be giving away our younger daughter in marriage a mere three weeks after saying goodbye at the grave of our older daughter, I never would have believed them. I never would have thought that I would have the kind of strength required to endure a funeral and a wedding in such a short period of time. I had often heard that during difficult times in our lives, we receive the strength we need just when we need it. This proved itself true in the spring of 2011.

The swirl and excitement of bridal showers and wedding planning for a soon-to-be June bride came to a tragic standstill on the eleventh day of May, when our older daughter passed away unexpectedly from an unknown heart condition, just four months after giving birth to our first grandchild.

Those first few days following the loss of our precious twenty-two-year-old were passed in a strange mix of disbelief and going through the motions of making all the necessary arrangements. Through all the grief and emotions that our family was experiencing, we were aware of a chapel that would be filled with wedding guests in a few weeks. We never considered postponing the wedding. We knew that one of the best ways we could honor Ashley was going forward with the plans to celebrate her sister's wedding day.

So we found ourselves in a surreal mix of planning a funeral and finishing last-minute wedding preparations. One day I would be sitting at a table at the funeral home picking out memorial cards and discussing the arrangement of photographs that would represent Ashley's life; then the following day I would be with Caitlin at her final dress fitting, with tears running down both of our faces. I remember thinking how unbelievable it was that just a few weeks earlier Ashley had sat in this same room with us while we laughed and joked during the first fitting.

The floral shop was the hardest. The same florist who was handling the floral arrangements for the funeral was also doing the flowers for the wedding. At the same time we were picking out a gorgeous array of lilies and roses to adorn Ashley's casket, we were also discussing that we needed to switch the maid of honor's bouquet of Gerbera daisies to a floral arrangement for a memorial vase to be displayed at the wedding.

At some point in all of the chaos, I half-jokingly remarked that we could have Olivea stand in for her mommy as the maid of honor. Her Aunt Caitlin loved the idea, so we put our heads together to figure out how to include a four-month-old maid of honor in a wedding ceremony. When the day finally arrived, there was not a dry eye as the best man walked down the aisle carrying a beautiful sleeping baby, dressed in pink satin from head to toe. We had worried that she would cry or be frightened by all the people, but we had not imagined that she would sleep through the ceremony. The precious little sleeping beauty was so worn out from the pre-wedding festivities and photo sessions that she didn't wake up until halfway through the receiving line.

That beautiful June day holds such special memories for me. The smiles on the faces of my daughter and new son-in-law, the coming together of family to celebrate such a special occasion after having gathered three short weeks previously to mourn the passing of a young woman who had touched so many lives. A sense of Ashley's spirit being present with us and smiling down on us seemed to permeate the entire day.

I'm sure there are some who would choose to view the timing of these two significant events in a negative light. I choose, however, to believe that a sunny day in June and a sleepy maid of honor taught me that life and, yes, even joy, can still be found in the midst of suffering.

~Julie Cole

No Longer the Ugly Stepmother

Mother love is the fuel that enables a normal human being to do the impossible.
~Marion C. Garretty

"Jimmy's coming to live with us!" I was so excited! My husband Roy's six-year-old son was coming to live with us full-time. His mom was doing a very noble thing. Jimmy had some unique learning requirements and needed special attention and therapy—something I could help with, as I had a very flexible work schedule. Not able to have my own children, I was delighted to be able to help raise this delightful, blond, happy little boy.

Over the years, little Jimmy became James. By the time he was sixteen, he was a surly, obnoxious, foul-mouthed teenager. Oh, how I wished for that cuddly boy in pajamas to return. Why did I ever think I could cope with a boy? When did he transmute into "The Enemy" and I into "The Ugly Stepmother"?

Roy was often out of the country on business. I was coping the best I could with James, but I was really struggling. I functioned as Mom's Taxi Service. Once he called me to pick him up with his best friend, Colin, at their favorite skateboarding place. But when I got to that location—no James, no Colin. Finally my cell phone rang.

"Where are you, Mom?"

"I'm right where you said you'd be—where are you?"

"Oh, Colin and I decided to get a hamburger—we're down the hill at Burger King."

This scene was followed by James yelling and swearing at me when I confronted him with my frustration. The argument that followed I imagine takes place in many a stepparent's household:

"As long as you are in our house, you will obey our rules!"

"This is my dad's house and I don't have to listen to you!"

"I am your father's wife and I am in charge while he is gone!"

"I'm leaving this 'f---ing' place!"

James uttered those words to me and stormed downstairs to his room. In a panic, I locked the door to downstairs and frantically called his father.

What would I do if James ran away while Roy was gone?

Thank goodness I reached Roy. As calmly as I could, I explained what had happened. He asked to speak with James. I called James to the phone and left the room. Later Roy called me back and said it was okay and that he'd be home the next day. I found out when he arrived that he'd placated James and sided with him on the argument.

From that point on, I had no control over James or any say in what he was or wasn't allowed to do. I felt like an unwelcome stranger in my own home.

The year James was a senior in high school he was assigned to the "worst" English teacher. All of the kids had to do a research paper, which would extend over most of the school year. Roy pleaded with me to help James with the project. "You're so good at writing—you'll know just how to help him put it together. You know how he struggles with things like this."

Flattered at being asked to help for a change, I agreed. The first part of the project was to pick a book. James picked *Deliverance*. Then he picked a thesis and scoured the library and the Internet for research. The night before his research cards were due, he was up until 3 a.m. finishing them. He then drove them to a friend's house for her to deliver in class, as we were going away on a trip and he had an excused absence. When he returned to class after the trip, the teacher ridiculed him about having someone else turn in his cards: "You just wanted to play hooky!"

The outline and thesis statement were next. James and I worked for hours to get it just right. Finally, I went to bed while he finished. The next morning, I found on my desk one of the rewards a step-mother often dreams of but seldom receives. A letter from James read:

> Mom,
> Thanks so much for helping me on this project. I just know that we'll get a really high grade on it. There isn't any way to tell you how much I appreciate it.
> Love, your son, James

I cried as I showed Roy the letter.

We anxiously awaited his grade on the outline — it came back 0! And next to his thesis statement was the scrawl, "Who cares?" James was demoralized and I was furious! "What kind of a teacher is this? Does he call this a critique? How is James supposed to know what is wrong? And besides, there isn't anything wrong with this!"

My husband was equally incensed. He wanted to head into school to confront the teacher. James told us about all the negative and slanderous comments the teacher had been making about him in front of the class, as well as several inappropriate stories the teacher had told the students. "In fact," James told us, "several times he's said in front of the class that no matter what I do, I'm not going to pass!"

Now deadly calm, I told my husband that confronting this particular teacher would not help — I would go and talk to the principal.

A day later I was in the principal's office armed with my arguments on James's behalf. The principal made the major mistake of trying to patronize me. I assured him that I knew what I was talking about — that I'd been an English major in college and had my MBA — in addition to being a published author. He backpedaled frantically. I told him we wanted James transferred to another section of English with a different teacher. He assured me that was not possible and that James had probably just overreacted. This teacher, he related, was one of the best, though on the tough side.

I asked him if he thought constructive criticism was part of a teacher's job on a project such as this. "Oh, it's one of the most important parts!"

"Then explain to me how this fits with constructive criticism?" I showed him the outline with the teacher's comment. "And let me show you how James felt about it before he got this back." I showed him my prized letter.

Crestfallen, the principal admitted there was nothing constructive in what James had been given. I repeated our desire to have James transferred. He reiterated that it was not possible. I told him that all James needed to graduate was a passing grade in English. I was not going to allow him to prevent my son from graduating even if I had to pull James out of school and home-school him! I further informed the principal that I was sure the PTA would love to hear about this teacher and that I had other parents who were willing to testify about the treatment their kids had received when in this teacher's class. Finally he capitulated and agreed to move James to another class.

While relating my conversation to Roy and James later, I could see the incredulity on James's face. His stepmom had done the impossible! No one went up against this teacher and won—no one had ever been transferred out, despite frequent attempts.

At that point a transformation occurred in our relationship. I started to see James as a person trying very hard to succeed given the obstacles he had to overcome. He started to see me as a person who loved him and really wanted to help and to be a part of his life.

While our relationship did not become smooth overnight, things did become better. He became a bright young man earnestly working to be a success at his job. Another "reward" I received occurred when James was building his first house and he called me to ask, "Mom, will you come and meet with the designer with me to pick out the options? You're so good at that." We spent a delightful morning doing the planning for his house and then had a very gracious lunch.

I saw my son as a very special person and not "The Enemy." He saw me as a friend and not "The Ugly Stepmother." In fact, the birthday card I got from him that year states: "For My Mother. One kindness follows another, and you are the source. You give advice when it's asked for, encouragement when it's needed, and kindness when it means the most. I hope you'll always know how much that means to me."

Yes, James, I knew. I hope you knew how much you mean to me. I am proud to have been considered your mother. You were one of the greatest challenges of my life, and you were one of its greatest rewards.

James was killed in an automobile accident when he was just twenty-four. The night before he died, my husband and I were with him at a restaurant where several of his friends also were. We asked him if he was coming back with us—he grinned his infectious grin and allowed he'd "hang with the young folks!" That was the last time we saw him alive. I am so glad we'd become Mom and Son and knew the love each had for the other.

~Deb Haggerty

Two Again

He spake well who said that graves are the footprints of angels.
~Henry Wadsworth Longfellow

stood at the foot of my husband's grave. It still showed signs of the recent burial.

"Now what?" I asked myself for the hundredth time. Fifty-seven years can't be brushed aside like it never happened. Plans were made, babies were born, and memories were set. What was I supposed to do with the rest of my life? How could he leave me?

There were no more tears. Anger had replaced the heart-tugging sorrow. We had unfinished business. Some arguments were not resolved. Questions were unanswered. Emotions not expressed. Trips not taken. To many "I love you's" left unsaid.

"How could you leave just when life was getting good?" I yelled.

"Were you talking to me?" a voice came from behind me.

I immediately shut my mouth. Evidently this conversation had gone beyond my husband and me, and was now open to the public. I turned to look around me. Two rows behind me a gentleman was sitting back on his heels staring at me. He was dressed in Levis and a long-sleeved shirt. His head was covered with a canvas hat that had seen better days and he wore dirty leather gloves.

"No," I said in a slightly raised voice. "I was just—ah—talk-ing—ah—to—to my husband." I finished in a soft apologetic voice. "Sorry if I bothered you. I didn't realize I was talking out loud."

"Not to worry," the man said, returning to his hands and knees, and brushing debris from a gravestone. "I do it quite often myself, but I usually wait until I'm at home — ah — alone."

He bent his head to finish his task and I returned my focus to my husband's grave. The mood was broken. I was no longer talking to my husband; I was talking to a plot of earth. I stuffed the flowers I had brought into the metal container that protruded from the top of the headstone and returned to my car without a backward glance.

"Stupid woman!" I said out loud as I drove away. Turning the corner I glanced back to see if the man was watching. He was not.

The next several weeks were filled with the challenges of fixing meals for one, finding someone to talk to, calling my children several times and reminding myself to sleep on each side of the bed so the mattress wouldn't become lopsided.

On a bright sunny Monday, I drove to the grocery store and ended up at the cemetery again. When I reached my husband's resting place, I saw the same man again tending to the grave two rows back. He looked up, sat back on his heels and took off his canvas hat, which he waved at me.

"I see you're back. I was going to clean off your husband's headstone if you didn't come today."

I walked back to where he was working and offered my hand.

"I'm Audrey. I promise I won't be so loud today. Whose grave is this?"

"Hi, Audrey, I'm Anthony and this is my wife. She went ahead of me two years ago. I celebrated our fiftieth anniversary by myself two days after she died."

"Do you come up here often?"

"Not as much as I did at first. I used to come every week because I was so lonesome, but now I can go a month or longer."

I settled myself on the ground sitting cross-legged in front of him and asked, "Do you mind if I join you for a minute?"

"Not at all," he said as he sat back on the grass and crossed his long legs in front of him.

"What do you do when you are not here? How do you stand to look at the days stretched out ahead of you alone? Does it get any easier?" Anthony didn't seem to be too startled by this semi-hysterical woman who had invaded his privacy so I continued. "Do you ever get mad at her for going first?"

"Sure," he sighed. "We planned to do lots of things when I retired, and we could have done them, but I wanted to work a few years longer. She couldn't wait. She was gone three months after they found the cancer."

Anthony and I talked a while longer and when I rose to leave, he said, "Next time you're here maybe we could have coffee and just talk some more."

Six weeks later we had coffee on the patio of a small café and talked for hours. A week after that we had dinner, and the following evening we saw a movie together. Don't ask me the name of it. I was just content to have someone to talk to and share the problems of living alone.

Anthony and I have wonderful times together. We sing the songs that we grew up with. Neither of us can carry a tune, which makes it all the more fun. If one can't remember the words, the other can. We hold hands, we walk in the park, we laugh out loud and we kiss goodnight in my doorway.

Two elderly people, who met in a cemetery, found their young hearts and are enjoying what the rest of their lives have to offer.

I think my husband was looking out for me again, and I hope Anthony's wife is happy for him.

~Ruth Smith

Simple Words

Shared joy is a double joy; shared sorrow is half a sorrow.
~Swedish Proverb

"**S**he's never told you?"

I shook my head. "And I've never told her."

My boyfriend gave me an incredulous look. He just couldn't believe that my mother and I had never said "I love you" to each other. He and his family members said it to each other all the time, usually accompanied by hugs and kisses.

But Greg's upbringing was radically different from mine. My parents had an unhappy marriage, and both of them had come from families that weren't very demonstrative. Mom and Dad were rarely affectionate with one another, and were even less so with my brother and me. It just didn't seem to be in our family makeup.

I knew my mom loved me. And I loved her. But we didn't express it verbally. It's not that I didn't want to, but whenever I tried, I just couldn't seem to do it.

"You have to tell her. You can do it," Greg urged.

"I'll try."

But I never could seem to find the right time.

Only a few months later, tragedy struck. Greg passed away unexpectedly. It was the worst time of my life. I didn't know if I would survive. I felt that my past, my present, and my future had all been taken from me.

But my mom was there for me. She spent hours listening to me talk about my pain and my regrets. She was sympathetic and reassuring. We went for long walks. I talked and I cried.

Then, one day, I spoke with her on the phone. At the end of the conversation, I said—the words flowing easily—"Thank you for taking such good care of me. I love you."

She said, "I love you, too."

Just like that. I had done it. We had done it.

Six years have passed since Greg died. My grief, while now an integral part of me, is manageable. I know that I have made it through. My mom and I are closer than ever. We talk every day on the phone, e-mail every couple of hours, and go shopping and to the movies together.

I know that Greg would be proud. He would know, as I do, that I was granted something special. I may have lost my boyfriend, but I found my best friend.

~Carol E. Ayer

From Lemons to
Lemonade

From Bleak to Blessings

73

Love Lids

When you forgive, you in no way change the past—
but you sure do change the future.
~Bernard Meltzer

t was early fall and the kids and I were looking for a new house, closer to the city where we drove almost an hour every day for school, church, shopping... everything. We had found the perfect house in the perfect location at the perfect price. And then I got the phone call.

It was my husband, from whom I was separated. "What would you think about you and the kids moving into my house and then I could get a smaller place?" His place was big and roomy and way too large for a man living alone. And it had land: my secret heart-of-heart desires. A place in the country with acreage.

A deal was struck—he would stay a couple of months in the lower level of the house and the kids and I would have the main floor. We would make the best of things, pool our finances, and put our differences aside until he found an apartment.

At first it was weird. We hadn't shared a home in years. We hadn't shared more than an argument in years. The months stretched out and he stayed. Financial burdens became a financial crisis and stressed us both to our limit. We had no choice but to learn to share.

Over time, we adjusted to living under the same roof and the kids had their dad with them to say goodnight and good morning and to join us for Family Night and family prayer. We all worked together in the yard and jumped together on the trampoline. We planted a garden and took pictures of every new vegetable as if it were a new baby in our family. One day it hit me: the kids were happier having both their parents with them. My own fog of worry and frustration at the situation lifted as I marveled in this blessing. We began to feel like a family again. Except for the tiny little detail of Mom and Dad not being together and not really even liking each other.

The financial struggles worsened and it seemed as if no end was in sight. Strangely though, this tremendous stressor began to create in me a compassion for my husband that I hadn't felt in years. There was no way we would ever get back together, but a new sort of friendship and kindness began to blossom. My heart softened; his heart softened.

After two years of learning and struggling and changing, one summer evening my husband came to me. He was humble and gentle and I could see his heart was truly hurting. He entered my room and asked if we could talk. I immediately felt nervous. It's never a good thing when someone says that. He perched on the edge of my bed, the pine canopy bed with the cutout hearts he surprised me with fifteen years ago when I was carrying Noah.

"I think we should try to see if we can fix our marriage."

My mouth dropped open. I never saw this coming and refused to open my own heart.

"No."

The conversation deepened and the pros and cons were discussed, but inside I was terrified to trust this man again. The conversation continued for days but I couldn't bear to crack my heart open to him, not even to let the teeniest ray of hope in. I had wanted this change and now that it was here, it was too late. Years too late.

About a week later, Marty suggested that we begin praying together. Just the two of us, like we used to back when we were happy. Eons ago. I agreed that this would be a good idea. What was the harm in prayer? I kept my heart firmly clamped shut and that night we prayed together.

I listened to my husband's humble words, felt his good, strong spirit and something inside me thawed. Each night we prayed and each night I felt something shift more and more between us. I started to believe that maybe we could be a family again. I prayed hard in private for guidance. If this was God's will for us, then He would have to help me find the faith. I needed proof.

The proof came in small, unexpected ways. Ways that showed me two stubborn people really can change. Each of us began to make changes within ourselves, not putting pressure on the other to change, just focusing on what we needed to improve on our own. Marty wasn't the only one who needed to change, I knew that. I began to be kinder to him, letting go of years of hurt. I felt peace inside at this change in myself. The change affected him, but it healed me. As I let go of my hurt, the walls I put up between us began to come down. Little, everyday things helped pave the way for big changes.

Marty stopped doing little hurtful things and replaced them with loving, thoughtful gestures. Flowers arrived from him weekly. Also gone were the snide remarks about my daily Diet Coke. In their place arrived a giant Diet Coke in our fridge every morning, the lids decorated with little love notes. The first one shocked me. I opened the fridge and couldn't believe my eyes. Not only had he bought me a soda that morning, but he wrote "I love you" on the lid in bright colors with little hearts. The second one surprised me and the third one had me eagerly anticipating what was on his next "love lid." His little notes made me smile all day. I secreted the lids away in a drawer and pored over them again and again. My husband is not a demonstrative man, so this was a tangible change that showed me he really was trying. I needed to try too. My faith began to grow with each "love lid."

As part of our self-assigned "marriage homework," we watched the movie *Fireproof*. It opened my eyes to the realization that the sacred vow of marriage is not about how much the other person deserves love, or how happy he makes you. My vow was to love unconditionally.

We had decided to attend any conference or marriage retreat we could find. Marty searched far and wide, but they were all too far away and we had no one to take the boys overnight. Finally he gave up, frustrated. One night on a whim, I thought maybe I should try too. The little seed of faith was growing in me. I scoured the Internet and I found an all-day Saturday conference called "The Marriage You've Always Wanted" taught by none other than Dr. Gary Chapman, author of *The Five Love Languages*. It was only an hour away and tickets were not too expensive. I felt my heart speed up at this stroke of luck.

I surprised Marty with the tickets, excited and nervous and proud of my find. It ended up being the turning point for our marriage and one of the best days of my life. We took notes and listened raptly, soaking in a million lessons and reminders about how to be married and how to be good at it. Sitting next to my husband, watching the tears slide down his handsome face, I realized I was head over heels in love with him again. He was a strong, beautiful, loving man and a truly wonderful father. I felt so very, very blessed. My eyes filled and my heart overflowed at this gift of a second chance. Leaning on him, I knew we could actually put our marriage back together. And my fear evaporated.

I have a drawer full of love lids and it's still growing every day. We are renewing our wedding vows on the weekend of our anniversary next month. The road is still bumpy at times. Like a delicate flower, it needs care and attention. We nurture it with nightly devotionals geared for couples and supported by scripture and prayer. We have actual dates where I shave my legs, wear jewelry and he opens doors for me and makes me feel like a teenager again. We play question-and-answer games that help us learn about each other's dreams, hopes, fears and the things that make us feel happy. The nurturing part is new for us and takes work. But the reward is greater than I ever imagined. My heart is full again and our children are happy.

I know that without the financial crisis we faced, we never would have healed our marriage and our family. We were forced to depend upon each other and learn to work as a team to get through that crisis. The financial stress itself was horrible. But without it, we would still be a broken family.

Sometimes it takes a crisis to create a miracle. But it is worth every moment of pain, of worry, of fear. You just have to have the faith to walk through the fire, look for the path God wants you to be on, and get to the other side. Where the miracle is waiting.

~Susan Farr Fahncke

74

Embracing My Life Just the Way It Is

As you embrace the here and now, don't be surprised if you suddenly feel lucky — lucky to be blessed with a good mind, lucky to have friends who love you for who you are, lucky to be living in such an interesting time.
~The Art of the Moment *by Veronigue Vienne*

My father lay in the hospital bed, his labored breaths creating a plume of white on the oxygen mask. His skin, once deeply tanned, hung in sallow folds on his face. I could make out the shape of his legs under the blanket, toothpick-like. His bony chest peeked out from the top of his johnny shirt.

"The surgery to remove the umbilical hernia went well," the doctor was saying. "However, he had a heart attack at some point in the days following the surgery and has developed pneumonia. There is a strong possibility that he has a blood clot in his lung. We're also very concerned about his prostate cancer. His PSA level indicates the cancer has spread to the bones."

I swallowed against the painful lump in my throat as the doctor went on to discuss DNR orders. A mixture of shock, grief and sadness washed over me, capped by an odd sense of relief. Relief that I was at last able to feel emotion. I had been going around in a numbed state, unable to feel anything since I found out for certain that I would not have any more children.

Six months earlier, my ninth and final attempt to conceive a second child through artificial insemination had failed. Due to a condition called polycystic ovarian syndrome, I was unable to get pregnant naturally. The fertility treatments had taken an emotional and financial toll on my husband and me, and we had decided that the ninth round was to be our last. We had ruled out adoption, as there was an eight-year waiting period to adopt in our province, and the more invasive in vitro fertilization procedure was financially out of our reach at $10,000 per round.

I felt like I had been cheated. I had so much love to give, and yet God had not seen fit to give me another child. I had lain awake many nights during the past six months, wondering how I had gotten pregnant so easily five years ago with my son, on treatment round number two, but this time I was being denied. I had fallen into deep despair, shut in at home like a hermit while my husband took our son to preschool, play dates and skating lessons. I could not bear to see all the multiple-child families. I was wallowing in self-pity, angry and bitter at the world.

Now I listened as the doctor talked about the possibility that my father's heart could stop. Overcome with the knowledge that his life hung in the balance, nothing else seemed to matter. I pushed aside the haunting knowledge that my dreams of having more children would never be realized and focused solely on Dad. I sat for several days at his bedside, praying that he would pull through, but not holding out much hope. The combination of emergency surgery and rapidly spreading cancer had severely weakened his body.

I had a lot of time to think during those long, anguished days. What if he didn't get better? What if his heart did stop? What if I didn't get the chance to tell him all the things I wanted to say? I had thought I would have so much more time with him. I hadn't even finished the short stories I had started for him a few years ago. He had always told me I was a great writer and wanted me to write something for him. But I had been so busy trying to beat infertility that I had given up writing completely. Actually, I had given up a lot of things on my mission to expand my family. As I looked at the gaunt man in the bed, for the first time it really hit me just how fleeting life is. And I had stopped living mine.

That night I cuddled next to my son as I read him bedtime stories, something I hadn't done in months. At one point, he gave my arm a squeeze and said, "I love you, Mom. You're perfect."

I looked down at him in surprise and hugged him back. My inability to have another child had made me feel like a colossal failure, but I suddenly realized that I wasn't one in my son's eyes.

One morning, as I was getting up, Mom called. She greeted me with a choked voice, and I knew immediately that something was wrong.

"What is it?" I asked.

"I just heard from one of the nurses," she said slowly. "Your father is bleeding internally. They're giving him a blood transfusion."

I rushed to the hospital to meet her and the rest of my siblings. We took turns sitting with him. When my turn came, I stifled a gasp at the sight of the bag of blood hanging on a pole next to the bed, three-quarters full. Dad's eyes flickered open as I sat down beside him. "How long do I have?" he whispered hoarsely.

"A very long time," I assured him, patting his cold-as-ice hand. He fell back into a restless sleep, and I buried my head in my hands. Of course I couldn't be sure of that. No one knows how long any of us have. I was quickly realizing just how important it is to treasure our loved ones while we have the chance, and to make the most of the life we've been given. I promised myself then and there, that no matter what happened, I would hold my son closer to my heart. And I would stop looking at secondary infertility like it was the end of the road.

A couple of days later when I visited Dad, I was shocked to see a healthy flush on his cheeks, the oxygen mask and blood bag nowhere to be seen. He was eating from a tray of food that sat in front of him. My heart leaped with joy and relief. He had made it.

A couple of weeks later, Dad was released from the hospital. He had gained his strength back, along with some much-needed weight. He gets a hormone shot once a month to treat the cancer, and complains of only minor bouts of pain. I am so grateful I've been given more time with him.

After Dad's health scare, I began to embrace the life I've been given instead of looking at it like it was a curse. I no longer mourn the children I didn't have; instead I thank God for the one beautiful miracle child I do have. I cherish the time I spend with my son, with whom I have a close, loving relationship. I've come to see that I don't need more children to be happy. Having an only child has enriched my life in ways I never thought possible.

My dream of having more children may have ended, but I am living a new dream now. And it's sweeter and more fulfilling than I could have ever imagined.

~A.M. Miller

A Turkey of a Thanksgiving

Enjoy the little things, for one day you may look back
and realize they were the big things.
~Robert Brault

I grew up with the crazy notion that cancer is 100% survivable. My mother's first bout with cancer came only a few weeks before my fifth birthday. She was diagnosed with thyroid cancer, and the surgery meant my mother missed my first day of kindergarten. My cousin Charlotte was the one who put me on the bus that morning. I don't really remember the day. My cousin's picture of me standing in my blue dress in front of the house is the only proof I have that my mother wasn't present. And the scar along the crease in my mother's neck is the only proof she'd had a tumor.

Mom survived the thyroid cancer, but as the years passed, the doctors kept finding skin cancer on her face and back. She'd have minor surgery to remove the malignant moles, and life would go on. Cancer didn't seem like such a dirty word to me. Just a nuisance that left my mother with another scar.

And then came my freshman year of college. I was home one weekend when my mother sat on the edge of my bed to tell me she had breast cancer. In hindsight, I should have been terrified, but my fear was tampered by Mom's track record for kicking cancer to the curb. Mom had survived thyroid cancer once and skin cancer more times than I could count. Surely, breast cancer would be just another bump in the road.

The impact of my mom's diagnosis didn't hit me until my dad called my four brothers and me together to discuss Thanksgiving. "Your mother's surgery is just a few days before Thanksgiving. She won't be able to lift anything heavy for a while."

I scratched my head. Why was he telling us this? And why would a mastectomy make it hard for her to lift things? Oh, yes, I was that blissfully ignorant. It wasn't until years later when a tumor was removed from my own breast that I understood how much even a small incision could impact arm movement.

"So..." Dad continued, "there won't be a Thanksgiving dinner this year."

"Wait. What?" My jaw hit the floor. Mom had cancer—again—and Thanksgiving was cancelled?

"What are we going to do instead?" my oldest brother asked.

Dad shrugged. "We'll go out to eat."

I had visions of the family in *A Christmas Story* eating Christmas dinner at a Chinese restaurant. My family would be doing the same for Thanksgiving? Inconceivable!

Apparently, my four brothers felt the same way. I don't remember which of them came up with the idea first, but one of them said, "We'll do it. The five of us kids will make Thanksgiving dinner."

Did I mention I was the only girl in this family with four boys? And none of us had any real cooking experience at this point?

It didn't matter. We quickly jumped on the bandwagon.

"Yeah. We'll each make a part of the meal."

"Mom can just sit in a corner of the kitchen and direct us."

"And tell us where she keeps things. Anyone know where the big roasting pan is?"

"Mom won't have to lift a thing."

"We'll do it all."

I saw the concern in my father's eyes. Could four young men and an eighteen-year-old girl make Thanksgiving dinner on their own? My two oldest brothers were just starting their careers in computer-related fields. My third oldest brother was in his first year of medical school, and my younger brother was a sophomore in high school. Although I'd done a bit of baking, none of us really knew anything about cooking, much less a Thanksgiving feast for seven.

But we were determined we'd have a traditional Thanksgiving dinner with all the fixings. Being techy nerds, my oldest brothers decided to make a Gantt chart for the meal. For the less nerdy, a Gantt chart is a type of bar graph that illustrates the development of a project. The project is broken into smaller elements, and the start and end times of each element are displayed on the chart.

Thus, the Thanksgiving feast was broken into parts and tasks were divvied up. I would make the pumpkin pie. Mike would make the apple pie. Dave was in charge of cranberry sauce and bread. Steve would make twice-baked potatoes. The youngest, Tom, would make the stuffing, and with Dad's help, get it and the bird into the oven.

Then each of the cooks was assigned a time to work in the kitchen. It was absolutely imperative that each cook finish his or her task on time, so the next cook could step in. Mom was deemed Executive Chef, but her tasks were purely supervisory.

Working backwards, with an expected dinnertime of 5:00 p.m., my brothers filled in the Gantt chart.

On Thanksgiving morning, I made two piecrusts. I filled one of these with pumpkin pie filling and got it in the oven. The other I left for my brother's apple pie. He began work on his as soon as I'd finished the piecrusts. After clearing off my end of the kitchen table, Tom stepped in to prepare the stuffing.

By the time my pumpkin pie came out of the oven, Mike's apple pie was ready to go in. By the time his pie came out, the turkey was ready to go in. And so the day continued, each of us taking our turn in the kitchen.

At four o'clock, we set the dining room table with Mom's good china, wine glasses, water goblets, and silverware. At 4:30, the turkey came out of the oven. It was the most beautiful golden brown bird I've ever seen. At five o'clock on the dot, exactly the time prescribed on the Gantt chart, all the food was displayed on the table, and the candles were lit. It could have been a scene from a Norman Rockwell painting. We took pictures so we'd never forget.

We sat down to that Thanksgiving table thankful for so many things. Mom's surgery had gone well. She'd still have chemotherapy and radiation treatment, but she'd survive. Yes, we were also thankful that we'd saved Thanksgiving dinner, but that was part of Mom's doing, too. She had taught us not to fear trying new things. She had instilled in us the importance of family. She had raised us to work together to solve our problems.

Over twenty years have passed since that Thanksgiving. Mom has battled breast cancer two more times. She's had numerous more incidents of skin cancer. She is the very definition of a cancer survivor.

And to honor our mother, my brothers and I still aid in the making of Thanksgiving dinner. Sometimes Mom makes the green bean casserole and helps with the turkey if her health is good. My brothers and I stick with our traditional roles. What had once seemed like it would be a turkey of a holiday has become our standard for the perfect Thanksgiving dinner.

~A.J. Cattapan

There All Along

What greater thing is there for human souls than to feel that they are joined
for life — to be with each other in silent unspeakable memories.
~George Eliot

I wasn't sure what to think about my stepmother. She came into
my life when I was a teenager, when I had more important things
on my mind than becoming friends with her. I liked her and was
always polite to her and we would chat at family gatherings, but
I had friends and a social life miles away from where she and my dad
lived. I was happy my dad had found someone who loved him as
much as I did, but I really never took the time to really get to know
her. Any communication she and I had was done through my dad.
While he retired early, she continued working in a high profile career
that left her very few free hours. This was just how it was and I never
gave it a second thought.

As the years went by I would meet my dad for lunch during
the week while she was at work. I would fill him in on the events in
my life. I know he relayed my news to her but she and I never had
one-on-one talks.

Then the unthinkable happened… my dad was diagnosed with
cancer. Before we knew it, the cancer had become aggressive and my
dad's remaining time with us was limited. I spent many long hours
in my dad and stepmother's home those last few months, but most of
the time it was to tag team with my stepmom so that she could run
errands, take care of business, or just go get her hair done.

I know my dad worried that my stepmom would be alone once he passed away. He expressed his hope to me that our family would stay intact and that we would still look out for one another since he would no longer be able to fill that role. I told him we would. My stepmom and I sat together on either side of the bed and held my dad's hands as he took his last breath and died peacefully.

The turning point in our relationship came on the night of his death. I remember it as clearly as if it were yesterday. We were sitting at her kitchen counter waiting for the coroner to arrive when I finally asked, "Why did you not have children of your own?" With sudden clarity I realized that, although she had been a part of our family for more than twenty years, I never took the time to truly get to know her. Her goals, her dreams, her past. It was clear that we loved and cared about each other but did we really know each other? I stayed with her that night and we talked, laughed and cried.

Since that night she has become my biggest cheerleader and I hers. She is the person I call to discuss hardships, frustrations and joys and she listens. She encourages my son to achieve his goals and dreams and never misses an opportunity to tell me how proud she is of him and how proud she is of the job I have done as a parent. When I need advice or just a sympathetic ear she is always there. Our lunch and dinner dates are cherished moments that don't happen often enough.

It has been almost eight years since that night. Rather then look back on what we missed those early years I am so grateful for what we have created since then. I hope my dad is able to look down from heaven and be proud of the relationship we have created on our own. A terrible time in my life brought a blessing I never knew existed.

By the way, her response to my question that night so long ago was, "I never thought I would be any good at it." How wrong she was.

~D'ette Corona

My Rocky Road to Menopause

A baby is God's opinion that the world should go on.
~Carl Sandburg

I am a farmwife. I bake rolls from scratch. The rows in my vegetable garden are straight. There is no time in my life for nonsense. Why then, I wondered, was this tiny man with the ridiculous horn-rimmed spectacles standing in front of me, arms crossed, smiling like a bad poker player holding a straight, telling me I'm pregnant?

"Doctor," I argued, "you told me to expect early menopause. Next month I will celebrate my fortieth birthday."

"I know," he laughed, slapping his knees. "I wish I could see your husband's face when you tell him the news."

"But, what about menopause? What happened to menopause? You promised me menopause," I whined.

"It will wait." He put his arm around my shoulder. "When this is all over, we'll have a conversation about menopause. Right now, the 'birds and bees' seem more relevant."

Sitting tall, looking as righteously indignant as anyone can in an open-down-the-back examination gown, I tried one last-ditch approach. "I can't be pregnant! None of the forty-year-old women I know are pregnant."

"Humm." He smiled. "I can't vouch for them, but you, dear lady, are pregnant."

I should have known. All those familiar symptoms: throwing up breakfast... throwing up lunch... throwing up dinner... throwing up. Because I had been told to expect the "change" early, I had thought that these symptoms in addition to nearly passing out in the garden were my imagination or simply the normal gateway to senior citizenship.

Farmwomen are not ignorant of natural cycles. Clearly tulips do not bloom in the fall. My friends and I had our children raised. I could imagine their delighted sarcasm but the really big conundrum was what my mother would say.

The world was tilting and everything I knew or, thought I knew, about middle age was turned upside down.

I raced across the plowed field to tell my husband the news. I figured he should be the first to hear since it was entirely his fault.

He grabbed me in a great bear hug and showered me with affection, which was exactly the response I should have expected from him, and is precisely why I am in the "delicate" condition I am in. Well, why wouldn't he be excited? I'll be the one doing all the breathing, holding, and pushing.

"Well," said my almost-twenty-year-old daughter. "Let's have it. What did the doctor say?" She had been filled with dread, and had urged me to see the doctor.

I paused dramatically and answered in an ominous tone, "You'd better sit down."

She sat, her expression reminiscent of a passenger aboard the Titanic.

I took a deep breath and blurted it out. "I'm pregnant. We're going to have a baby."

The sudden change in her expression might have caused an earthquake. She doubled over with laughter. I thought she was having a stroke. Her face was red; tears filled her eyes. Rasping, choking sounds came from her throat. I've never witnessed anyone having so much fun. For weeks she had flashbacks whenever we came into contact.

"It's not that funny," I said. "I'm not that old, you know."

Everyone in town thought I was. They had the same reaction. I met a friend in the grocery store. He saw me coming, did a double take, and ran into a stack of canned veggies. News travels fast in a small town, and this was big! I half expected to hear my name mentioned in the evening news broadcast of our local radio station. I could picture headlines: Sarah and Abraham Revisited, or Wrinkled Woman Risks Massive Stomach Stretch.

As my pregnancy continued I began to see the wonder of it all. I began to relax and enjoy the experience along with my family and friends. Mother turned out to be my staunchest supporter. It was evident that this was a very special blessed event, though a little tardy.

When the baby girl was about ten, the jaws of menopause actually did grip me in unending crescendos of hot flashes, night sweats, and emotional craziness. I wept over cosmetic commercials and laughed hysterically at *Blondie* and *Dagwood*. My husband begged. "Woman, have mercy on us; take your medication."

I now have nine grandchildren. Familiar names do not roll off my tongue as in the past. Sometimes I forget appointments and where I put my glasses. At any rate I am in the last lap of my race, headed for the finish with a flourish. My advice is: Life is good! When it deals you a curve, put some gravel on it and go!

~Kay Thomann

Joy in Service

How wonderful it is that nobody need wait a single moment
before starting to improve the world.
~Anne Frank

hated everything about my life that summer. I hated my job. I
hated my roommates. I hated being around my friends, who
seemed to live perfect lives. I hated being around people who
were cheerful and I wanted them to be as miserable as I was. But
mostly, I hated that I was filled with so much hatred.

Looking back, I still can't figure out what made me feel so much
animosity towards everyone and everything. All I know is that I was
mad and that I was sick of being mad. One day, I vented my frustration to my younger sister. I knew my overall attitude towards life was
damaging my relationships with everyone and that I just needed to
get over whatever was bothering me. But it seemed like the harder I
tried to "be happy," the more things would just anger me.

After listening to me bemoan my rotten attitude for half an hour,
my sister said to me, "Have you tried praying?"

I couldn't believe she would suggest something so stupid. I had
just expressed a deep, unexplainable rage to her, and her advice was
to pray? After glaring at her for a few moments, I regret to report,
I responded with, "Prayer? That is the stupidest thing I have ever
heard!"

My sister looked at me sadly for a few seconds and then said,
"Perhaps this is the reason why you are struggling right now."

Even though I initially reacted to my sister's advice with scorn, I did think about what she had said to me. I realized that she was right. I had let my church attendance slip that summer. Even when I did go to church, I didn't pay much attention to what was said. I couldn't remember the last time that I had read the scriptures. I had let my spiritual life come to a complete halt. So I finally swallowed my pride and knelt down in prayer.

A few days later, I was talking to a friend and she mentioned how sad she was feeling over the recent death of her grandmother. The day after that, another girlfriend was saying that she didn't feel like she belonged in our community. I suddenly felt the strong urge to do something kind for these two friends that were feeling so down. I talked to my sister, and we decided to "heart attack" these friends. We cut out paper hearts and wrote kind messages on them. As we were preparing the surprise for the two friends, the names of five other people came to mind. So then we cut out more hearts and wrote more messages. Later that night, we placed the hearts on the vehicles of our friends and also left a dozen cookies or a bag of candy for each of them.

As the days went on, we heard from each person who we had "heart attacked" how much they appreciated whoever had done this for them. They said they had been feeling as if no one cared. It felt so good to know that I, being as angry and hard-hearted as I was, had made someone else feel special. And suddenly, just like that, I realized I wasn't angry anymore. Whatever horrible thing had managed to capture my heart for that summer was gone. By forgetting myself and serving others, even in a way that some might think is silly, I had forgotten that I was angry. I had found joy in service. And now, whenever I find myself getting a little angrier than I ought to, I know that it is time for me to do something for someone else.

~Nicole Hone Webster

Hope from the Ashes

Dare to reach out your hand into the darkness,
to pull another hand into the light.
~Norman B. Rice

I kept screaming, "Help me" and "Save my family!" But the roaring inferno around me was much louder than the sound of my voice. In this nightmare I saw my own skin melting off my arms and legs as I crawled away from my family. They were trapped in the fiery inferno. I asked myself over and over, "When will I wake up from this nightmare?" But after a few days I realized that it was not a nightmare at all. My husband, daughter and I had been in a horrendous motor-home accident. It truly was a reality.

We all lived, but my husband and I were severely burned. We had a long journey ahead of us. My husband lost the left side of his face, his eyesight, and four fingers on his left hand, and had a nine percent chance of living. Our daughter was severely injured but not burned.

Each day I lay in a hospital bed looking out the window, watching the world go on around me. Everyone and everything but me seemed to be moving. I was trapped inside a severely burned body and my backbone had been shattered. The pain was like no other in this world. I now understood the term "racked with pain." I cried constantly, but my burned arms and hands could not reach up to wipe the tears away.

As I watched the seasons change, I realized my life would never be the same. I was facing the biggest challenge of my forty-seven years, and I was falling into a deep pit of despair and depression. In her book, *A Gift of Mourning Glories*, Georgia Shaffer captured this dark time in my life as she wrote, "Winter existed both on the inside and outside of me."

Encased in bandages from head to toe, my first few weeks consisted of five skin grafts and one surgery to repair my broken back. My stomach had become my donor site. Skin was harvested every three to five days, and it was stapled in place. I had to stay still those days, and my muscles forgot how to move. I literally had to learn to bend my fingers, and go through rehabilitation to learn to feed and take care of myself again.

My dreams of making a difference in people's lives seemed impossible when, at this time in my life, I could not even take care of myself. I wanted most of all to have something good come out of this tragic incident.

The one thing that helped me most during my hospital stay was when a former burn patient came to see me. He shared his story and showed me pictures of when he was in the hospital. Standing before me he looked like a normal person. He did not look at all like the monster I pictured myself to be. He gave me a spark of hope that everything would be all right someday.

That glimmer of hope carried me through those early days and thereafter. I clung to my faith like never before. I listened to music that helped to lift my spirits. Each time a therapist entered the room I repeated Phil. 4:13, "I can do all things through Christ who strengthens me." And each time I repeated the line I felt more hopeful.

After two months of extreme pain and therapy I was able to take six steps with a nurse on each side of me. I could sit in a chair for an hour at a time. I was learning to feed myself. I still had a hard time emotionally; I cried continually. And then it was time to go home. Leaving the hospital was another major adjustment, but with it came the realization that there was a bigger plan for me. My purpose now would be to touch and inspire others.

After a year of recovery I was ready to start giving hope to others.

I began visiting burn survivors and their families in the hospital and encouraging them. In the beginning it was very difficult going into the burn unit. The stark white surroundings, the ticking sounds of the machines keeping people alive, and the smells of burned skin reminded me of the most painful time in my life.

I felt overcome with emotion each time a new family entered the burn unit. Even though we had traveled the same road, my heart would go out to the people who were just beginning. To be burned is one of the most devastating things that can happen. Within seconds your outside appearance can be stripped away. It affects all parts of your humanity—spiritual, physical, intellectual, and emotional. Each part malfunctions and needs to be rebuilt. Many patients want to die rather than endure the pain and face the reality of their new lives. By my living example, I wanted them to choose life.

Today my life is fuller than I could ever imagine. My husband, daughter and I are healed. I am grateful for every part of the changes it took to make me the woman I am. Without this experience, I would not have met some of the greatest and bravest overcomers on this earth.

My purpose is to give inspiration not only to people disabled by accidents, but to all of us who have suffered setbacks. We feel that fate has treated us unfairly but still believe that we can make something of our lives if we only know how. I did learn how, and I am grateful I can share that with others.

~Susan Lugli

My Father's Gifts

A daughter may outgrow your lap, but she will never outgrow your heart.
~Author Unknown

Over the years my father gave me many gifts, ranging from the fees for a university education to a very generous down payment on my first house. However, there was one thing he always wished he could take back: an inherited medical condition called polycystic kidney disease. Over time, this disease will cause my kidneys to stop functioning, leading to dialysis and eventually to congestive heart failure.

After my father's diagnosis, his doctor recommended my sister and I go for testing as we had a 50/50 chance of inheriting the disease. We resisted at first, waiting almost two years until the anxiety of not knowing outweighed the fear of knowing. My sister's tests came back negative. Mine didn't. I wasn't exactly thrilled to receive that particular inheritance, but we don't get to choose our families or our genetic makeup. Sometimes, though, what seems like a lousy legacy can bring unexpected benefits.

When I received my official results, I did the hardest thing I'd ever done: I called my parents and told them. Silence greeted the news. "Think of it as a family affair," I said, desperate to lighten the mood. "Tiger's had kidney disease for years and the vet says she's doing fine. Maybe we should sprinkle some of her special cat food on our cereal."

My mother tried to laugh. My father could barely say goodbye to me before he hung up.

A few days later my mother called. "Your father is having a tough time dealing with your diagnosis. He's upset he passed the disease on to you, but he won't talk to me about it." She took a moment to steady her voice. "Maybe you can do something."

Dad and I had always been close, but he wasn't much of a talker, especially on the telephone. When worried, he became even quieter. Telling him that I was fine with my newly discovered disease wouldn't work. We both knew it was a lie. I wasn't fine. I was scared. I thought of telling him that passing on the disease wasn't his fault. He didn't know about the disease when he decided to have children. While that was the truth, I knew it wouldn't change how he felt. His genes. His daughter. His guilt.

Knowing he'd shy away from any direct talk about my condition, I looked for ways to show him how I felt. He loved the Internet and his computer. So, I surfed the web to find things that would interest him and e-mailed him daily jokes and information about the stock market. Every so often, I'd throw in an article about kidney disease.

The same man who might call me twice a year, always leaving the mushy stuff to my mother, began to type short e-mails back to me. "Good joke." "That stock looks interesting." "Maybe they'll come up with some new wonder drug for kidney disease in the next ten years." Since we both knew my father didn't have ten years left, we understood any wonder drug would be for me. That was as close as we ever came to verbally acknowledging that we shared the same disease.

Along with my daily e-mails, I increased my trips home to visit my parents. To give my mother a break from her constant vigilance, I accompanied my father to the hospital for his dialysis treatment to keep him company and monitor his vitals.

The first time, the sights and smells of the hospital punched me in the gut. I struggled not to throw up, seeing my future in the faces of the people on the dialysis beds. It didn't help that one of those faces was my father's. The matter-of-fact way he sat on the chair, letting the nurses hook him up to the machine that would function as a surrogate kidney, removing excess fluid from his blood, helped calm my nausea. He introduced me to some of the other patients he had gotten to know. We chatted for a while before he would nod off.

By the third treatment, the process had become familiar enough that I barely reacted to it. When my turn came, I knew I'd be able to face dialysis. My father had shown me how in his quiet, uncomplaining fashion.

Back at their home, some days we just sat silently together, some days he'd sleep, and other days we'd chat. We became more and more comfortable with each other. Even the silences felt familiar.

Over the next three years, as his kidneys continued to fail, causing more and more heart problems, his world contracted to his bedroom, the kitchen and the dialysis room at the hospital. His doctors added a fourth dialysis session per week, but just the effort to get dressed and go to the hospital tired him out.

He no longer used his computer, so our communication was solely face-to-face. I made the trip home more often, knowing that one of those visits would be the last time I would see him.

While he wanted to be strong for my mother, over time he allowed himself to relax with me and express his fears. "I don't have any energy," he said, sinking into his chair, gently petting the cat that had become his constant companion. "Even my mind is slowing down. What will happen to your mother?"

I reached over to stroke his hand. "She'll be fine." I paused, realizing it was time to acknowledge what lay between us since my diagnosis. It was my turn to give him the gift he needed. I leaned toward him and whispered, "I'll be fine, too, Dad. I promise."

He looked at me and smiled. "You're a good kid." Then he sighed and dozed off. A month later, he died the way he'd lived, with dignity and grace.

My father gave me so much more than an education, a house and yes, even kidney disease. He gifted me with the love and courage to deal with whatever my future brings. For that, and for those last years in which we became closer, I will always be grateful. Thanks, Dad.

~Harriet Cooper

Family Ties

To us, family means putting your arms around each other and being there.
~Barbara Bush

My dear neighbors sat in my sunny breakfast room, clutching cups of coffee as they explained their dilemma to me. Their foreclosure notice had finally arrived. Mark looked at me with tears in his eyes. "It's unbelievable. All these months we've searched for work. All the prayers and hopes. We've decided there's only one thing to do. I hoped it wouldn't come to this."

They asked me to watch their kids while they pursued their last hope. Liz's parents lived in typical suburbia: a three-bedroom ranch-style home with a fully finished basement, shady fenced yard and no mortgage. They had reared Liz to be frugal; Mark's parents had done the same with him. That made it worse in some ways. When the couple picked up their two lovely children that evening Liz explained what had happened:

"My mom opened the door with Dad close behind. I could see that they suspected why we had come. They were aware of some of our problems, but had no idea foreclosure was certain.

"I told them, 'You know we've both tried to get jobs. As soon as Mark got laid off we cut our expenses to the bone. We eked by on my salary. The school downsized. I thought I had tenure. Mom, you taught me how to cook cheaply. We did everything we could think of to save money. Our mortgage payment ate up most of our savings and we had to default on our loan. Unemployment checks barely covered expenses for food and utilities and insurance. Now Mark's and my unemployment has run out. We were served with the foreclosure notice this morning.'

"With no suggestion of recrimination, Dad had said, 'How can we help?'

"Before I could speak, Mark blurted, 'We're asking you to let us move in with you until we can get jobs. We have a little savings left for dire emergencies. This can't last forever.'

"Before he could say more, Dad looked at Mom and they nodded. 'Of course, you can stay here. Let's go look at this house and plan for the best way two families can co-exist.'"

And just that quickly Mark and Liz had a new home.

I met Liz in the grocery store weeks later. Liz was eager to continue her story, much to my delight.

"Mark and his brother borrowed a truck for us to move. I followed in the van with the children and unfastened seat belts for two laughing kids. They hit the ground running and threw themselves into the arms of their doting grandparents.

"'Grannie! Poppa! Can we come live with you?'

"'That's a good idea, Ellen. Do you want to live here, too, Rich?'

"Richard gave his grandfather a big kiss. 'Yes I do!'

"Mom took the kids into the back yard out of the way of the men. She showed them their swing set and toys we had moved after they went to bed the night before. I heard Mom explain this, invoking the time-honored story about fairies doing magical things. I directed the placement of boxes I had spent most of the week packing and labeling. We'd all sleep upstairs, but the basement would be our refuge and the kids' playroom and the storeroom for all the things I'd not unpack. The washer and dryer were there. We stored things in the garage that we had not been able to sell.

"'Mom, I think this is going to be better than living in the van. What do you think?'

"'Silly girl,' she said. 'How could we visit our grandchildren if you lived in the van?'

"I hugged her one more time. 'This is so wonderful of you and Dad. I'll put our computer downstairs and Mark and I can take turns job hunting online. How can there not be any jobs for someone as smart as he is?'

"'Sweetheart, how can schools complain about test scores, then lay off good teachers?'

"Dad followed me to the basement one day as I began another load of laundry. 'I heard two old geezers talking in the barbershop this morning about the senior citizen center. The manager left and they were hunting for someone. I don't know what it pays, but it might be worth looking into.'

"'Dad! Let me get into some decent clothes and you can come show me where it is.'

"I abandoned the washer, dressed, grabbed a copy of my résumé and dragged Dad off to Shady Dale Center. I wasn't the only one who had heard of the opening, but I had the best credentials. The pay was pathetic, of course, but it was still a job. I'd start Monday.

"The enormity of what I had agreed to do hit me on the way home. 'Dad, do you think Mom can take care of the kids while I work and Mark hunts for a job? What I'm going to make won't even pay for decent day care.'

"'Liz, I can help your mother. Ellen will be in kindergarten in the fall. Rich and I are big buddies. You've got good kids, honey. Let's see what Mark says.'

"Mark was pleased—with a few reservations. 'How are you going to get to work?'

"I glanced at Dad and we grinned. 'I'm going to ride my old bike. The Center is six blocks away. You can use the van. Oh, Mark, I know this is penny ante compared to what we used to make, but it'll take some of the burden off Mom and Dad.'

"Mark came in the next day wearing a smile. He said that he had been hired at a construction site to hang dry wall and paint.

"'Do you know how to do that sort of work?'

"'Sure. I worked summers in high school and college with Uncle Gus. The contractor said he knew Gus. That was all it took.'

"Now we had two very low-paying jobs and a touch of self-respect back.

"Two months later, my dad called a family conference. 'Dad, are you throwing us out?' I said half-jokingly, but with a twinge in case it was true.

"'In a way, Liz. The bank had your old home for sale. I talked to them. They're asking about half of what you paid for it ten years ago. And...' he smiled, 'I bought it.'

"I didn't understand. He waited for a reaction from Mark and me.

"'Why would you buy it, Dad?'

"Mark asked the obvious question, 'What on earth are you going to do with it? The resale value would be pitiful.'

"'I thought I might sell it to a couple of good people who've been down on their luck lately. People I love.'

"By this time I was bawling on Mark's shoulder and he was struggling to hold back the tears.

"'But Dad, you know we don't have much money. We give you and Mom nearly every cent we make.'

"'Well, Liz, I think I could be your ideal landlord. Something tells me we can cut a deal that would be fair to all concerned. Now, blow your nose and let's go look at your new home. I had the utilities turned on. In fact you can take a load of your stuff now if you want to. You'll have a little yard work to do, but I think the house is as you left it.'"

I had my good neighbors back! Mark and Liz would continue to hunt for better jobs and find them in the future. In the meantime they would be in their dream home again. I gave Liz a hug and welcomed her and her family back.

~Nancy Peacock

Already Blessed

Reflect on your present blessings of which every man has many, not on your past misfortunes, of which all men have some.
~Charles Dickens

lost my job on a November Wednesday, from a company that I worked with for almost thirty years. The position was one I earned through a culmination of hard work, great results and good timing. I loved it, and in the blink of an eye, it was gone.

The human resource director tried to sugarcoat the whole situation. I remember his ridiculous words to this day. "You've always done a great job, and you shouldn't view this as a dismissal. Our company, like many today, is going through major restructuring. We're giving you this small package. This is not a termination; it is more of an early retirement."

Leaving the meeting, I wondered how in the world I was going to tell my wife. Within the past week, we had discussed how our lives were really coming together. We had finished paying for our daughters' weddings and didn't have a kid in college. Finally, we were going to have time and money for ourselves. It was fun to talk about our plans, places to see and things to do. Now I was going to have to tell my wife that we had to put our dreams on hold.

I was embarrassed to go home early. Arriving home at the normal time, my wife greeted me at the door. I got right to the point. "I hate to tell you, but after almost thirty years, I was let go today."

I looked right into her eyes as I said this, not really sure what the reaction would be. It was immediate. She gave me a hug and a loving kiss, and simply said, "I wonder what new adventures God has planned for us now."

As we were sitting by our fireplace, sipping glasses of wine, the phone started ringing. The word was getting around quickly, and many friends were calling. It was heartening. They all offered support and many promised prayers.

I have to admit that Thursday and Friday were really bad days. I was doing my best to stay positive. My résumé needed to be updated and I was networking with people I knew in the industry. It had been a long time since I've had to look for a job.

Saturday, I was reading the newspaper. There was a terrible story about a helicopter crash in Iraq. Almost twenty soldiers died. Many were on their way back home for their first leave. I was brought up as a military brat and was in the military myself. I've seen firsthand the devastation brought on by the loss of a friend or family member. I know it's the same everywhere, but there is a feeling of extended family in the military. A brother in arms is still a brother.

I had to stop and think. I lost a job and people are praying for me. They really should be praying for these soldiers and their families.

Sunday, I arrived early for church, as is my habit. The priest greeted me. She had heard my bad news and invited me back to her office. We talked for a few minutes, and then holding hands, got on our knees and prayed. As we got up, I looked at her. Her hair was nicely coifed and in place. The sad thing was, I knew it wasn't her hair. She was in the middle of her second round of treatment for ovarian cancer. Her own, beautiful, thick, wavy hair was gone. Here she was, devoting all of her strength and energy towards me.

I had to stop and think. I lost a job and people are praying for me. They really should be praying for this wonderful woman.

After the service, we drove to another church to attend the funeral of a friend's father. I didn't personally know the father. That quickly changed as one person after another spoke of him. He was obviously loved and cherished. Most of the stories were funny and everyone was laughing between the tears. It seemed he was a man with many hobbies and interests and most clearly a man with a wonderful sense of humor. The pastor pointed out that not only had the gentleman selected all the songs to be sung; he even planned the food to be served after the service. My friend told me his father was a member of the choir. Apparently, he was a horrible, yet joyful singer, singing off-key at full throttle. In honor of him, I sang the same way, my usual practice as well.

I had to stop and think. I lost a job and people are praying for me. They really should be praying for this man and his family.

I can't say that my personal angst was over by Sunday night. Losing a job is high up on the stress scale and can bring anyone down. With time and reflection though, something had become very clear to me. Yes, I lost my job, but along the way, I found my faith, my family and my friends. I appreciated the prayers, but asked that they be directed towards others. I was already blessed beyond belief.

~William Hogg

Push in the Write Direction

It is often hard to distinguish between the hard knocks in life and those of opportunity.
~Frederick Phillips

"W e're letting you go," my boss said. My mouth fell open and I stared at him blankly for a few seconds. Then I burst into tears, right there in his office.

I was an experienced business professional, and I'd never been fired before. He was a good, kind man, but he had a job to do. "It's not personal," he said, handing me a Kleenex. "You know we're downsizing. You'll get a severance package to help you bridge the gap till you find a new job."

He continued to offer comforting words, thanking me for my years of service, but I was lost in my own thoughts. I was forty-seven, divorced, with a teenager at home, and a mortgage to pay. Now what?

After taking a little time to compose myself, I reluctantly headed to my office. Not that I wanted to remain in my boss's office, but walking out meant passing the desks of co-workers who would see my tear-stained face.

Heartsick and humbled, I drove home, stopping twice to cry. This was difficult, but it wasn't really a surprise. Rumors of cutbacks had been flying around the office for months, and my job was a prime target. But even more than that, I had come to hate the work I was doing and it probably showed. It wasn't my employer or the conditions that I didn't like. After many years as an accountant, I was just burned out. I wanted to quit, but didn't know how else to make a living.

The only thing I could imagine worse than crunching numbers was starting over with a new employer, still as a number cruncher. Now that I'd been fired, I feared that was exactly what I would have to do.

Like any avid job hunter, I pursued every lead for accounting work. But the economy was slow and nobody was hiring. I didn't get a single nibble. So when I could, I indulged in the hobby I loved most, writing.

Before I'd lost my job I'd managed to write and sell a few small articles. I'd even sold a story to a popular anthology and was published in a book. There was nothing I loved more than writing. I'd been able to make a little extra money that way. If only I could make a full-time income as a writer—preferably without leaving home. When rumors of cutbacks at work had started circulating, I enrolled in an online editing class. The goal was to increase my side income by adding this writing-related skill, and improve my own writing in the process. The instructor gave us tips on how to find short-term freelance writing work, but while I was still at my day job, there wasn't enough time to pursue editing work too.

Then the axe fell and I was fired. With time on my hands, I landed a few freelance editing jobs, mostly for PhD students and also for a book in process. The money was good, but sporadic—not nearly steady enough to depend on.

I continued to check online jobsites and one day I saw it: A business-to-business online publication was seeking someone with three overarching qualifications—paid experience as a writer, as an editor, and with a background in accounting. That was me! With great excitement, I applied. I was sure I was the person they were looking for, but I heard nothing. Eventually I forgot about it.

Then one day the phone rang. It was the executive editor of that business publication and she wanted a phone interview. She was on the East Coast; I was in California.

"We need a writer and editor who also knows accounting," she explained. "The trouble is, accountants generally don't like to write, or they don't have talent for it. All of us work from our homes, so it doesn't matter where you live." Perfect! She asked me to write and submit a feature article as an audition. Then I had to meet the boss, on the phone.

A few weeks later, I was hired. That was nine years ago. Not every day has been exciting and fun, but overall, I can't imagine a better position for me. No more number crunching. No traffic. No corporate life. No panty hose, no business suits, and no heels. Each day I work in my own home, surrounded by my dog posse. Life is good. One year, the company even took us on a Caribbean cruise.

Being fired was a devastating experience. But in retrospect, I'm so thankful it happened. It's true I had prepared myself for my current job by learning to edit and improving my writing skills. But without the push of being fired, I lacked the courage to make the change. And most importantly if I hadn't needed a new job, I would not have been looking in the right direction when this wonderful opportunity presented itself.

~Teresa Ambord

A Mom's Blessing

One must be poor to know the luxury of giving!
~George Eliot

In the late 1960s, I was a single mom of four children five years apart in age. My husband was an alcoholic and upon leaving home, told me "I'll see you living in a slum. The kids won't know the difference, but I know it will bother you." I understand he wasn't in his right mind at the time, but I never forgot those words. Determined never to fulfill his parting wish, I was lucky enough to find a part-time job in a law firm that allowed me to work until the kids came home from school. Needless to say, I lived paycheck to paycheck, struggling to raise the kids in a nice neighborhood. They wore hand-me-downs, but always had a roof over their heads and nourishing food to eat. I could only afford the basics, so I made it a point to be sure that they always had fruit, ice cream and home-baked cakes—there was no money for potato chips, soda or fast food (lucky us!).

I always taught them to respect each other's personal things. That meant they didn't take each other's things, and my pocketbook was also one of my "things" that was off-limits.

Bill was able to have a paper route when he was twelve years old, which he and his eleven-year-old brother Michael shared. They delivered papers seven days a week, worked out the responsibilities and finances (learning to record collections and share profits) together. It was their only way of getting "spending money." Often when there was a snowstorm, the neighbors would call to see if one of the "boys" could shovel their walk. If, for some reason, the boys were not available, my daughter Debbie would beg me to send her in their place. The first time, our neighbor was so excited, I heard her say with glee, "Honey, this time we're getting a girl!" Stephen, the youngest, was responsible for taking his grandfather for a walk around the block each day after school. Pop had a stroke and the doctor wanted him to get up and out. Stephen took this responsibility very seriously and would always give Pop whatever he made in kindergarten that day, and then insist they go for their walk.

I could not afford to give them an allowance or even buy school lunches. I packed lunch for the four of them every day — snacks from the outlet store usually came in packages of twelve, which meant divided by four, those snacks were good for three days of packed lunches. I often went to work with just a dime for a phone call, should it become necessary. I really didn't care — we were in a good school district, unusually healthy and happy.

I thought I was successful in not worrying the kids about money, although apparently they knew it was an issue. Due to the circumstances, I always knew exactly what I had in my purse — to the penny. I had to be careful not to overspend at the grocery store because in those days, cash was the only method of payment — there was no credit card or overdraft protection.

Then came a day when I looked into my purse, knowing I was broke but hoping for a miracle, and finding one. I went from penniless to having four dollars. I couldn't imagine how I could have forgotten those four dollars. When it happened a second time, I was truly at a loss, until the day I came upon the kids whispering around my pocketbook (where they were not supposed to go). I surreptitiously watched and discovered four sneaky little angels putting their hard-earned money into my wallet. The next day when I made a point of exclaiming about the money, no one said a word. I almost admired their ability to keep the secret as I much as I did their unselfish love.

I often regret not being able to give them more, but it was a blessing in disguise—it somehow made them into confident, responsible and caring adults. I am grateful for the lesson to us all. God balances hardship with blessings. We need only the capacity to recognize them when they arrive.

~Maureen T. Cotter

Chapter
9

From Lemons to
Lemonade

From Apprehension to
Appreciation

The Truck

Be content with what you have; rejoice in the way things are. When you realize there is nothing lacking, the whole world belongs to you.

~Lao Tzu

Being ten years older than my brother Sammy, I played a huge role in his care and have always shared an unbreakable bond with him. When he was an infant, I would marvel at him while he slept, in awe of how little and perfect he was. I admired this little being with all my heart and daydreamed about what he would be like when he was my age. When Sammy was diagnosed with autism around three years old, my world crumbled. I remember feeling angry, confused and afraid for him. For days after his diagnosis, I could not look at my little brother without a flood of tears. My greatest concern was how he would be accepted by others. I wanted people to see Sammy just as I did, not labeled by autism.

One day, shortly after his fourth birthday, Sammy walked over to me with a new toy truck in both hands and said, "Break it!" He handed me the small toy truck.

My grandfather walked up to us and with a screwdriver in hand said, "Give it to me, he wants us to break it for him." I looked at them both with confusion. My grandfather then said, "He's been having me break all of his toys. I think that's how he understands them. How they're built, what they're made of." I handed him the truck and watched as my grandfather unscrewed the pieces. When he got to the parts with wheels and gears, Sammy's eyes lit up with wonder. His gaze was focused on the pieces coming off the truck one by one. He took each piece in his hands as it came off and examined it thoroughly. It was clear to me now that my brother saw things so differently than I did. He knew that the pieces worked together harmoniously, but also that each part was unique. He saw that each part had its own special purpose.

It occurred to me that just like the truck, all of the "pieces" that fit together to make Sammy were pieces placed together perfectly for him. Each piece together created my brother, who sees the world in a different light than anyone I have ever known. His actions at four years old helped me to understand that we are all fit together in a different way for our own specific purpose. I now see the beauty in these differences.

Now, whether he is telling me about math and numbers, presidents, or demonstrating his exceptional memory, the many special qualities my brother has inspire me. Since his diagnosis I no longer cry when I look at my little brother—I smile. I don't see a scary thing called autism. What I see is my brilliant brother Sammy who lights up my darkest days and teaches me new things every day.

~Olivia Mitchell

The Right Move

Change always comes bearing gifts.
~Price Pritchett

"Then you will have to go without me!" was my first reaction when my husband Rob announced that the company we both worked for wanted him for an assignment in their headquarters in Cincinnati, Ohio. Moving from our home in Rome, Italy to the United States—a nine-hour flight away from my parents and my friends—was unthinkable for me. And I was convinced that if I just protested long enough and kept saying, "I'm not going," it was somehow not going to happen. I knew his career was important to him, but I also knew he wasn't going to sacrifice our marriage for it—at least not knowingly.

I told myself that I had the last word on this matter and pretended the decision to stay in Europe was a done deal. But Rob continued to bring up the subject at regular intervals. He tried to convince me that this was a great opportunity for both of us. "Imagine visiting all the great places in the U.S. You won't have time to feel homesick. And if you do, there are direct flights to four European cities from Cincinnati every day." Given our company's dual career policy, I knew I would find an appropriate assignment in the same location. But nothing could persuade me. I tried to talk him out of the idea. I pulled every string I knew. I pouted. I cajoled. I threatened to leave him. All to no avail. I felt helpless. Of course, I did not want him to go alone. Despite my repeated threats to this effect, it had never really been an option.

After a couple of months, Rob's management confirmed the plan for the dreaded move. By then, the fear of living on another continent almost suffocated me. I was also worried about my parents' reaction. They would be horrified by the prospect of having their only daughter live on the other side of the world.

I resorted to my typical reaction when I felt powerless and out of control. I fell sick. I developed severe colitis. In the beginning, I just felt an odd pain in my lower abdomen. Then it turned into more frequent cramps until a couple of weeks later I was in constant excruciating pain. I tried painkillers, but to no effect. My family doctor was worried by the severity of my symptoms and prescribed a long list of diagnostic exams. The results were clear. There was no detectable physical cause to my condition. Nevertheless, the pain got worse by the day. My doctor, now out of ideas, sent me to a specialist. She was a middle-aged, motherly woman and I trusted her immediately. She put me on a strict low-fiber diet to give my body a rest, and conducted more tests. All of them confirmed that my intestines were healthy — except for the constant spasms. Fortunately this wise doctor helped me make the connection that I had ignored.

"Your body is perfectly fine," she said. "So what is happening in your life that causes you so much pain?"

"I don't want to go to America," I confided in her. "My husband's next assignment is in the United States and I don't want to go. I told him he should go without me, but I don't want that either. He wants to go, but I am terribly scared."

She quietly read my face for a while before she concluded: "Well, dear, you have to make up your mind; either you go or you don't. But whatever you do, you have to come to terms with your decision. You cannot continue to put your head in the sand. Your body has been trying to tell you this for a while. It's time to listen."

I nodded. It sounded so plausible and straightforward.

"I will prescribe some injections for the pain. They are easy to administer yourself. Every morning…" I stopped listening. My practical side was taking over. I was not going to give myself injections for a pain that was so obviously psychosomatic. That would make no sense at all. And then it came to me in a flash. I had covered up the anxiety of moving abroad with the unrelenting pain in my abdomen. It was time I accepted reality and took charge of my life again. As hard as it was, I had to make my own decision, take responsibility for it and live with the consequences.

Outside the doctor's office, I tore up the prescription for the injections and let the bits of paper fly off in the wind. I didn't need it anymore. I needed a good book about the United States, so I could prepare for my new life overseas. Within a week after I decided to give Cincinnati a chance, the pain stopped and never returned.

A few months later, we arrived in Cincinnati—in a thunderstorm. I had still been crying during the flight and I was not sure at all if I had done the right thing.

"So this is where you brought me?" I said in my most reproachful voice. Why in the world had I given in?

A cab took us to our temporary apartment in downtown Cincinnati. It was bright and spacious and the large windows provided a magnificent view of the Ohio River. I started to feel a bit better. The next morning, we went for a walk to explore the city. I had to strain my neck to look up at all the skyscrapers. Everything was so clean. There were huge colorful flowerpots everywhere. People smiled and greeted us. I told myself that these were all good signs—the sun, the smiles, the blue sky, the flowers, the beautiful architecture—that maybe, just maybe, I could really like it here.

That was twenty years ago. At the end of the initial two years, we agreed to add on another year, then another... and so on. To my complete surprise, we had both fallen in love with the United States. When our visas ran out, we applied for permanent residency and celebrated the big event of receiving our green cards. We still went back to Europe several times a year to stay in touch with family and friends. But now we had made even more friends in Cincinnati. Now I would get homesick for Cincinnati when I was away. When we retired four years ago, we knew that the United States had become our home and that this is where we wanted to grow old. We moved from Ohio to Florida, bought our retirement home and even became American citizens.

To this day, I reproach Rob that he would have gone to the United States without me. But he swears that he was always sure it was the right move for us and that I'd eventually come around. He was right.

~Rita Bosel

Just for You, Teacher

The road to success is dotted with many tempting parking places.
~Author Unknown

"You've got to be kidding! That's your teacher?" As I approached my classroom, I immediately knew something was wrong. My students clustered around the door to the room where our Tuesday evening Grammar Basics course met at Tidewater Community College in Virginia Beach. A tall middle-aged man stood in the center, looking down at one of my students as she pointed down the hall towards me.

I fought back the embarrassment I felt warming my cheeks. I was only thirty-two, but even with my hair pulled back, I looked much younger—much younger, in fact, than most of my students. The male instructor chuckled as I approached. I took a deep breath.

After finishing graduate school, my salary as an editor with a non-profit organization wasn't enough to pay the bills, so I decided to moonlight as an adjunct instructor in the English department of the local community college. When I was a child, I always wanted to be a teacher. I imagined a class of young, eager elementary-aged students, but not this. I had no clue what to do with adults.

Only entering freshmen who failed to pass the written portion of the entrance exam were required to take one of the two preparatory, no-credit prerequisites for English Composition I. Half of my class didn't think they deserved to be there. The other half didn't seem to care. Teaching was difficult enough. Now I had to deal with other instructors?

As I approached the door to my classroom, even my own students overshadowed me. I found myself looking up at a man at least a decade older and a full head taller than myself.

"Is there a problem?"

Yes, his class needed to run over time tonight, and he needed our classroom. "You'll have to find another room, Miss... ?"

"That's Ms. Bennett." I was flustered but tried to hold my head high. "I'm sorry sir, but our class has this room booked every Tuesday night. You'll have to find another room to meet in."

As I busied myself preparing for the class, he found a room, but my confidence was damaged. I wasn't sure if I had enough left to deal with the reluctant students sitting before me. I forced a smile and jumped into the lesson.

There were days like this when I didn't want this job. I was tired, overworked, and didn't feel like I was making a bit of difference to any of the students. By the time finals rolled around, more than half my class had dropped. Out of the few who remained, half were failing.

I felt like a failure. What was I thinking? I was a writer, who worked in solitude. Words rarely had attitudes and never spoke back. What ever made me think I could teach? My first class reviews were brutal.

My advisor comforted me over the phone one evening. "Don't worry about it. You accomplished what you needed to with the class. Some students just aren't going to be happy with it. That's normal."

Well, it didn't feel normal. I second-guessed my decision to teach another semester. After grades had been submitted I made one last trip to the mailroom to drop off my contract and clear out my mailbox before the Christmas holiday. Under the recommended syllabus for the spring course was a red envelope.

I sat down in my car, put the paperwork aside, and opened the envelope. Inside was a Christmas card with a cartoon illustration of Santa on the cover. At the top were the words: "Just for you, Teacher."

It reminded me of the kind of card a child might pick out, but when I opened it, I immediately recognized the handwriting… Anna.

Anna had approached my desk when I dismissed the first class of the semester. Tears had filled her eyes. Her hands shook, and her voice trembled as she spoke in a heavily accented broken English.

"Ms. Bennett, I don't think I can take this class. I don't take tests very good."

I looked at the syllabus in her hand. I had scheduled five quizzes and two tests (a mid-term and a final). I listened as Anna told me about moving to America from the Ukraine earlier that year. She wanted to study here, but just didn't understand the proper sentence and paragraph structure. By the time she was finished, tears streamed down her face, and her voice was barely audible.

"Sit down." After the other students left, I tried my best to assure Anna that the quizzes and tests were not meant to trip her up. They were simply a way for me to keep track of how each student understood the material throughout the semester and help those who were struggling. "If you understand the weekly homework exercises, you'll do fine on the quizzes. And if you need extra help, I'm available before and after class to answer any questions."

When Anna left that evening, she had wiped the tears from her face and promised me that she would be back for the next class. Throughout the semester, I never saw a student work harder. If she missed one question, she asked me to clarify it for her. She passed the course with a strong "B" average.

The thought of Anna's success made me smile. I had been so focused on all the other students, I had almost forgotten about her first-day fears. Then I read the note she wrote inside the card:

Dear Ms. Bennett,

I really enjoyed having you as my teacher this year. English isn't one of my favorite subjects, but you make the class fun and exciting. I really hope that my other teachers are just like you.

I believe that I learned much more than just English... I learned not to give up and to try again if I fail. I wish you the best and hope to see you again one day.

Anna

As I watched Anna struggle through each quiz that semester, I never realized that she was learning an even greater lesson than English grammar. And in that moment, she taught me something greater than my own fear of failure. If Anna didn't give up, why should I?

I've kept that Christmas card to this day to remind me that feeling like a failure is rarely a true test of reality. I proceeded to teach another semester at the community college before taking another position. Today, in addition to writing, I teach creative and academic writing workshops regularly to children, elementary through high school.

If I ever saw Anna again, I would thank her for teaching me not to give up and to keep trying, even when I feel like I've failed.

~Carolyn Bennett Fraiser

Sudden Clarity

My cancer scare changed my life. I'm grateful for every new,
healthy day I have. It has helped me prioritize my life.
~Olivia Newton-John

"How can you possibly consider yourself lucky?" my friend asked me. "You have breast cancer!"

Well, she was certainly right about that. I'd just been diagnosed and was facing a bilateral mastectomy followed by chemotherapy, so I could see her point; it was hard to see where there was any good luck in my life at that point.

A few weeks before, I had found myself sitting on a hard plastic chair in a crowded waiting room at the diagnostic clinic. My breast cancer had been confirmed by a core biopsy and the next step was to scan and X-ray the rest of my body to see if the cancer had spread. Just when I thought my life couldn't get any worse, I realized that it definitely could. If you're going to get cancer, then breast cancer is a "good" one because early detection and advances in treatment mean about an eighty-percent chance of survival. In short, while the diagnosis wasn't good, it would certainly be a whole lot worse if doctors discovered the cancer had spread.

At that time, I was forty-three years old, with a seven-year-old son and three-year-old daughter. My worries about mastectomies and chemo were bad enough, but my fear for the children if something happened to me was devastating. I would wake in the morning with acid churning in my stomach. Thoughts about Charlie and Lucie and what the future might hold for them as well as me heightened my fears. Every moment, more worries surfaced and I found myself fighting back tears practically all the time.

If I died, my children would grow up without a mum. Who would ever love them unconditionally like me? How vulnerable would they be without me to protect them? Who would they turn to when they hurt? I imagined their grief, their tears and a life without me there to watch their backs. It was simply unbearable.

With yet more tears streaming down my face, and facing the prospect of more bad news, I started to think. I had accepted my diagnosis of breast cancer and knew that in order to give myself the best chance of survival, I would have to sacrifice both breasts. I had also reluctantly agreed to chemotherapy for the same reasons, knowing that no matter what horrors it involved, research showed it was my best chance for long-term survival. But this treatment was based on the assumption that no other nasty little tumors were lurking elsewhere in my body. If the cancer had spread, then my chances of survival were about to take a nosedive.

As I thought about that prospect, I pictured myself riddled with cancer and with perhaps only a short amount of time left for me on this earth. I didn't know how I would bear it if I wouldn't live long enough to care for Lucie and Charlie until they were grown up. As I sat in the chair, my head in my hands, I remembered the advice a nurse had given me a when I was first diagnosed: Be strong and pray. I closed my eyes and spoke to God, praying for my children.

And so the day stretched out, full of poking, prodding and seemingly endless tests from blank-faced technicians who refused to comment on what I was sure was the worst news possible. I sniffed and snuffled, eyes puffed and red, nose sore and heart shredded with fear and pain. And then it happened: Confirmation that the cancer hadn't spread! My breasts had betrayed me but the rest of my body was free of anything malignant. I had the all clear and my battle would be solely with breast cancer.

With sudden clarity, it dawned on me. It was all about perspective.

Yesterday, having breast cancer felt like a death sentence. Today, a mere twenty-four hours later, having just breast cancer felt like a gift. I had been so overwhelmed with fear that I saw my situation as the worst possible scenario. It had taken the prospect of an even worse diagnosis to make me realize that if the cancer hadn't spread, my prognosis was good and the odds were in my favor that I would survive.

Four years later that moment still lives with me. It colors every thought and influences my attitude in a positive way that has given me strength to cope in other difficult situations. Through the death of my beloved mother and a painful divorce, I was able to cope so much better by putting my situation in perspective.

When I tell people I've had breast cancer and been lucky, they often think I'm mad. But I know differently. I am lucky. Not just because I beat it and have so far enjoyed four years cancer-free, but because the battle gave me the knowledge and clarity to face life and whatever it may throw at me with a smile on my face and the ability to put it all in perspective.

~Briony Jenkins

Beth's Prom

We achieve inner health only through forgiveness—
the forgiveness not only of others but also of ourselves.
~Joshua Loth Leibman

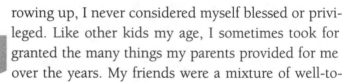

rowing up, I never considered myself blessed or privileged. Like other kids my age, I sometimes took for granted the many things my parents provided for me over the years. My friends were a mixture of well-to-do, somewhat poor, and yes, snobby. That's when I noticed the shy girl, who didn't have any friends. Seeing her when she walked past would give me this lonely feeling that made my heart ache.

I found out that her name was Beth. She didn't really go anywhere, attend school functions, play sports, or participate in any activities other than her schoolwork and her chores at home. I learned early on that her mother passed away when she was very young, so it fell on Beth to take care of all the chores, her siblings and even her father at times.

She seemed very lonely, taller than most girls her age and very quiet. While everyone was talking about prom night, buying fancy dresses, shoes, and hairstyles, she never said a word or joined in the chatter. All of us were driving our own cars by then, but she would gather her books every day, walk with her head down and climb onto the school bus. To this day, I don't understand why I didn't speak to her other than to say hello. All I would feel was loneliness when I thought about being around her, and I know I was being snobby, just like the rest of the kids.

I could see she didn't have many changes of clothing. She wore plain knee-length dresses every day. She had long straight stringy hair and she never wore even a hint of make-up. It was obvious to me that she could barely afford what she had. I often pitied her when I saw she was forced to wear the same black dress and shoes day after day, with just a hint of a heel on the bottom, worn out at the toe. Her outdated Coke-bottle glasses weighed heavy on her face. As they would slide to the end of her nose, she would take her index finger and push them up in their rightful place, doing so while never missing a step. Beth was heavier than most girls her age—big-boned is what I would call it—with a lot of muscle. Her appearance was the brunt of many jokes, and though I never participated in the teasing and laughter, I certainly made no attempt to defend her either. I just quietly felt sorry for her.

Prom night finally arrived. Pictures were taken, music played, and laughter was in the air. It was a festive occasion and everyone was enjoying it to the fullest.

All of a sudden there was a communal gasp from almost half the room—the half that consisted of the clique of snobs. It sounded as if they all lost the power to breathe at the same time. Then I heard the usual whispers, laughter and snickering that was usually reserved for Beth. As if their actions weren't bad enough to begin with, some actually pointed. My eyes followed the direction of their fingers and that is when I saw her.

The poor, motherless girl who had never been anywhere special in her life had come to the prom. She was wearing what looked like a new (used) dress, with different shoes and her hair pulled up into a bun. She was even wearing a corsage. She seemed to glow with a confident serene beauty that I suddenly envied. She was beaming. I saw a different Beth! Tonight, she was holding her head up high with so much happiness I felt myself fill up with pride for her. My boy-friend and I had already settled down at our table watching everyone get their prom photos, so we had a front row seat.

Her date was a true gentleman, pulling her chair out for her, and taking her by the hand to go to the front of the room for their prom pictures. Their smiles only became brighter as the people in the room ridiculed them and laughed out loud. I felt the heat rush across my face and my palms start to sweat. I was so embarrassed for her, but angry at the same time. I wanted to stand up and scream, "Leave her alone," but nothing would come out. I just sat there and listened and watched it unfold.

The music started with a slow familiar song. As we started to get up to dance, Beth's date glided her to the dance floor. She still held her head high, as if speaking to the crowd of onlookers. I was mesmerized by the pride in their eyes and the smile that never once wavered. I remember the happiness that filled my own heart and the admiration I felt for the statement she and her date were making. Beth didn't care about what others were saying and thinking. She simply got lost in the joy of attending her first prom. I didn't feel sad or lonely when I saw her that night. I felt proud.

There were many people who continued being mean and nasty that night as they mocked Beth and her escort, but I suspect many of them wished they had done the same thing she did that year. Despite their cruel snickers, they must have realized, as did I, that Beth had the person she obviously loved most in the world sharing her unforgettable experience, and the memories to go along with it.

Her very special date proudly dressed up in his best suit and tie. He put his dress shoes on and escorted his daughter to the prom when no one else had asked her. What a blessed memory she would always have because of this night. All because of a father's love! I felt honored to have witnessed it and went home with a new attitude. I no longer pitied Beth for the material things she didn't have. I knew she was rich beyond words in the things that truly mattered.

I don't know where Beth is today. I wish I could thank her for the positive impact she made on my life that night. A simple, quiet, hardworking girl touched my heart in a way that changed my life forever, teaching me to make the best of what life hands you, and to cherish the true riches in your life. That night I also learned that material things do not bring you happiness. The people in your life do.

~Deana J. Scott

Positive

Babies are such a nice way to start people.
~Don Herrold

Positive, positive, positive. The word repeated over and over again in my head as I stared down at the pregnancy test. Why in the world does a positive pregnancy test have to be called "positive"? In my mind, there was no way this news could possibly be "positive." I was seventeen, I wasn't living at home, had no relationship with the father of the baby growing inside of me, and to top it all off, I was in a whole other relationship with someone new. This situation was not positive. Or at least that's what I thought at the time.

After two months of being completely in denial, after two months of being sick all the time, after two months with no period, I knew before I even took the test that I was pregnant. But yet those two pink lines and that dreaded positive sign still sent my entire body into shock. A million questions ran through my head. What was I going to do? How could I raise a child? As I dialed my ex-boyfriend, my hands shook uncontrollably. "I'm pregnant," I whispered as he answered the phone. And in that moment, as I said those words out loud, I knew my life would never be the same.

I chose to become a young mother, despite all of the pressure I had from others telling me I couldn't do it. Support was minimal from the people I believed were my friends, except for a few. However, the support from my family was certainly comforting. I had moved out of my parents' home to live with my aunt, believing it would be an easier life. I had broken my mother's heart; her only daughter had abandoned her, giving someone else the responsibility of caring for me. I did not understand how much this affected her at the time, until I became a mother myself. Despite her heartache, she welcomed me back with open arms. Easily forgiving me, because "that's what mothers do," she had said.

The new boyfriend I had been with for less than a month quickly disappeared from my life as the news of my pregnancy became public knowledge. The old boyfriend and the father of my baby struggled to cope with the news. He was not speaking to me, and school was becoming harder to go to each day. As my belly grew, so did the whispers and rumors. People asked questions that they had no business asking. "Who's the father?" "Are you going to graduate?" Countless stares and questions led to severe stress.

Because I was able to complete all of my courses a semester early, I knew I would finish before my baby was due. I knew I had to, for myself and most of all for the little one who would soon be mine to hold. Classes dragged. When other students were discussing the next party or who had slept with whom, I was silently going crazy. These things didn't matter to me anymore. What mattered was finishing the assigned work for the day, planning for the future, budgeting, fearing I wouldn't be a good mother and learning how to become one.

I could feel myself maturing and growing up. After every rude comment, every snicker or eye roll, I would close my eyes, blink away the tears and slowly, tenderly caress my belly. I felt my baby kick, roll, move inside my growing stomach, and that was all I needed to stay strong. Each day my stomach, my strength and my love for this child grew.

I finished that semester with all nineties, proud and relieved that I would graduate with my class that year and excited to meet my baby. Things were looking up. The father was talking to me again, accepting that he would, in fact, be a dad. I was slowly filling up the house with baby items, passed down from others whose little ones were growing older. As my belly grew, so did the support. Despite all of my hardships, I managed to get through my pregnancy.

As motherhood approached, I spent two long days in labor and delivery. Every little struggle I had faced in those nine months disappeared as I looked down into my baby boy's eyes. Tears fell uncontrollably, just as they had the day I looked down at that pregnancy test, except this time they were tears of total and complete joy. The moment I held my baby, my heart fluttered out of my chest and found its place in my beautiful son. My heart was his. Forever. And I knew that was where it belonged.

Eight months later, as I sit here writing this story, and my baby lies on my lap napping, I cannot help but cry. These eight months have been joyous, frustrating, and heartwarming. I wanted to rip my hair out multiple times. I wanted to give up plenty of times, but in those moments, all I had to do was look up at my innocent, beautiful, adorable little boy and those feelings melted away. It all became worth it.

They say no one will understand the love a mother has for her child, what they will give up, and I don't believe you can until you experience it. As I looked down at that pregnancy test months ago, I believed that I would never see this beautiful baby as something positive. Until I chose to take the situation, accept it and make the best of it. Now, as I smile down at my child, I know that my life would not be complete without him. Now, as I hold him close and smell his fine, blond hair, feel his soft skin and look into the eyes I see when I see myself, I know that I could not have any better life than the life I have right now, as a mother. I unconditionally, unquestionably, love my child and motherhood. I would not take back any of the hardships I faced, because seeing my child, laugh, smile, reach out for me, I know that it all turned out to be a positive, beautiful, glorious thing.

~Maitland Mullen

From Worker to Owner

Choose a job you love, and you will never have to work a day in your life
~Confucius

Hot, humid summer days turned to cool, crisp fall nights. Heavy frost covered the ground at sunrise. Apple trees laden with ripe fruit were ready for picking. Like the changing weather, this busy harvest season would bring changes in my life.

The first day back to work at the apple orchard consisted of preparation for school tours. School children of all ages accompanied by adult supervisors participated in the daily routine of a working apple orchard. Groups of curious children and eager adults travelled from station to station and experienced apple picking, sorting, polishing and packaging. The tasting table offered a variety of apples for sampling. Apple peelers clamped onto a picnic table removed apple skins that looked like snakes, leaving a coreless apple sliced to resemble an accordion. The stationary bike, when ridden by eager students and willing adults, turned an apple press producing fresh squeezed apple cider. Employee-driven tractor and wagon tours, a favourite of most participants, travelled through the orchard. Students learned the history of apples and the orchard. The tour ended with a trip to the old, wooden outhouse before boarding the school bus.

Larry, the orchard owner, asked all employees to meet for lunch at the house. The usual spot for lunch was a wood picnic table located in the steel apple shed. Eating indoors in the warmth and comfort of Larry's home was a treat. Jackets, sweaters, toques and mittens formed a pile inside the rear door of the house. Before lunch boxes were unzipped and paper bags unfolded Larry spoke. "You're probably wondering why I called you all in here. I have decided to sell the orchard. This will be the last season." A brief discussion followed Larry's announcement. With an uneasy feeling in the pit of my stomach, I found it difficult to finish my lunch. Head hung low, fighting back tears, I walked slowly back up the hill to the orchard.

Last-minute jobs needed to be completed before the first tour of the season began. The usual laughter, teasing and playful nature of all the employees, including myself, did not surface. At closing time, we all gathered around the sales desk to talk. Eyes filled with tears as everyone agreed on how much of a privilege and pleasure it was to work for Larry.

The orchard's sale happened quickly with a closing date of January 5 the following year. A workforce would not be needed by the new owners as they planned to employ family members. Apple products would not be sold at the local market. Other ventures were being considered by the new owners. I was saddened by the ownership change but happy the orchard's sale came together promptly for Larry.

The last apple was picked, pressed and bottled as cider by the end of November. Larry asked Bonnie, a long-time employee, and myself to stay through to the end of December to help with clean up and moving preparation. Each day Larry, Bonnie and I sorted, cleaned, packed and reminisced. Within a few weeks Larry found a home suitable for his family. He looked forward to the move and to semi-retirement.

The weather turned from the frosts of fall to winter's snow and extreme cold. Larry asked Bonnie and me to meet him in the house after we had finished lunch. All I could think about was that I was going to get my pink slip and lose my job. I was stunned when Larry asked, "How would you two women like to take over the stand at the market and sell cider? With the new owners not interested in pursuing that part of the business, there is an opportunity for you two to make some extra money." Bonnie and I sat speechless as Larry explained his proposal further. After an hour-long discussion Larry suggested taking some time to think about it.

Bonnie and I spent the afternoon discussing Larry's potential business opportunity while we worked. A business deal signed two days later between the three of us was celebrated over a glass of fresh apple cider. The new business, named after the apple orchard where it all began, became established.

Final days at the orchard came to a close as the last boxes were packed, floors swept clean, memories shared and photographs exchanged. Sales of apple products at the market grew steadily over the first year. The new business grew with the addition of baked goods. Out of necessity the business kitchen relocated from Larry's basement to a larger space in Larry's new shed. Baked goods sales branched out to include fundraising sales in local schools and non-profit organizations. Demand for catering services in the third year allowed for a second expansion of the kitchen facilities. Hard work, long hours, sacrifices, tears, laughter and growing pains were the norm. Larry supported the business every step of the way with words of encouragement. Pay cheques grew in numbers as business increased.

Life changed the day I turned a pink slip into a pay cheque. From an apple orchard worker to a small business owner. Thanks Larry.

~Caroline Sealey

Rebuilding

Our brothers and sisters are there with us from the dawn of our personal
stories to the inevitable dusk.
~Susan Scarf Merrell

W hen my only sibling, Scott, came home in late
February, we had spoken just a handful of sentences in nearly seventeen years. Now he was
dying of AIDS and we had little time left to mend
our relationship. I wasn't even sure we could, yet I was determined
to give it my best.

Our first meeting happened while he was hospitalized a few
days after he came home. Having smoked heavily for years, his lungs
were weak. I walked into his hospital room to find him asleep and the
color of the bed sheets. He had the skeletal features of a Holocaust
survivor and the distended stomach of a starving African child, the
results of a bone-eating disease and Hepatitis C, I later discovered. I
had been told he had over a year to live. Seeing him, I doubted he
had half that. I went back out into the hallway, sobbing. I quickly got
control of myself and entered his room a second time. He was awake
and grinned when he saw me. We were off to a better start than I had
hoped for.

A couple of days later, we took a trip out to the bus station
shelter across the street from the hospital so he could smoke, his IV
mix of medication, including a good dose of morphine, in tow. There
were several people sitting there when Scott said, "Did you see that

blue elephant just pass by?" Everyone turned to look at him, a mix of expressions on their faces, ranging from shock and fear to amusement. No one quite knew what to think. I scrambled for something to say for a couple of seconds and then popped out with, "Nope. No blue elephants here, bro." The entire crowd giggled and the tension was broken.

By the second week of March, he was strong enough to go out to dinner and on a shopping trip with me. He, the guy, loved shopping much more than myself, the female, who hated it. But off to the local Big Lots store we went. Now understand, he didn't really need anything: he simply liked to shop. After we wandered around the store for ten or fifteen minutes, he found a stack of huge wall mirrors he wanted to look at. These were about 4' x 2' but he pulled one toward his frail body. "For heaven's sake, don't break one of those," I practically shouted. "It'll be about twenty-one years of bad luck." He looked at me with a grin and said, "Just transfer it all to me. I don't have that long to live." And he went back to his browsing. I wasn't sure whether to laugh or cry, until he looked back up at me, smiling. We both doubled over in hilarity. That was the moment I knew we could repair what had been broken between us. It was as if those seventeen years of near silence had never happened.

By the beginning of April, I was caring for my brother full-time in my parents' rural home. Part of the reason for Scott moving back to Iowa had been that he didn't want to die in a hospital. My brother was aware of the fact that, even as a child, when many girls were going through the "I want to be a nurse" phase, that option had never crossed my mind. Now, as an adult, I still had never done any kind of caretaking, nor seen anyone as sick as he was. Yet I promised to do everything I could to keep him out of the hospital, providing that whatever his care required was something I could learn.

As children and young adults, I had thought my brother and I were very different. He got along with my mother while she and I fought like cats and dogs. I liked to be out working on the farm while he'd rather help Mom with the housework. He was smarter, learned quicker and retained information longer. Even though he was two years behind me in school, I was intimidated by his performance in everything. In college, he graduated magna cum laude with two degrees. He was, quite simply, brilliant.

As we spent more time together during April and May, though, I discovered we were more alike than we were different. We loved science fiction and had watched many of the same movies and television shows as well as collected many of the same books. We loved writing: he made his living at it and won national awards for newspaper articles, while I had published fiction. We had similar senses of humor—a bit offbeat and laced with sarcasm—and we both found it difficult dealing with our mother: he was just better at it than I was.

During the last four months we were together, the long period of silence between us was never discussed. Except for one occasion: an interlude that spring when he was in the hospital for pneumonia. We were out in the courtyard so he could smoke. In the middle of a discussion, and without looking at me, he said, "I'm sorry I didn't get to know you all these years. I missed out." Before I could work through my shock, however, he went on with the previous conversation we'd been engaged in. I whispered thank you under my breath and went on, as well.

All during his illness, my brother had continued doing some editing for the last newspaper he'd worked at. But one day in late May, he called me into the back room where his computer was set up. He looked at me with blank eyes and said, "I can't remember how to log onto the computer." I did it for him and then fled the house so he wouldn't see me cry. I had clearly seen his physical deterioration, but it had never occurred to me that his mental faculties were being impacted by the huge amounts of morphine in his system, too. He was my brilliant brother. How could this happen?

Scott died, in my parents' living room, on June 9th. We buried his body three days later, but he had one final gift for me. A week after he left us physically, a psychic friend came to me. "I don't know if you're ready for this yet or not, but your brother visited me last night." Shocked, I asked her what he had said. "He wants you to know that he's okay. He's no longer in pain, and he presented you with a rose. I don't know what it means, but he said you would understand." Tears poured down my face. Deb had no way to know and I had never shared with Scott that roses were my favorite flower. "Thank you," I whispered. "Thank you for telling me."

Had someone asked me before Scott came home whether I could do what I did for him, I would have said a definitive "no." And if they had asked whether we could repair our long neglected relationship, I would have said "no" as well. But his illness gave us four months of a bittersweet, but rebuilt, relationship that I will always treasure. It was a beautiful gift.

~Robyn Rae Ireland

93

The Bonus Child

Age is a question of mind over matter. If you don't mind, it doesn't matter.
~Leroy "Satchel" Paige

Ah, June! The month of orange blossoms and brides. When our daughter became a June bride, I was in the front row of the chapel—crying. I was happy for the couple, but I had mixed emotions; our bonus child had grown up and was leaving home.

When I became pregnant at forty-three, I hesitated to tell my friends. I could almost hear them say: Don't the Johnsons have enough kids to support? Now they're having their sixth one!

I was four months pregnant when I finally dared tell a friend about the baby. "Great!" Mary said. "In a big family there's always enough for one more. Relax. This will be just fine."

Lee, my husband, also had a positive response. "This child will be our bonus baby. Just wait and see," he said with a twinkle in his eye.

But when I told Bryan, our seventeen-year-old son, he said, "Man, will I ever look stupid to my friends. I'm a senior in high school and my mom is having a baby? That's dumb!"

I had my own worries. When I did the math, I came up with frightening figures. I would be forty-eight when this child started kindergarten. That's nearly a half-century old. When she graduated from high school, I'd be sixty-one. And on our child's college graduation day, I'd be nearing seventy—if I lived that long. What if Lee or

I died before she graduated or was married? What about her? How would she feel about parents as old as some kids' grandparents? And when I picked her up from school, would she ask me to park a block away so her friends wouldn't see me? In spite of the nagging worries, I was happy to be pregnant. I loved children and couldn't wait to hold this new life in my arms.

We named her Ann Marie. Her siblings, with the exception of Bryan, were thrilled to welcome her home. But that problem soon took care of itself. When Ann Marie was a few weeks old, Bryan came from school one day for lunch and found me in a frenzy.

"There's no lunch," I said. "I haven't had time because the baby's been fussy."

"Give her here," he said, taking Ann Marie from me. She promptly went to sleep in his arms. Bryan was instantly smitten. From then on we heard no more about being embarrassed by a new baby sister.

When Ann Marie potty trained herself at an early age, Lee reminded me, "See, I told you. She's our bonus baby." By the time Ann Marie started kindergarten, I was relieved to see that my fear about being the oldest parent of a kindergarten child was unfounded. Several of the mothers looked as old as me. But who had time to worry about our ages? In the next years Lee and I kept busy driving Ann Marie to softball practice, flute and voice lessons, school activities and her friends' homes for sleepovers.

During those years I began to see the advantages of being an older parent. At five, when Ann Marie asked to carry two purses to church—hers plus my large, old bag—I didn't protest. And I raised no red flags when as a fifth-grader she wanted to wear my clothes to school. We had a free spirit on our hands and allowed her to be her own person, something younger parents might not have tolerated.

The miracle of it all: Ann Marie didn't view us as older parents. Never once did she mention our ages and neither did we. Occasionally I stopped to wonder why I'd believed the myth that older moms and dads can't cope with the rigors of parenting. We were doing just fine.

Lee and I were there when Ann Marie graduated from high

school and college, but on that June day when her dad walked her down the church aisle, I felt a twinge of sadness. Now our mother-daughter relationship would change. With a twinkle in his eye, Lee again reassured me, "We've had her for twenty-eight years, a gift we didn't deserve. Just the Lord being generous, I guess."

I agreed. God was so good to give us our bonus child.

~Jewell Johnson

94

Hidden Treasure Finder

It's not what you look at that matters, it's what you see.
~Henry David Thoreau

"Here you go," the auction coordinator said. "Everything in this cargo container is yours and must be moved out." She looked over at our Ford Expedition and back at the cargo unit.

"I hope it all fits," she said, with a shake of her head that indicated she was doubtful. I looked in at all the junk and thought, "I hope it doesn't!"

How did we get there? It didn't seem that long ago that my husband Jeff and I were working hard at our real estate business and doing okay; then the market took a dive and we found ourselves needing to get creative about other ways to earn income. Jeff took the initiative by bidding on an auction lot of items from an area community college with the intention of reselling the items to make some much-needed cash.

So there I stood, staring into a cargo container full of old, stinky, dirty junk, not knowing where to begin. I could feel some anger toward my husband building up. What was he thinking? What were we going to do with all this stuff except go straight to the dump and pay to get rid of it? What a racket. We just paid the school eleven dollars for the pleasure of removing their trash! As though reading my mind, my husband began to load our newly bought "treasures" into the SUV without saying a word.

It was a quiet, hour-long drive home. I didn't have the heart to share with Jeff how I really felt. I knew he was trying his best. Besides, I sensed that he felt the same way I did—that buying this auction lot was a big mistake. We got home and gradually began to unload the Expedition. It was obvious that some of the items needed to go straight into the recycling bin. But other items, though old, appeared to be in decent shape.

"Hey," my husband called out from our home office. "You know that Altec microphone in the box? I think it might be worth some money."

"Really?" I asked. I knew the item he was talking about. To me it looked like an old microphone in an old box—nothing special.

"Yeah, I think I am going to list it on eBay as an auction and see what happens."

We waited excitedly to see if someone would bid—and it didn't take long before someone did! I couldn't believe it! Someone actually wanted to buy some of the junk from that old container. The day the auction ended, my husband rushed over to the computer to see the final result.

"You aren't going to believe it!" he said.

"How much? How much?"

"Almost $300!"

"Are you kidding? For that old microphone?" I quickly learned that we don't refer to things as "old" but "vintage"—vintage has value! Our eleven-dollar auction lot had already more than paid for itself. And another great benefit to the whole process was that someone on the other side of the country found that one treasure he had been looking for. There's truth to the saying that one man's junk is another man's treasure!

There were many other treasures in that cargo container that we were able to sell to people eager to buy them. It seemed my husband had a knack for seeing value in things that others, including myself, would dismiss as trash. I now had a new nickname for him—my Hidden Treasure Finder.

Each time we would go to pick up an auction purchase, I would have the same thoughts as the first time — great, more junk. But I was wise enough not to verbalize my thoughts after the results of the first auction. One purchase found us emptying an old school laboratory in downtown Los Angeles. A little wiser this time, I took special care with some of the equipment that looked particularly intriguing, like the metal dome containers with the classic leather handles. Under the dome lids were what appeared to be some kind of technical survey equipment. It turned out that the lab contained quite a bit of this vintage geological survey equipment that ended up being worth thousands of dollars. Cost of the lot? Five dollars!

Every once in a while I have the opportunity to turn trash into treasure. Once we bought a box of old, or should I say vintage, silver plates. None of them were much to look at, suffering from years of tarnish. I became a quick study on cleaning silver and what emerged from the black tarnish were beautifully engraved pieces of art. These sold quickly and easily, and are sure to be treasured heirlooms for their next owner.

A downturn in the real estate market and less than promising job prospects for two middle-aged people made our financial future seem bleak. But my husband chose to look outside the box and found a new, perhaps somewhat unconventional, way to pay the bills. I am now in charge of shipping our treasures. Even though I may not always know or fully appreciate what I am shipping, I appreciate that it has value to the person receiving it and value to our household.

There has been another positive outcome from this new business venture. Early on my husband realized that many of the items we collected didn't have any resale value, but it bothered him to just throw them away; so he began to investigate the possibility of recycling all of the unwanted waste. Now, in addition to the resale business, we have a thriving electronic waste recycling business. We are living the "reduce, reuse, recycle" philosophy.

It has been several years and many eBay sales since that first auction. There are times I still question the value of some of the things my Hidden Treasure Finder brings through our doors; but, more often than not, I have learned that someone out there will be happy he found it and glad to pay for it. It seems that one man's trash is indeed our treasure!

~Lynne Leite

From Lemons to
Lemonade

From Fear to Faith

Two Sides of the Coin

Fear knocked at the door. Faith answered. And lo, no one was there
~Author Unknown

In the spring of 2011, my husband (then an active duty Airman in the Air Force) was deployed to Afghanistan. We had an eight-month-old baby boy. At the time, I was also working part-time as a youth mental health therapist, finishing up a master's degree, doing a part-time internship as an adult mental health therapist, and going to class. Two weeks before my husband deployed, we found out I was pregnant with our second child! I was going through my pregnancy, taking care of my eight-month-old baby son, working, interning, and finishing my graduate degree all while dealing with the heartbreak of being separated from my husband.

To top it off, I had an intense fear of something happening to my husband during his deployment. I had to seek my own therapy. I had to turn this situation into a positive one and I couldn't let my fear and negative thinking win. I needed to stay positive for my eight-month-old son and the child in my womb while Daddy was gone.

Weeks into therapy and discussing my fear, my therapist, gave me a coin. One side said "fear" and the other side said "faith." My therapist told me, "Every time you feel afraid or overwhelmed, flip the coin from 'fear' and focus on the 'faith.'" I put the coin in front of my mirror and looked at it every time I felt afraid or overwhelmed. That coin gave me the boost to carry on with those difficult days and move forward!

I later realized that the coin was not the thing keeping me strong, it was me! I was the one who turned my negative situation into a positive one by focusing on my "faith" rather than "fear." My faith took over my fear and I knew everything was going to be okay! We survived the deployment. My husband came home early that summer. Our son is now two years old and our daughter is one. I hope to inspire other military wives or family members who are separated from a loved one by deployment to stay strong. I hope they look for the sunshine in their days and have "faith" that everything will be okay!

~Bernadette Fleming

Remembering My Passion

When we learn to say a deep, passionate yes to the things that really matter,
then peace begins to settle onto our lives like golden sunlight
sifting to a forest floor.
~Thomas Kinkade

" I really hate this," said my boss as she scooted a manila envelope across her desk, "but we've had to cut back. I'm sorry to tell you that you're being laid off." She continued talking, but I didn't hear anything else. Fired? Me?

We'd worked together for a decade in the marketing department of an Oklahoma City hospital. For the last few months, rumors of layoffs circulated, but our vice president assured us that although the hospital was experiencing a reduction in force, our division would be spared. Numbly, I fumbled with the envelope.

"It's your severance package," she said looking at me hopefully, like she expected me to thank her.

But the words wouldn't come. My heart pounded and emotions swirled around my mind. Anger, hurt, rejection, humiliation, resentment, confusion. I stood and left her office. Why me?

I had a cushy job in corporate community relations. Flexibility, wonderful benefits and my best friend was my boss. I didn't think it could get much better! A single woman in my late-thirties, I promoted the hospital and its programs. Though routine, my job was simple and the salary was excellent. Still, I had to admit that for the last year I'd felt an emptiness. A restlessness. It started right after my pastor's wife cornered me at church.

"Stephanie, we need to start a women's Sunday school. With your public relations background, we hoped you could get it going."

Sure, I'd organized corporate parties and other events. But a Sunday school class? And for women only? I reluctantly agreed. She was the minister's wife, after all.

A few of us got together and called potential members. Married and single women flocked to our room. An associate minister led our studies for the first few months but then she was needed elsewhere. We didn't have a teacher. I stepped up, because no one else would.

I chose a study on Knowing God's Will, a subject that always had puzzled me. The words in the book sizzled in my soul as I prepared for Sunday. Could God really have a plan for each of our lives?

At the end of the first lesson, I handed each woman a note card. "Finish the phrase, Lord I'm ready for you to show me…"

I scribbled the words "a career that glorifies You and fulfills me" on my two cards, then dropped one into a Styrofoam cup.

"Choose a card, ladies, and pray for your secret prayer partner when you pray for yourself." Glibly, I added, "And God will answer our prayers!"

That was eight weeks ago. And now I was jobless.

What was I going to do? How would I break it to my Sunday school class? Did my secret prayer partner forget to pray for me?

I cleaned out my desk, drove home, and cried the rest of the afternoon and evening.

The next morning, music blared at 5:30 a.m. I forgot to turn off the alarm. I rolled over and pulled the covers up to my neck. It had been years since I slept in. Saturdays were busy with chores and errands. But now…

I lay there a few moments, but couldn't go back to sleep. Something was bothering me. I padded into the kitchen, put on a pot of coffee, and sat down at the table with my Bible, as usual. I ran my fingertips over the note card stuck between the pages. Lord, I'm ready for you to show me a career that glorifies You and fulfills me. A shiver ran down my back.

Maybe my prayer partner was praying for me. Could a layoff be God's will?

I read my Bible and prayed. After breakfast, I sucked up the courage to open the manila folder. Just seeing the words "Severance Package" made my stomach turn. I took a deep breath and read through the pages. Six months salary, plus a couple weeks of vacation pay would certainly provide time to find another job. But where?

If I were honest with myself, I had to admit that my duties at the hospital were mundane compared to the exhilarating career I'd had in journalism and broadcasting when I first graduated college. Interviewing interesting people, reporting stories that made an audience think—I loved the challenge of writing catchy copy. Even working under a deadline appealed to me. I had put aside my dreams of a competitive career in media and focused on a safe, uncomplicated, mediocre life. Regret and shame bubbled up.

Later that week, I made myself unpack the boxes from my office. Photos, framed diplomas, personal books. I stacked files into the metal cabinets. At the bottom of the box, a man in a business suit smiled at me from the cover of a motivational goal setting series. I'd purchased it at a conference, but never had the time to listen. I shrugged. Now, I had time. I loaded the first CD and sat at my computer desk.

Hours flew by like they were minutes. I paused the recording to make lists and answer the speaker's questions. My fingers flew across the keyboard. I remembered my passion as I typed about the regret of giving up on the gift God had given me—the ability and desire to write. As my words jumped onto the screen, it became evident that my destiny was to go back into the field I'd abandoned fifteen years earlier. The career I'd enjoyed. It was where I'd felt the happiest. Broadcasting and journalism. But not the way I'd done it before, reporting news and negative events. My focus was clear because of my prayer—a career that glorified God and fulfilled me. I'd serve God as a Christian communicator, telling people how God yearns to be part of our daily lives. How he wants us to hear His voice and know His will for our lives.

I sat back in my chair. I wasn't an evangelist. There were no religious organizations with radio or TV shows in my town. For the next weeks I prayed for clarity.

While I waited, I typed. Stories about the difference God had made in my life. Articles about interesting people who'd had adverse circumstances, but still trusted God. Narratives about church friends who served by volunteering. Even devotionals. I'd forgotten how much I loved to write.

I felt energized by my passion. What a contrast from the lethargy and apathy I felt at the hospital. Never again would I comb the want ads and accept an easy or meaningless way to make a living. No longer would I hide my talent and desire to write.

Four months had gone by when a friend invited me to a business club luncheon. "You need to get out and meet people." She raised her eyebrows. "Network. You're unemployed and single."

The next week, I smiled nervously as I scanned the hotel conference room. I made small talk with tablemates while we waited for our meals. The speaker stepped to the podium. She spoke about her radio show and how she made a living by selling advertising. My heartbeat quickened. That's the key! Advertising sales would generate revenue to pay for the airtime and provide a salary for me. I talked to a couple of friends who owned businesses. They were excited to be a part of my adventure and support the show as sponsors.

Two months before my severance package ended, I put on headphones for my first radio talk show broadcast. The response was so great that six months later, I added a newspaper column featuring stories from my inspirational guests.

Working for God was exciting, rewarding, and scary. Whenever I had a need, He provided. Sometimes it was leading me to a person to interview, other times it was directing me to a new business for advertising. One appointment for a potential guest took me two-and-a-half-hours away from my home in the city to a ranch in the middle of nowhere. The handsome house manager extended his hand and introduced himself. But I didn't end up interviewing him. Ten months afterward, I married him!

I firmly believe it was God's will for me to be laid off that July day a decade ago. Had I stayed with my company, I might have built up my pension. Instead, God built my dream job.

~Stephanie Welcher Thompson

Four Weeks Without Pay

When someone you love becomes a memory,
the memory becomes a treasure.
~Author Unknown

"'m so sorry, but we have found cancer throughout the entire abdominal area. I would classify it as Stage 4." It had all happened so quickly. My husband finished the school year by teaching until the end of May. He was diagnosed on June 18th (our 41st anniversary), and he died on August 1st.

It all occurred within a period of six weeks. I had noticed that he seemed unusually tired and had stopped working on his street rod, but each time I asked, he assured me that he was okay.

I had spent four decades with a man who could do everything from repairing the family automobiles to constructing a bedroom from a bare storage room in our home. How would I cope without him? The day after his funeral, I collapsed into a heap of terrified tears, suddenly overwhelmed with fear and anxiety, trying to imagine how I would keep everything up and running in a large house. Who would I call when I had an electrical problem? Who should I contact when a plumbing problem occurred? What if a pipe burst in the middle of the night or on a weekend? Did I know the location of the main water shut-off valve? I was overwhelmed with the realization that I was now responsible for either caring for our one acre of property or finding someone else to do it.

The shock of my husband's death was almost paralyzing at times.

I was a widow after forty-one years of living with a man who had never been ill—had never known what it was to even have the common cold. Nevertheless, I managed to return to my demanding job after three weeks.

My stressful days at work were often offset by my son's enjoyable phone calls during my lunch hours and his company on many evenings and most weekends. Mark had his own apartment but frequently came by the house either to visit or stay overnight because he knew how much I missed his father. We had always enjoyed each other's company because of our similar personalities.

From the time he was a young boy, Mark had been a people person who enjoyed spending time with others—especially his family. He had always shown a compassion and consideration toward older folks and those with disabilities, and he would go out of his way to help neighbors by cutting their grass or shoveling snow, never asking for payment.

During the time I was dealing with grief and loss and the stresses of a demanding job, yet another difficulty came my way. A situation arose at work in which I was lied about and treated unjustly. I had always felt it was best to resolve conflict with kindness and conversation. I had seen the negative effects of hostility between workers in other situations, and I knew the damage that festering anger could cause in the workplace. Surely we could work this out as reasonable adults. Imagine, then, my surprise when the person responded to my rational approach with an irrational attack of shouting and physical violence.

My employer decided to handle the shocking attack with no regard for my innocence and my attacker's guilt. The resulting judgment was that both of us would be suspended without pay for thirty days. Never before, in all my years of employment, had I been involved in any type of altercation, and now I would have a month with no income.

During the days that followed, I endured the frustration of no one wanting to listen to what I had to say about the incident. I endured threats from my employer. My director talked to me as though I were an unruly student rather than a professional adult woman who had exemplary employment there for ten years.

It seemed as if this thirty-day sentence was the proverbial last straw. Little did I know that these thirty days would prove to be one of the most priceless gifts God has ever given me. Well-meaning friends and supporters suggested many avenues for obtaining vengeance and vindicating myself, yet every time I considered these possibilities, I would hear the Lord say within my spirit, "Don't do that. I will take care of things."

The first time or two that I heard His voice, I questioned it. I was now a widow on one income, and I knew that the month's loss of pay would also affect my retirement that was coming up shortly. I chose to leave it in the Lord's hands and decided not to pursue any further action. I would return to work on my appointed date and go from there.

During this unexpected vacation, Mark visited more often, and I came to appreciate him more each time he stopped by the house. Mark had always been truly "all man," but he could be so tender toward those he loved. He showed that sensitivity during those difficult four weeks. I loved the sound of my front door opening and hearing the words, "Hi, Mom!"

He would come by with a bouquet of flowers or my favorite candy bar. When I would remind him that he did not have to do that, he would respond, "But I love you, Mom, and I wanted to do this."

At the end of my second day back at work, I returned home to find my apparently healthy six-foot one-inch, 190-pound, thirty-two-year-old son dead. Mark had died in his sleep of natural causes during the day. The official cause of death was pulmonary edema—fluid around the heart. No one had even known he was ill, but while I was at work, Mark had stepped into God's presence. In the months since his dad's death, Mark had grieved deeply and often commented, "I wish I could just go to sleep and wake up in the presence of the Lord and my dad." In His own timing and for reasons known only to Him, God had graciously granted my son's request.

Those thirty days, which caused me such pain, were actually a gift from God. He, who could see the beginning from the end, knew that my son was in his last thirty days of life on this earth. Knowing what was ahead, God had graciously permitted me to spend my son's last month of life with him, rather than at work. As my son was pronounced dead in the emergency room, I cried through my tears, "Thank you, Lord, for the last thirty days!"

~Carol Goodman Heizer

The Spider that Saved My Life

Let food be thy medicine and medicine be thy food.
~Hippocrates

June 19th dawned bright and beautiful. It was the day before my birthday, and I was humming to myself as I got ready for work. I knew my employees had something special planned for me, and I couldn't wait to get to work. I was off the next day, for my birthday. My husband was going to take the children and me to a local water park during the day, and we were going out for a "fancy" dinner that night at one of my favorite restaurants. I could hardly wait!

As I got ready for work, I admired my newly pedicured toenails. I noticed that one of my toes had a large black bruise on it. I must have stubbed my toe on the treadmill, I thought.

Later that day, at lunchtime, my employees brought in a beautiful cake, flowers, and presents. I was jubilant, but I just didn't feel right. I attributed it to a strenuous workout at the gym, and continued to enjoy my pre-birthday festivities.

As the day wore on, I felt worse and worse. I finally headed home and passed out in bed. The next thing I knew, I woke up in the emergency room, feverish and incoherent. I learned later that I had been bitten on my toe by a brown recluse spider and the poison had spread rapidly through my body.

The doctors gave me an IV antibiotic and covered me with

blankets. My toe and leg was swollen and black, and I overheard the doctors telling my husband that amputation of my toe was a possibility.

My birthday was officially ruined!

Luckily, my toe began to heal but I still felt lousy. After five rounds of antibiotics, I still could not regain my health. Working, taking care of my family, and doing household chores simply wore me out. I became sick and tired of being sick and tired.

About three months after my spider bite, I was surfing the Internet, one of the few activities that didn't wear me out. My church had started some small groups, and I began looking for a group to join. As I browsed through the groups, one caught my eye. It was a health and wellness group, located not too far from my office. I could hardly contain my excitement as I e-mailed the leader, Debra, to see if I could join.

Soon after, Debra e-mailed me with details about the group. I could hardly wait for the first meeting, and prayed that somehow I would learn something to revitalize my flagging health and my depressed spirits.

The next Thursday I pulled up in front of Debra's health food store. I was anxious and hoped the meeting would be beneficial. I walked in the door and was met with the loving and welcoming faces of Debra and Sharae, the co-leaders of the group. An intoxicating smell emanated from the kitchen at the rear of the store, and I could see a delicious lunch spread out before us.

I met the other ladies, and we dug into the sumptuous feast. Our leaders began teaching us about health, nutrition, and the human body. We learned about eating properly, drinking enough water and getting proper activity for our body. These ladies truly believed that our bodies were God's temple, and taught us to treat them with the respect they deserved.

Each week, I looked forward to attending the meetings. I devoured the books we were instructed to read and completely revamped my family's eating habits. Soon, I noticed, I was regaining my energy and the spring in my step. I began feeling better than ever before. Even though I was close to fifty, I felt better than I had in my twenties. My skin began to glow, and family and friends wondered if I had had "something done." I chuckled to myself as I explained to them that I was regaining my beauty and health from the inside out!

As I began to feel better and better, my sister, Victoria, who suffered from a severe kidney disease, noted my greatly improved health. I began teaching her how to eat the way I did, with organic fruits, vegetables and vitamin and herb supplements. Slowly, she also regained her health. She began helping our dad, who had health issues, and began drinking healthy smoothies and juices. My passion for health had spread to my entire family.

Because of what I had learned in my small group, I made the decision to return to school to obtain a degree in nutrition, and become a Certified Health Specialist. My dream became to minister to others the way I had been ministered to, and to help others obtain optimum health and wellness. My sister and I even made plans to open a health food store when we retired from our jobs.

Today, I am ministering to others who are in poor health, and seeing them restored to health and happiness. Nothing gives me greater joy than assisting others and seeing the glow come back to their faces and the sparkle back in their eyes, as they begin to feel and look their best.

I thought my spider bite was one of the worst things that had ever happened to me, but it truly became a blessing in disguise. I realized that my health was my most valuable asset, but I had not treasured or appreciated it until I became ill. Thanks to that spider I took control of my health, my life, and my future, and found a new passion helping others do the same!

~Melanie Adams Hardy

Victorious Val

You gain strength, courage and confidence by every experience in which you
really stop to look fear in the face.
~Eleanor Roosevelt

Reeling from the news, I hurried home and climbed into bed. Those words, "Vallory, I'm sorry, you have breast cancer," invaded my thoughts and nagged at me. Pulling the covers up to my chin, I considered my options. Should I call my friends? Should I keep it a secret? My whole life I had been the girl with a plan, and now, suddenly, I found myself completely plan-less.

I gathered my composure and called one of my girlfriends. That seemed like a good place to start, but after going through the details of the last hour, I realized informing all of them was going to be emotionally exhausting. How many times would I be able to rehash all of this? I made it through four more calls before finally giving up. As I lay there, my faced stained with tears, it felt as though my airway was blocked and a very large person was sitting on my chest. I wondered how advanced my cancer was, whether or not it was anywhere else in my body, and if this was "it" for me.

"This is draining," I thought. So I did what any fitness freak would—I went to the gym. I may have cancer, I rationalized, but I still need my cardio. I got on the Stairmaster and lost myself in a good, old-fashioned sweat. I climbed until my legs were heavy lead objects. By the time I couldn't go any further, I'd made a decision. Cancer, you will not get the best of me.

Invigorated from sweating my frustrations out, I returned home to make a video announcement for friends and extended family. It seemed like a natural way to tell everyone since I'd already been filming *TRuDaT*, my amateur video series, for two years. Sweaty, I blotted my face and applied some mascara, eyeliner, and lip gloss. I laughed at myself, but like I always say, there's never a good excuse for ugly—not even cancer. I sat down at the kitchen table and, unscripted, poured out my feelings on camera until I felt purged. The burden lifted, and surprisingly, I felt emotionally energized.

I posted my finished episode, "It's Official: I'm Pink," on Facebook—forty-eight hours after my diagnosis. In it, I confronted cancer, channeled my strength, set my focus, and flexed my biceps a few times. My sense of humor has always been the way I choose to cope with difficult experiences, and if there was ever a time to exercise lightheartedness, it was definitely upon me. Looking back, that video served three very important purposes. Providing me with a means to inspire myself, it forced me into character and psyched me up for the journey of a lifetime. It reassured the people around me that I was "fully gloved" and poised to put up one heck of a fight. And most importantly, it eliminated the endless retelling of events to others and thereby preserved my sanity. For weeks, I played that video every day so that I could maintain focus and fight like the girl on film who boldly talked smack about cancer.

Comments and personal messages of support flooded my wall and inbox. I noticed my supporters were drawn to one particular quote from my video: "I'm not in this to be all Sad-Sally-Sappy-Sue. I'm all about being Victorious Vallory." Many began addressing me as "VV" or "Victorious Val," and it resonated with me. That one line became my anthem, and that's how Victorious Val, my superhero alter ego, was born.

I immersed myself in anti-cancer diet books, breast cancer research, and worked with an amazing cancer care team, but truly, the self-talk made the biggest impact on my journey. It was in that spirit that I posted a significant status announcing to 575 of my friends that I aimed to change my Facebook name to Victorious Val until I kicked cancer's butt. But long after the butt kicking, I'm still Victorious Val, and I really don't see that changing. Of course, along the way, I learned that dubbing myself "victorious" didn't magically exempt me from tears and sadness. I kept it real, though, sharing every last detail with my Facebook crew, even when I had an emotional meltdown. I learned it takes courage to face fear head-on, and because I was willing to walk through it, when I did break down, I was rebuilt stronger.

Like any other survivor, I would not have chosen this particular road to travel, but I found myself forced onto cancer's tollway. I won't lie, this journey has been full of potholes, but I've found the blessings in it, and I celebrate the newness it has produced in me. Breast cancer was a character builder—a test of my physical and mental strength—and as a result, I acquired a profound appreciation for even the smallest of life's moments and an incredible sense of self.

~Vallory Jones

Sticking Together

You don't choose your family. They are God's gift to you,
as you are to them.
~Desmond Tutu

M y eyes brimmed with tears as I focused on the unresponsive body of my daughter. The lead trauma
doctor cautioned, "This is serious, very serious. She
needs brain surgery immediately." He paused and
dropped his head before looking me directly in the eye. "I have to
warn you, even with surgery, her chances are not good, and if she
does survive, there may be brain damage… to what extent, I can't
tell you."

I left the room shaken. The lonely hall echoed with the sounds
of my sobs. My body shook uncontrollably. Why? It simply wasn't
fair. Penny was in the prime of her life, a single parent and a good
person. And me? Well, I was already in a funk. I'd taken Penny, her
son and the dog into my home to live after the struggling economy
caught up with them. My recent retirement was becoming a chore,
and my emotions bounced between resentment and compassion.
Still, we were making it, and having my grandson so close was a real
blessing.

Then the unthinkable happened. In a freakish accident, Penny
fell down the basement stairs and suffered a brain bleed.

Now, as I paced the halls of the hospital's ICU unit, the limitations of my usual "I can do this alone" and "don't show emotion"

attitude became obvious. I was scared and needed family and friends. Oh, I had plenty—but they weren't allowed to enter my emotional sanctum. It was only on holidays that our small family really connected, and even then discussions bordered on superficial behavior at best. Our lives ran on automatic, never taking time to call and chat over mindless things as well as the challenges taking place in our lives.

I braced and signed the consent for surgery, then headed for the waiting room. I had a choice to make. I could wallow in fear and self-pity while shouldering all the responsibility or I could reach out and share my need for support.

My fingers trembled as I punched in my oldest daughter's phone number. "I need help. I'm at the hospital with Penny. Can you come?" She was there within minutes. I called my youngest, 150 miles away, and told her to prepare for the worst, then called my sister, 3,000 miles away, and blurted out the situation. She was on the next plane out with my brother-in-law in tow.

My emotions were set free as our small family cried together, prayed together and leaned on one another. Miraculously, our Penny survived surgery. Now for signs of recovery. My sister and brother-in-law stayed for days that stretched into weeks. My brother, miles away, called daily and set up prayer chains in his church. My close friends brought food and gave tons of moral support, not to mention hours babysitting me in the hospital.

The hours stretched into days and then into weeks. I took the day shift at the hospital; my oldest daughter, bless her, took the night shift and then worked all day, and my youngest spent as many weekends as possible without her business crashing. Everyone now talked daily, sometimes hourly. We had lunch with each other, and spent endless time together willing our Penny to recover.

Friends appeared out of the woodwork. I was amazed at how many true friends I had. Never again, I thought, will I be too proud or too stubborn to ask for help. It felt good. I wasn't alone.

Months sped by and with each passing day, my daughter improved. Little did she know the transformation going on inside her family. I began to really know my adult daughters all over again, and they me. I puffed with pride realizing that in spite of my clumsy attempts at parenthood, they'd turned out pretty well. My sister and brother-in-law became a source of unparalleled guidance. We leaned on each other and commiserated. What to do, where do we go from here, and all the business details of guardianship, finding the best rehabilitation hospitals and researching similar cases.

Goodness, these people, family to boot, are okay, I thought. They were caring, unselfish and even fun. I'd missed so much over the years.

It wasn't all rosy. I agonized and finally broke, lashing out at anyone who would listen, not sleeping and worrying that I wasn't doing enough to help her. All inhibitions were placed on hold and my exterior walls fell under the weight of my emotion. My family suddenly began to see the person inside.

There have been disagreements as we all struggle to find answers, but more importantly, we stuck together, cried, laughed and reminisced. When Penny passes another milestone, we are on the phone within minutes telling each other the news.

Today, looking back at that fateful year, I know it wasn't only her life that changed, but ours—and for the better. We are going to be fine, because we learned the importance of family. I watch as Penny tries to communicate with her once distant sisters, who are now her closest allies. Me? I've learned it is okay to let down my shield and allow people inside.

It will be a long haul before Penny will be able to lead a normal life, but as a family, we know it will happen and in the meantime, we are sticking together.

~Arlene Rains Graber

The Buck Stops Here

The human spirit is stronger than anything that can happen to it.
~C.C. Scott

CANCER. First my mother. Then my brother. Followed by my sister. All in eighteen months. Then, finally, a breather.

During that time, my husband and I decided to move from our beloved Michigan to Texas, despite the fact that most of our family lived near us in Michigan. We found a lovely home in Texas and put our Michigan home on the market. But no one made an offer. Thank God they didn't, because two years after my sister died, my husband was stricken with cancer, too. He had been complaining about having a pain in his side. At first, the doctor diagnosed it as an infection and gave him a prescription for antibiotics, which he took for about a month. When his condition didn't improve, he had a biopsy. That's when we discovered that he had Stage 4 cancer and only had four to six months to live. He was a health-conscious person and it was difficult for us to understand how his condition could develop to Stage 4 without us knowing something was terribly wrong. He passed away just five months after his diagnosis.

My husband's passing left me in utter shock. But the transition from wife to widow wasn't the only major crisis I had to deal with. Before I could catch my breath, I was diagnosed with cancer. I'd always been faithful about my annual mammogram, and this time the test showed something "abnormal" on the film. The biopsy came back Stage 1 breast cancer. Naturally, I was panic-stricken. I thought about my mother, my brother, my sister, and my husband—all dying from this awful disease.

Once I got over my initial fears, I rose up and prepared myself for battle. I have always been a fighter and it's a good thing. Enough was enough!

Being a writer, I have a very creative imagination. Immediately, I began to see myself healed—instead of dead. Instead of writing out my obituary, I wrote out my goals for the next five years. And I wrote my autobiography. I also designed and posted signs all over my home. One of the signs said: "THE BUCK STOPS HERE!" Another one depicted the word CANCER with the "R" crossed out and replaced with an "L."

When it came time for my surgery, I can truthfully say that all my fear was gone. Although I had to go back twice for the disease to be removed (it was so small that it was hard to pinpoint), it was on an outpatient basis!

Looking back, I am not only grateful to God that my life was spared, but for the tremendous lesson I learned from this defining moment: the importance of praying the right prayer. Eddie and I never asked God's permission to leave Detroit. What we prayed was that God would bless us to sell our home and move to Texas. Now it's clear to me how devastating it would have been had we left Detroit, left all of our family and friends (especially our grandchildren). I would have been like a ship without a sail. And I would have never started my widows' ministry here in Detroit, where I have had the opportunity to serve hundreds of widows.

Yes, I've lost my dear mother, all of my siblings, and my husband to cancer. But today, I'm cancer-free and it stops here. I am the only member of my immediate family still living today after being stricken with this disease. I plan to live long and finish my story. I just celebrated my seventieth birthday, which is longer than any of my family members lived.

~Minister Mary Edwards

From Lemons to
Lemonade

Meet Our Contributors
Meet Our Authors
Thank You
About Chicken Soup for the Soul

Meet Our Contributors

Debbie Acklin is a frequent contributor to the *Chicken Soup for the Soul* series. She lives in Alabama with her husband, two children, and Duchess the cat. She loves to travel and read. She is currently working on her first novel. E-mail her at d_acklin@hotmail.com.

Teresa Ambord is a full-time business writer and editor working from her home in rural far-northern California. When she's not writing for business she writes personal stories about her family, her faith, and her posse of small dogs (mostly rescued). Her dogs inspire her writing and decorate her life.

Max Elliot Anderson grew up as a struggling, reluctant reader. Using a lifetime of experience in dramatic film, video, and TV commercial production, he brings that same visual excitement to his adventures and mysteries for readers eight and up. He has ten published books, and ten additional books are contracted.

Jennifer Arnold, MD is a new mom, a neonatologist at Texas Children's Hospital in Houston, a Simulation Educator, and also co-stars with her husband Bill Klein in the TLC series, *The Little Couple*. Follow her on Twitter @JenArnoldMD.

Carol Ayer has been published by *Woman's World*, *The Christian Science Monitor*, *The Washington Pastime*, and in several titles in the *Chicken Soup for the Soul* series. Her romance e-novella, *Storybook Love*, is available at Amazon.com. Visit Carol's website at www.carolayer.com.

Glynis Belec, a freelance writer, author and private tutor, faces each day with hope and thanksgiving. She rejoices daily that she is on the right side of the grass, and counting blessings is getting to be a daily addiction. Glynis loves capturing life in words and can't wait for tomorrow so she can feel inspired all over again. E-mail her at gbelec@bell.net.

A three-time pancreatic cancer survivor from Atlantic Beach, FL, **Alicia Bertine** is a model, businesswoman and motivational speaker. In 2012, she was honored as the Pancreatic Cancer Action Network's "Champion of Hope," and inspired viewers each week on the OWN TV show *Lovetown, USA*. Contact Alicia through her website AliciaBertine.com.

M. Binion enjoys writing and reading. She likes reading inspirational stories of how people are able to turn seemingly bad circumstances around and achieve positive results.

Jeanne Blandford is a writer/editor who, along with her husband Jack, is currently producing documentaries and creating children's books. When not in their Airstream looking for new material, they can be found running SafePet, a partnership between Outreach for Pets in Need (OPIN) and Domestic Violence Crisis Center (DVCC).

While **Harris Bloom** is a writer and stand-up comedian in New York City, he is most proud of founding and running Stewie to the Rescue, the subject of the essay included in this book. Well, he's also REALLY proud of his daughter Zadie and his wife Josie (and his dog, River).

Rita Bosel, a native of Germany, has lived and worked on three continents. Now residing in Palm Coast, FL, she enjoys life in the Sunshine State and capturing—and thus reliving—the defining moments that shaped her life's stories.

Robert Brake, Ph.D., is a retired college teacher, freelance writer, jazz musician, and member of several non-profit boards. He, his wife, and four furry friends reside at "the end of the world," Ocean Park, WA. E-mail him at oobear@centurytel.net.

Lorraine Cannistra received her Bachelor of Science in English and Master of Science in Rehabilitation Counseling degree from Emporia State University. She enjoys advocating, cooking, reading, writing and motivational speaking. Her passion is wheelchair ballroom dance. Read her blog at healthonwheels.wordpress.com and e-mail her at lcannistra@yahoo.com.

Elaine Cartwright received her associate's degree in Applied Science of Paralegal Technology and is a student at North University of Alabama earning her bachelor degree in Criminal Justice. She enjoys reading her Bible, swimming, and spending time with her family. Elaine plans to pursue a career as a crime investigator or parole/probation officer.

A.J. Cattapan holds a bachelor's degree in English Education from Marquette University and a master's degree in Language Arts Instruction from Northeastern Illinois University. In addition to being a middle school English teacher, she enjoys writing magazine articles and stories for children. Learn more at www.ajcattapan.com.

Elynne Chaplik-Aleskow is a Pushcart Prize nominated author and award-winning educator and broadcaster. She is founding general manager of WYCC-TV/PBS and distinguished professor emeritus of Wright College in Chicago. Her stories and essays have been published in numerous anthologies and magazines. She has performed her work nationally. Learn more at LookAroundMe.blogspot.com.

Cindy Charlton is a professional speaker and published author. She lives in Colorado with her two sons and adorable pooch, Lilly. Cindy invites you to visit her website, www.cindycharltonspeaks.

com. She also writes a monthly blog, "The Survivor's Handbook," thesurvivorshandbook@blogsport.com.

Julie Cole received her Bachelor of Integrative Studies degree from Ferris State University in 2010, where she is employed in the admissions office. In her free time Julie enjoys blogging, crocheting, and spending time with family. She and her husband reside in the Stanwood, MI area. Please visit Julie's blog at wheretrustbegins. wordpress.com.

Harriet Cooper is a freelance writer and has published personal essays, humour and creative nonfiction in newspapers, newsletters, anthologies and magazines, and is a frequent contributor to the *Chicken Soup for the Soul* series. She writes about family, relationships, health, food, cats, writing and daily life. E-mail her at shewrites@ live.ca.

D'ette Corona is the Assistant Publisher of Chicken Soup for the Soul Publishing, LLC. She received her Bachelor of Science degree in business management. D'ette has been happily married for twenty years and has a sixteen-year-old son whom she adores.

Maureen Cotter received her MBA degree from Mercy College and retired as a legal administrator after working in the same law firm for almost fifty years. She lived in Zaire (Belgium Congo) for two years and has traveled to more than forty countries and five continents. As a former Garden Club Member, she also enjoys gardening.

Maryanne Curran is a writer from Lexington, MA. This is the third essay published in the *Chicken Soup for the Soul* series.

Barbara Davey is the director of community relations at Crane's Mill, a retirement community located in northern New Jersey. She is also an adjunct professor at Caldwell College where she teaches business writing. She received bachelor and master's degrees from Seton Hall University. E-mail her at BarbaraADavey@aol.com.

Linda C. Defew writes from her home in Salem, KY. She started her own writers' group in 2009 with five people, which has grown to ten. They critique as well as inspire other writers to keep on keeping on. E-mail her at oldest@tds.net.

Donald Quinn Dillon, RMT is a practitioner, national (Canada) speaker and author of two books in the massage therapy field. He lives in Niagara with wife Cheryl, sons Noah and Gabriel.

Jo Eager is a broadcaster, writer, reporter, and fitness instructor. She's worked in radio, television, newspapers, and magazines. Last year Jo had a story featured in *Chicken Soup for the Soul: The Magic of Mothers & Daughters*. She currently covers news and traffic from a news helicopter in San Diego.

Minister Mary Edwards is founder of The Called and Ready Writers, a Christian writers guild and Widows With Wisdom, a support group for widows. Edwards is a book coach and editor and has appeared in *Who's Who in Black Detroit*, *Black Enterprise* and *Gospel Today*. Learn more at www.thecalledandreadywriters.org; www.widowswithwisdom.org.

Karen Ekstrom received her Bachelor of Communications degree from the University of Texas, where she majored in Chi Omega and fun. Karen has just finished her first novel, a cozy book for women who are more inclined to slap a bodice ripper than embrace him. E-mail her at kcekstrom@gmail.com.

Susan Farr Fahncke has been published in over seventy books and is the author of *Angel's Legacy: How Cancer Changed a Princess into an Angel*. Her volunteer group, Angels2TheHeart, supports people battling cancer and other serious illnesses. Learn more or take an online writing workshop at 2TheHeart.com.

Judith Fitzsimmons lives in Middle Tennessee and enjoys writing, teaching yoga, and spending time with her daughter (when she is not traveling the world). With love to her mom, Marie, and her precious daughter, Chelsea.

Bernadette Fleming received her bachelor's degree in psychology from the University of Arizona and master's degree in counseling from the University of Phoenix. She is currently a stay-at-home mom to her two-year-old son and one-year-old daughter. She loves the beach. E-mail her at bduenas81@yahoo.com.

Jess Forte is a sophomore in college studying creative writing. When not sitting at her laptop working on one of her novels, she enjoys traveling and spending time with friends. Follow her on Twitter @ authorjessforte.

Carolyn Bennett Fraiser is a graduate of Regent University's School of Journalism and has more than fifteen years experience writing for non-profit organizations. Carolyn currently lives in Asheville, NC, where she works as a freelance writer and teaches children the art of creative writing. E-mail her at carolynbfraiser@gmail.com.

Ken Freebairn has written several articles and was an international Christian motivational speaker. He has been married to his lovely wife Noreen for over forty-one years, and has two wonderful children and three grandchildren.

Jody Fuller was born and raised in Opelika, AL. He is a comedian, speaker, writer, and soldier with three tours of duty in Iraq. He currently holds the rank of Captain in the Alabama National Guard. Jody is also a lifetime stutterer. E-mail him at jody@jodyfuller.com.

Claire Fullerton is an award-winning essayist whose first novel, *A Portal in Time*, will be published this year. She is a contributor to numerous newspapers and magazines, and is an avid ballerina who loves walks on the beach with her husband and two German Shepherds.

Paul George received his Bachelor of the Arts degree from the University of Nevada, Reno. He is a freelance writer. Paul is currently working on a novel and enjoys writing non-fiction and fiction and loves swimming.

Nancy B. Gibbs is a pastor's wife, mother, and grandmother. She is the author of ten books. She has contributed numerous stories to the *Chicken Soup for the Soul* series, newspapers, and magazines. She speaks at churches, businesses and civic organizations nationwide. Contact her at www.nancybgibbs.com or nancybgibbs@aol.com.

Writing is one of **Nancy Gilliam's** many gifts. Her stories have been included in *Chicken Soup for the African American Soul*, *Chicken Soup for the African American Woman's Soul* and *Chicken Soup for the Soul: Teens Talk Middle School*. Learn more at nancygilliam.webstarts.com.

Arlene Rains Graber is an award-winning journalist, novelist, and devotional writer in Wichita, KS and is the author of four books. The newly released *The Cape Elizabeth Ocean Avenue Society* is the second novel in the *Plane Tree* series, and is available on Amazon.com. Learn more at www.arlenerainsgraber.com.

Esther McNeil Griffin, a graduate of SUNY Geneseo, volunteers at the Ross Park Zoo in Binghamton, NY. She has written *Alex, the Lonely Black-Footed Penguin*, and written and illustrated *Which Witch is Which, Today?* and *My Mom Hates Violence*. E-mail her at Eltiemblo@aol.com.

Deb Haggerty writes, speaks, and coaches people to Positive Health.

She and Roy have been married for thirty years and live in Plymouth, MA with her mom, Shirley Ogle, and Coki the Dog. Currently she works with people who want to lose weight and gain optimal health. Learn more at www.PositiveHealth.TSFL.com.

Dr. Rita Hancock is a board-certified pain management specialist, a national radio and TV guest, and the author of several books on the faith and health connection—especially in regard to pain management and weight control. Find out more about Dr. Rita and learn about her books at www.RitaHancock.com.

Mary Hansen has a Master's of Education degree and a Master's of Divinity (theology) degree. A former teacher, she now writes full-time and enjoys swimming, children's crafts and Mexican travel. She has written extensively about churches in Mexico. E-mail her at maryh6@live.ca.

Melanie Adams Hardy is an attorney, certified health specialist, and writer of short stories. She lives in Birmingham, AL with her husband and children. She enjoys cooking, Bible study, and working out. E-mail her at russymel@yahoo.com.

Jill Haymaker received her law degree from the University of Nebraska in 1995. She is a family law attorney in Fort Collins, CO. She enjoys outdoor activities and sporting events with her three grown children and three granddaughters. She also writes contemporary romance novels. E-mail her at jillhaymaker@aol.com.

Carol Goodman Heizer resides in Louisville, KY, where she received her Master of Education degree from the University of Louisville. She is a five-time published author whose books have sold both in the United States and overseas. Her writing has also been featured in *Chicken Soup for the Soul: Reader's Choice 20th Anniversary Edition*.

Marijo Herndon lives in New York with her husband, Dave, and two cats, Lucy and Ethel. She has written several stories in the *Chicken Soup for the Soul* series, NightsAnd Weekends.com, *Not Your Mother's Book* series, *One Touch from the Maker*, *Simple Joy*, and *The Daily Gazette*.

Karen Hessen is a speaker and author of inspirational nonfiction and humor. She is a frequent contributor to the *Chicken Soup for the Soul* series and writes the monthly column, "Out of the Ark." She and her husband, Douglas, live in Forest Grove and Seaside, OR. E-mail Karen at karenwrites@frontier.com.

Mary Hickey is the mother of four children, three of whom are on the autism spectrum. She graduated from Boston College and is a registered nurse in Boston. She has always had a passion for writing and hopes to share her experiences of motherhood and raising children with special needs. E-mail her at maryhickey_4@yahoo.com.

Southerner **Rebecca Hill** started life in a shoebox. Born premature, she's utilized this head start with verve and enthusiasm. In Los Angeles, Rebecca worked with *American Idol*, National Geographic, Warner Bros., and IMAX. Her stories have appeared in several *Chicken Soup for the Soul* anthologies, *Redbook* magazine, and for Hallmark.

Bill Hogg received his MBA degree from Auburn University in 1975. Upon retiring in 2011, he began writing, something had he wanted to do for a long time. E-mail him at bhogg6119@gmail.com.

Robyn Ireland is working on getting her first novel published and writing her second. She has published fiction and non-fiction regionally. Working in the aerospace industry by night, she enjoys reading, writing, and nature during the day. She has a BA degree in English Literature. E-mail her at writerrobyn@gmail.com.

Joelle Jarvis's passion has always been personal development. She has worked with many of the world's most inspirational names, including Tony Robbins, and now has her dream job as Vice President of marketing for Chicken Soup for the Soul. Her greatest love is her son Jackson. E-mail her at joellejarvis@mac.com.

Briony Jenkins was diagnosed with breast cancer at the age of forty-three while living in Barbados; her son Charlie was seven, her daughter Lucie only three. After a bilateral mastectomy, reconstruction and chemotherapy, Briony is now happy to count herself as a survivor of over five years. E-mail her at briony.jenkins@gmail.com.

Jewell Johnson lives in Arizona with her husband, LeRoy. They are parents of six children, and grandparents to nine. Besides writing, Jewell enjoys walking, reading, and quilting.

Vallory Jones, a published freelance writer, English teacher, and breast cancer survivor, took her "LIVE VICTORIOUSLY" motto to heart. Her life-changing journey inspired her to jumpstart her writing career. She currently freelances, volunteers in the breast cancer community, blogs at victoriousval.com, and seeks public speaking opportunities. E-mail her at victoriousval2011@gmail.com.

Kessie Kaltsounis received her Bachelor of Science degree and Master of Arts degree in Teaching in Education. Kessie volunteers in various groups in her city and was named Troy's Distinguished Citizen in 2008. Her most rewarding volunteer experience is with Blessing in a Backpack. She is filling her retirement years with writing.

Mimi Greenwood Knight is a freelance writer living in South Louisiana with her husband, David, and four spectacular kids. She enjoys gardening, baking, karate, knitting, Bible study, and the lost art of letter writing. Mimi is blessed to have two dozen essays in the *Chicken Soup for the Soul* series.

Miranda Koerner lives in San Antonio, TX with her husband and two Chihuahuas, Bitty and Bear. Previously published in *Chicken Soup for the Soul: Food and Love* and several magazines and newspapers. Miranda is also the author of *The Butterfly Dress* and *Blue Mermaid*. Learn more at www.wordsnwhimsy.com.

Ann Kronwald holds a master's degree from the University of Hawaii, and has a passion for writing. Her articles often highlight one of God's Old Testament names, or narrate a tale of the wee folk in her life. She received first place in the 2011 Writers-Editors Network International Writing Competition.

Tom Lagana is coauthor of *Chicken Soup for the Prisoner's Soul*, *Chicken Soup for the Volunteer's Soul*, *Serving Productive Time*, *The Quick and Easy Guide to Project Management*, and *Serving Time, Serving Others*. Contact him at P.O. Box 7816, Wilmington, DE 19803 or e-mail TomLagana@yahoo.com. Learn more at www.TomLagana.com.

Lynne Leite is a hidden treasure finder who is mining her life for precious stories. She believes life is a series of stories meant to be told. Lynne is a writer and speaker, wife and mother, storyteller and dreamer. Learn more at www.CurlyGirl4God.com.

California State Employees Association (CSEA) employed **Linda Lohman** for several years after her retirement from the State of California. Since retiring she has been published in several *Chicken Soup for the Soul* anthologies. Enjoying retirement, she writes extensively on grief issues. E-mail her at lindaalohman@yahoo.com.

Margaret Luebs is a graduate of the University of California, Berkeley and the University of Michigan. She has taught technical writing, and worked for several years as a technical editor. After spending four years in the Mojave Desert, she and her family recently returned to Boulder, CO, where she tries to find time to write.

Susan Lugli is a Christian speaker and author. Her stories have appeared in several *Chicken Soup for the Soul* anthologies. She is an advocate for burn survivors and speaks on their behalf. E-mail her at suenrusty@aol.com.

Renee Beauregard Lute's work has appeared in a variety of magazines. She holds an MFA degree in creative writing from Hamline University. She and her family are about to move from Rhode Island to Washington State, because there's no such thing as too much adventure. E-mail her at renee.b.lute@gmail.com.

Gloria Hander Lyons has channeled thirty years of training and hands-on experience in the areas of art, interior decorating, crafting and event planning into writing how-to books, cookbooks, newsletters, humorous short stories and blogs. Visit her website to read about them at www.gloriahanderlyons.com.

Christopher McDaniel is currently a dancer with the Los Angeles Ballet. He is simultaneously on the faculty at Lula Washington Dance Theatre. During his off time he enjoys going to the beach, going out dancing with friends, and seeing other forms of art. E-mail him at chrismcdaniel08@gmail.com.

A.M. Miller has a Bachelor of Journalism degree from King's College. She lives in Newfoundland, Canada with her loving husband, amazing son and two active dogs. This year she has rediscovered her passion for writing and is currently working on essays, children's stories and a novel. E-mail her at ams_miller@yahoo.ca.

Olivia Mitchell is a college student in New York. She has always had a love for writing and considers it a gift passed on by her mother Teri Fernandez Mitchell, a published poet. Olivia hopes to tap into her writing more and see where it takes her. E-mail her at itslivilove@gmail.com.

Maitland Mullen is from a small rural town in Nova Scotia, Canada.

She is a full-time mother, who has always loved writing. Although motherhood has become the main focus in her life, she enjoys writing short stories and poems in her spare time.

Margaret Nava writes from her home in New Mexico where she lives with a rambunctious Chihuahua. In addition to her stories in the *Chicken Soup for the Soul* anthology, she has authored six books and written numerous articles for inspirational and Christian living publications.

Sally Ness is a large animal veterinarian at Cornell University and a native of the rural Oregon Coast. She lives in upstate New York with her husband and their two dogs, Tucker and Dudley. E-mail her at sally_ness@yahoo.com.

Tina O'Reilly loves the ocean and writing. She resides in Rhode Island with her loving husband, four children and three dogs. She loves to hear from readers. E-mail her at tmoreilly68@aol.com.

Donna Palomba is the founder and driving force behind Jane Doe No More, Inc., an organization dedicated to improving the way society responds to victims of sexual assault. Her book *Jane Doe No More: My 15-Year Fight to Reclaim My Identity—a True Story of Survival, Hope and Redemption* was released by Globe Pequot Press in 2012.

Nancy Peacock is a retired librarian who loves to read and garden. She began writing novels and short stories when she retired several years ago. Her husband and three daughters are her best critics.

Connie Pombo is a freelance writer and the author of *Trading Ashes for Roses*. Her stories have appeared in several *Chicken Soup for the Soul* anthologies and *Coping with Cancer* magazine. She is a speaker for the National Cancer Survivors Day Network. Contact her or learn more at www.conniepombo.com.

Emily Raymond is a senior undergraduate history major at Hardin-Simmons University in Texas. She plans to continue her education in graduate school and earn a Ph.D. and teach at the university level. Emily enjoys reading, scrapbooking, gardening, writing letters, and having coffee with friends.

Stacey Ritz is an award-winning freelance writer and the Executive Director of Advocates 4 Animals, Inc. Stacey enjoys reading, writing, animal rescue/fostering, running and the arts. She is currently working on several fiction and nonfiction books. Learn more at www.staceyritz.com and www.advocates4animals.com.

Marcia Rudoff, a writer and retired educator, lives on Bainbridge Island, WA, where she teaches memoir writing classes and writes a monthly newspaper column. Her personal essays have appeared in newspapers, magazines and anthologies. She is the author of *We Have Stories — A Handbook for Writing Your Memoirs*.

Tammy Ruggles is a freelance writer based in Maysville, KY. She has had over 200 pieces published in print and on the Internet. In 2005, her first book, *Peace*, was published by Clear Light Books. Her latest project is an e-course for beginning writers, *9 Secrets To Getting Published*.

Loretta Schoen grew up in São Paolo, Brazil and Rome, Italy and now resides in South Florida with her husband, two cats and two dogs. She enjoys traveling, working with abused animals, and spending time with her grandson, Aiden. She is currently writing medical stories to inspire and empower patients.

Deana J. Scott loves writing and is very excited about this story! A mother of two daughters and a grandmother of two, she has been married for thirty-three years. Deana learned a lot from that prom and knows how to turn lemons into lemonade… that's for sure.

Caroline Sealey's life consists of the 4 Fs — faith, family, friends and farming. Her spare time is spent writing, reading, playing sports and crafting. In the future she hopes to write an inspirational children's farm book. E-mail her at baakfordyakers@hotmail.com or read her blog at afarmersheart.blogspot.com.

Ruth Smith was raised and educated in Golden, CO. She has three children, seven grandchildren and six great-grandchildren. Her husband Ralph passed away shortly after their fifty-seventh anniversary. She enjoys reading, writing, traveling and her family. E-mail her at msgslbc@bak.rr.com.

Tope Songonuga is at once a mother, a coach, a businesswoman, an IT manager, an author, all depending on the time of day. She has a passion and thirst for knowledge and growth, a hunger to give back, to inspire, equip and empower others to live their best life each day.

Diane Stark is a former teacher turned stay-at-home mom and freelance writer. She is a frequent contributor to the *Chicken Soup for the Soul* series, as well as dozens of magazines. She loves to write about the important things in life: her family and her faith. E-mail her at DianeStark19@yahoo.com.

Florence Strang is a registered psychologist. She enjoys blogging (www.perksofcancer.com), gardening and hanging out with her kids in scenic Lewin's Cove, Newfoundland. Her book, *100 Perks of Having Cancer Plus 100 Health Tips for Surviving It* (Basic Health Publications), co-written with Susan Gonzalez, is available in bookstores and online.

After recovering from burnout as a veterinarian, **Dr. Swift** redirected his life to writing and life coaching, becoming an expert on personal life purpose, founding Life On Purpose Institute (www.lifeonpurpose. com) in 1996. He is the author of several inspirational books, including *Life On Purpose: Six Passages to an Inspired Life*.

Kay Thomann uses her gift to write stories that inspire. Her love of family and farm life has produced many humorous accounts, which have appeared in local and national periodicals. Her novella, *Through a Glass Darkly*, was published in 2012. E-mail her at thomannkay@ yahoo.com.

Stephanie Welcher Thompson found inspiring stories for the *State of Change* radio show/newspaper columns for four years. Now a contributing editor at *Guideposts* and *Angels on Earth* magazines, she feels blessed to be included in more than a dozen *Chicken Soup for the Soul* books, but her favorite job is parenting ten-year-old Micah.

Jayne Thurber-Smith is an award-winning writer for various publications including *Faith & Friends*, *Floral Business* magazine and *The Buffalo News*, and is a sports contributor to CBN.com. She and her husband's favorite activity is being included in whatever their four adult children have going on. E-mail her at jthurbersmith@cox. net.

Nicole Hone Webster resides in Utah with her husband and three small children. She has been interested in writing since the age of eight, and focuses mainly on writing young adult literature. Other interests include scrapbooking, cooking, hiking and reading.

Kate White is a twenty-nine-year-old writer who lives just outside of Detroit, MI. Her previous work has been published in the *Floating Bridge Review*, *The Linor Project* and *Ink, Sweat and Tears*. She is currently working on her memoir and is expecting her first child in September.

Lisa M. Wolfe is a published writer and fitness professional. In her heart lies her passion for keeping her own health and improving the health of others. She is blessed to spend every day doing what she loves and to be a mother of two wonderful teenagers. Learn more at www.lisamwolfe.org.

Dallas Woodburn is the author of two collections of short stories, numerous plays and essays, and a forthcoming novel. She is currently a Steinbeck Fellow in Creative Writing at San Jose State University and is founder of the nonprofit organization Write On! For Literacy.

Greg Woodburn is a Rhodes scholar Finalist as well as Founder and President of Give Running. His social entrepreneurship has been recognized with prestigious honors including the Pac-12 Leadership Award and Jefferson Award for Public Service. He is a 2015 MBA candidate at the USC Marshall School of Business.

Melissa Wootan enjoys refurbishing furniture alongside her husband, Joey, but is most passionate about writing. Her stories have appeared in the *Chicken Soup for the Soul* series and *Guideposts*. She is currently working on her first New Adult novel. You may contact her through Facebook at www.facebook.com/chicvintique.

Amy E. Zajac lives in Encinitas, CA. Her first book, *It Started With Patton, Teresa Leska's Story, A Memoir*, released 2012, is her mother's compelling story as a Nazi political hostage. Amy's first novel, a story of enlightenment after global destruction, will be released late 2013. E-mail her at azajac10@yahoo.com.

Marilyn Zapata, along with her husband, Art, retired from court reporting in 2012, after forty years. They are headed to San Miguel de Allende, Mexico where they plan to build their dream vacation home. To view her other artistic pursuits, including a four-volume tome of their travels, visit marilynzapata.blogspot.com.

Meet Our Authors

Jack Canfield is the co-creator of the *Chicken Soup for the Soul* series, which *Time* magazine has called "the publishing phenomenon of the decade." Jack is also the coauthor of many other bestselling books.

Jack is the CEO of the Canfield Training Group in Santa Barbara, California, and founder of the Foundation for Self-Esteem in Culver City, California. He has conducted intensive personal and professional development seminars on the principles of success for more than a million people in 23 countries, has spoken to hundreds of thousands of people at more than 1,000 corporations, universities, professional conferences and conventions, and has been seen by millions more on national television shows.

Jack has received many awards and honors, including three honorary doctorates and a Guinness World Records Certificate for having seven books from the *Chicken Soup for the Soul* series appearing on the New York Times bestseller list on May 24, 1998.

You can reach Jack at www.jackcanfield.com.

Mark Victor Hansen is the co-founder of Chicken Soup for the Soul, along with Jack Canfield. He is a sought-after keynote speaker, bestselling author, and marketing maven. Mark's powerful messages of possibility, opportunity, and action have created powerful change in thousands of organizations and millions of individuals worldwide.

Mark is a prolific writer with many bestselling books in addition to the *Chicken Soup for the Soul* series. Mark has had a profound influence in the field of human potential through his library of audios, videos, and articles in the areas of big thinking, sales achievement, wealth building, publishing success, and personal and professional development. He is also the founder of the MEGA Seminar Series.

Mark has received numerous awards that honor his entrepreneurial spirit, philanthropic heart, and business acumen. He is a lifetime member of the Horatio Alger Association of Distinguished Americans.

You can reach Mark at www.markvictorhansen.com.

Amy Newmark has been Chicken Soup for the Soul's publisher, coauthor, and editor-in-chief for the last five years, after a 30-year career as a writer, speaker, financial analyst, and business executive in the worlds of finance and telecommunications. Amy is a *magna cum laude* graduate of Harvard College, where she majored in Portuguese, minored in French, and traveled extensively. She and her husband have four grown children.

After a long career writing books on telecommunications, voluminous financial reports, business plans, and corporate press releases, Chicken Soup for the Soul is a breath of fresh air for Amy. She has fallen in love with Chicken Soup for the Soul and its life-changing books, and really enjoys putting these books together for Chicken Soup for the Soul's wonderful readers. She has coauthored more than six dozen *Chicken Soup for the Soul* books and has edited another three dozen.

You can reach Amy with any questions or comments through webmaster@chickensoupforthesoul.com and you can follow her on Twitter @amynewmark or @chickensoupsoul.

Thank You

W e owe huge thanks to all of our contributors. We know that you poured your hearts and souls into the thousands of stories that you shared with us. We appreciate your willingness to open up your lives to other Chicken Soup for the Soul readers and share your own experiences, no matter how personal. As I read and edited these inspirational stories, I was amazed by the courage shown by our contributors and the resilience they have shown in their lives. Our assistant publisher D'ette Corona and I were in awe as we read your submissions and put together this collection. D'ette and I could only choose a small percentage of the stories that were submitted, but every single one was read and even the ones that do not appear in the book had an influence on us and on the final manuscript.

We also want to thank editors Kristiana Pastir and Barbara LoMonaco for their help with pre-production and proofreading, and we also owe a very special thanks to our creative director and book producer, Brian Taylor at Pneuma Books, for his brilliant vision for our covers and interiors.

~Amy Newmark

Improving Your Life
Every Day

Real people sharing real stories—for twenty years. Now, Chicken Soup for the Soul has gone beyond the bookstore to become a world leader in life improvement. Through books, movies, DVDs, online resources and other partnerships, we bring hope, courage, inspiration and love to hundreds of millions of people around the world. Chicken Soup for the Soul's writers and readers belong to a one-of-a-kind global community, sharing advice, support, guidance, comfort, and knowledge.

Chicken Soup for the Soul stories have been translated into more than forty languages and can be found in more than one hundred countries. Every day, millions of people experience a Chicken Soup for the Soul story in a book, magazine, newspaper or online. As we share our life experiences through these stories, we offer hope, comfort and inspiration to one another. The stories travel from person to person, and from country to country, helping to improve lives everywhere.

Share with Us

We all have had Chicken Soup for the Soul moments in our lives. If you would like to share your story or poem with millions of people around the world, go to chickensoup.com and click on "Submit Your Story." You may be able to help another reader, and become a published author at the same time. Some of our past contributors have launched writing and speaking careers from the publication of their stories in our books!

Our submission volume has been increasing steadily—the quality and quantity of your submissions has been fabulous. We only accept story submissions via our website. They are no longer accepted via mail or fax.

To contact us regarding other matters, please send us an e-mail through webmaster@chickensoupforthesoul.com, or fax or write us at:

Chicken Soup for the Soul
P.O. Box 700
Cos Cob, CT 06807-0700
Fax: 203-861-7194

One more note from your friends at Chicken Soup for the Soul: Occasionally, we receive an unsolicited book manuscript from one of our readers, and we would like to respectfully inform you that we do not accept unsolicited manuscripts and we must discard the ones that appear.